D1154178

PROPHETS IN BABYLON

PROPHETS IN BABYLON
Jews in the Arab World

Marion Woolfson

FABER AND FABER
London   Boston

First published in 1980
by Faber and Faber Limited
3 Queen Square London WC1 3AU
Printed in Great Britain by
Latimer Trend & Company Ltd Plymouth

British Library Cataloguing in Publication Data

Woolfson, Marion
  Prophets in Babylon.
  1. Jews in Arab countries
  I. Title
  909'.04'924   DS135.A68
  ISBN 0–571–11458–X

For Rosalind, Esther, David and Rebecca

Contents

Introduction

THIS book describes fully for the first time the events that led to the exodus of the Jews of the Arab countries from their homelands, and the conditions in which they lived. The story of these Jews, which is virtually unknown outside the Middle East, is a tragic one for, through no fault of their own, they became pawns in a conflict which did not concern them and in which, initially, the vast majority had no wish to be involved.

In a pamphlet which contains no documentation whatever, entitled *The Jews of Arab Lands*, statistics are provided concerning refugees from various parts of Europe, as well as Muslims and Hindus from India. The pamphlet states: 'All the above peoples fled or were driven from their homes, and few of them were allowed to take with them either money or possessions, or to retain any property rights. Most of them, but not the Arabs from Palestine, were resettled permanently in their new lands, accepted a new Statehood, and encouraged their children to take on a new nationality.' The pamphlet adds: 'The movement of more than five hundred and eighty thousand Jewish refugees from Arab lands to Israel, and of a similar number of Palestinian Arabs to Gaza, the West Bank, Jordan, Syria and the Lebanon, was typical of such movements [of population]. . . . But whereas the uprooted Jews strove to become an integral part of Israeli life, the Palestinian Arabs remained, often as a deliberate act of policy by their host countries, isolated, neglected and aggrieved.'[1]

It seems obvious that the author of the pamphlet either does not know, or does not wish to know, that the Palestinian Arabs adamantly refuse to settle anywhere except in their own country. But why, one might ask, does a publication concerning the Jews of Arab countries mention the Palestinian Arabs at all? The reason for this is simple. The existence of the State of Israel and the 'legitimacy' of the so-called 'Law of Return' which allows

Jews from every country in the world to settle in Israel rests on the denial of any right of return to their homeland to the indigenous inhabitants of the country, the Palestinian Arabs. Thus the absolute refusal of the Palestinians to be resettled anywhere else in the Arab world and their insistence on their inalienable right of self-determination must, somehow, be shown to be 'unreasonable' while 'the ingathering of the exiles' which is the Zionist term for the immigration of Jewish settlers to the country has to be made to seem totally justified.

To understand why this situation arose, one must go back to the end of the nineteenth century, to the time when Theodor Herzl, the founder of political Zionism, and other Zionist leaders who were non-practising Jews and, often, agnostics, decided to attempt to solve 'the Jewish problem' because, at that time, Jews in Eastern Europe were being cruelly persecuted. The Zionists believed—and they believe to this day—that persecution of Jews is inevitable and that it was, therefore, necessary to 'normalize the Jewish condition' by providing the Jews with 'a State like everyone else'.

Originally, the Zionists were prepared to accept any territory which was offered to them but, eventually, they decided to colonize Palestine, using certain passages in the Old Testament in order to justify their claim. It was, however, an extremely weak one because it rested on a promise made by God to Abraham that: 'I will give unto thee, and to thy seed after thee, the land wherein thou art a stranger, the land of Canaan. . . .' (Genesis 17: 8) In fact, however, the Arabs, who were the descendants of Abraham's son, Ishmael, were just as much his 'seed' as the Jews descended from his son, Isaac. Another contradiction was, of course, the fact that the Zionists whose claim to the land of Palestine was based on a Divine promise, made some four thousand years ago, were self-proclaimed agnostics.

A further problem was that, when the decision to colonize Palestine was made, the country already had a population of Arabs and only eight per cent of the country's inhabitants were Jews. The Arabs objected strongly to the proposed influx of large numbers of foreigners, and so the stage was set for a conflict which has continued ever since those days. As there were no moral, legal or historical grounds on which a firm claim to the land of Palestine could be made, it became necessary to re-write history, and this was done so successfully that many people now firmly believe that the Jews were the earliest inhabitants of Palestine and that the Arabs were merely 'invaders' thirteen hundred years ago.

In fact, however, when the Israelite tribes invaded the land of Canaan in the twelfth century B.C., after their exodus from Egypt, Palestine's settled population included the Canaanites, the Gibeonites and the Philistines. Apart from the Mediterranean coastal plain which was retained by the Philistines, the rest of the country was occupied by the Israelite invaders who established the kingdom of Israel; this lasted for two hundred years before being divided into the kingdom of Israel in the north and the kingdom of Judah in the south. In 721 B.C., Israel became politically extinct and never regained full independence. After the Assyrian and Babylonian conquests, Palestine was occupied by the Persians, the Greeks and the Romans, and between the fourth and seventh centuries of the Christian era the country became a centre of Christianity. The Muslim Arab conquest of Palestine took place in A.D. 637 when many of the indigenous inhabitants were converted to Islam so that the population which had been predominantly Christian became predominantly Muslim.[2]

Today's Palestinian Arabs are, therefore, the descendants of the earliest inhabitants of Palestine and of the Arabs because both groups merged and became one people. The Jews were the invaders and, in terms of world history, the Jewish kingdom only existed for a short length of time. Indeed, one Jew, Professor Erich Fromm, wrote that: 'The claim of the Jews to the land of Israel cannot be a realistic political claim. If all nations would suddenly claim territories in which their forefathers lived two thousand years ago, this world would be a mad-house', and he added that the Arabs in Israel had much more legitimacy to the rights of citizenship than the Jews.[3]

This writer was, of course, assuming that 'world Jewry' is descended from the early Jews of Palestine but there is much evidence to show that this is not the case. Although Jewish historians have, for centuries, described how the Khazars of Russia were converted to Judaism in the eighth century, this fact was not widely known until Arthur Koestler wrote a popular book[4] explaining that the majority of European Jews are descended from the Khazars, and he was attacked by the Zionists for making this revelation. Nevertheless, Koestler believes that the Jews have acquired a 'right' to Palestine because of what he terms 'a century of peaceful immigration and pioneering effort', but he is also of the opinion that the Jews made their own contribution to their suffering and persecution by their 'racialist' attitudes and their 'sense of superiority'.[5]

For their own purposes, the imperial powers supported Zionist demands for a Jewish state and, in 1917, the British Government issued the Balfour Declaration which 'viewed with favour' the establishment of a 'national home for the Jews' in Palestine. The attitude with which this step was taken may be judged by a memorandum written by the author of that document to Lord Curzon on 11 August 1919. He wrote: 'The Four Great Powers are committed to Zionism. And Zionism, be it right or wrong, good or bad, is rooted in age-long traditions, in present needs, in future hopes, of far profounder import than the desires and prejudices of the seven hundred thousand Arabs who now inhabit that ancient land.'[6]

Unfortunately, the Zionists seemed to share the attitude of the colonial powers which totally ignored the rights of the indigenous inhabitants of the countries which had been colonized. Thus one of their major aims was to create a Jewish working class as it was felt that this was the only way in which the Jews could become 'normal'. But Theodor Herzl was a reactionary who, four months after the pogrom at Kishinev in 1903, at a meeting with Vyacheslav von Plehve, Russia's Minister of the Interior, who had been responsible for the massacre, offered to rid Russia of its Jews. This, Herzl said, would end 'the defection to the Socialist ranks'.[7] However, the early Zionist pioneers in Palestine saw themselves as socialists but there was a conflict between the ideals of universal suffrage and the necessity to deprive Arab workers of a livelihood in order to provide manual employment in Palestine for Jews. From that time, when the requirements of socialism were opposed to those of Zionism, the latter was considered paramount, and the situation remains the same until the present day.

The most underprivileged Jews of the Arab world were those of Yemen, and there were some early attempts to encourage them to fill the void left by the Arab workers; but Zionism was very much a European movement, concerned solely with the problems of European Jews. Instead of recognizing the social and economic factors which led to the persecution of minorities and instead of encouraging Jews to fight for freedom and equality in their own countries, the European Zionists decided that the only way to combat persecution was to remove all Jews from the existing ghettos to what became, virtually, a large ghetto in the Middle East. The fact that the establishment of a Jewish State on territory wrested from its rightful inhabitants provided neither 'safety' nor 'normalcy' for the Jews seems to indicate that there was something very far wrong with the 'Zionist dream'. A major error, and one which caused much Arab bitterness, was the insistence on imposing Eastern European Jewish standards and habits in Palestine; these values were just as alien to the Middle Eastern Jews as to the Arabs, but the Zionists were unaware that the history, culture and economic situation of these Jews were entirely different from those of European Jews. In fact, the Zionists were unaware, initially, both of the presence of Jews in the Arab countries and of the fact that more than ninety per cent of Palestine's population was Arab, and it has been these two neglected groups which have suffered most as a result of the Zionist colonization of Palestine.

What is not generally realized is the part played by the Zionists themselves in the troubles which beset the Jews of the Arab countries and the methods used to force them to emigrate to Israel. Some of the facts have been revealed in Israel by writers expressing themselves in the relative privacy of the Hebrew language, but all the details are virtually unknown in the West. Israel requires the moral and financial support of Western Jews, and if certain alarming facts about the fate which befell once-prosperous Jewish communities were disclosed, a searching scrutiny might be directed towards, for example, the massive propaganda campaign concerning the Soviet Jews. Their immigration to Israel was considered essential by the Zionists in order that Jewish settlers could inhabit the huge areas of Arab territory seized in 1967 and thus provide some justification for the retention of this land. Admittedly, Jews had suffered from severe discrimination and persecution under Tsarist and Stalinist rule but, later, a large number of them achieved eminence in their chosen professions. The harassment which some of them suffered as a result of deciding to emigrate to Israel was labelled 'anti-Semitism' by the Zionists but, in fact, the Jews had become a privileged class because, unlike their non-Jewish fellow-citizens, many thousands of them were allowed to emigrate. On the one hand, Mr Beniamin E. Dymshitz, a Jew, was 'tipped to take over from Kosygin' (Prime Minister of the Soviet Union),[8] and another Jew, Colonel Boris Volynov, commanded the Soyuz-Two Soviet spacecraft launched in July 1976,[9] while, on the other hand, Zionist campaigners persuaded British churches to hold prayers in support of 'our Jewish brothers and sisters, the children of Rachel, the children of Israel, who live in the Soviet Union. . . . They are not free to practise their faith and are punished when they seek to leave to make a new home in the land of Israel. . . .'[10] As a correspondent to the *New Statesman* put it: '. . . the whole of the so-called "Jewish Problem in the Soviet Union" has developed into a farce. . . . A month ago, I read of prominent Soviet Jewish physicists, mathematicians, a cybernetist and sundry professors widely acclaimed for their work on liquid gas and high energy physics who had entered the stage. They were on hunger strike.

'Why do these men wish to leave the USSR? They have reached the top of their respective professions, and having done so it is inconceivable (perhaps laughable is more appropriate) to accept that they were being persecuted at the same time. I can just imagine the KGB whipping them up the ladder of success.

'Why do they wish to go to Israel? Do they think they will be better off under free enterprise. . .?'[11]

Zionist interest in the Soviet Union increased because, by 1967, the Arab countries had been practically emptied of their Jews; however (as will be explained in Chapter Six) the Zionists were not concerned with the 'saving' of Soviet Jews who were treated with great callousness if they chose not to settle in Israel. Although this work primarily concerns Jews in the Arab world, reference is made to the Soviet Jews because, in many ways, their problems are similar to those which have confronted Jews of other countries who found themselves hopelessly compromised by Zionism, a creed which may, one day, also cause difficulties for Western Jews who refuse to heed the lessons of the past.

The major problem of the Zionists has always been to find a sufficiently large number of Jewish settlers in order that Palestine would not only have a Jewish majority but would also fulfil its supposed role of providing a 'refuge' for suffering Jews. In many cases, however, it was Zionism which caused the discrimination that the Jews suffered in their own countries.

Even after the Nazi persecutions in Europe, comparatively few Jews settled in Palestine as most of them preferred to go to the United States or Western Europe. Notwithstanding considerable Jewish immigration to Palestine from the end of the nineteenth century onwards, the Jews numbered only thirty-three per cent of the country's population when the State of Israel was established on 15 May 1948. It was at this time that the Zionists began increasingly to turn their attentions to the Arab countries where there had been much anti-Zionist feeling for some years before the United Nations recommendation of November 1947, that Palestine should be divided into Jewish and Arab States. (Although the Jews were a minority and they owned no more than six per cent of the land, it was recommended that they should have the major and most fertile portion of the country.) Raphael Shapiro has written that a severe blow to the welfare of Jews in the Muslim world in general and in the Arab world in particular was the Zionist enterprise itself. Nationalists in the Arab countries were becoming enraged by the organized settlement of European Jews in the heart of the Arab world and the second holy place of Islam, under the protection of an imperialist mandatory power (Great Britain). The violent clashes between the Zionists and the Palestinians from 1922 until 1947—which claimed far more Palestinian than Jewish victims—were seen as massacres of Palestinians. The Jewish communities of Arab countries were not only the co-religionists of the Zionist aggressors but the Zionists actually claimed them as compatriots.

Another factor which led to the eventual exodus of the Jews from the Arab countries was the determination of the Zionists to settle Jews in the huge tracts of agricultural land which the dispossessed Palestinians, who were not allowed to return, had left behind. The Zionists also required military personnel and so they began to organize the large-scale immigration of Jews from Arab and other Islamic lands between 1949 and 1953.[12]

When the Jews of the Arab, and other Eastern, countries were hastily removed to Israel, they were not facing any imminent danger and this exodus could not possibly be described as a humanitarian rescue operation although the propagandists present it as such. The truth, however, is that Israel urgently required one million new immigrants because it had a very weak claim over those areas which it had occupied in 1949 and which were considerably in excess of the territory allocated to the proposed Jewish State by the United Nations partition recommendation. Israel not only required settlers for the territories but also manpower for the military settlements which were being built on the frontiers, not in order to repel any army but to prevent the Palestinian peasants, living in refugee camps outside the borders of their former homeland, from returning, which they tried to do persistently (usually at night), making attempts to go back to their homes or to work in their fields.

Although the immigration of the Jews from Arab countries was vitally important to the Zionist State for the reasons outlined above, they were in an invidious position from the beginning. Israel, as defined by the Zionists, is 'the State of the Jewish people', which means that the State is considered to belong to all the Jews in the world and, as the majority of these are European, or Ashkenazi, Israel is, therefore, an Ashkenazi Jewish state. The fact remains, however, that the majority of Israel's Jewish citizens are non-European, but Zionist doctrine considers them a minority. According to the Israeli 'Law of Return', every Jew in the world has an automatic right to become an Israeli citizen on arriving in Israel. On occasion, the rules have been changed and Israeli citizenship has been offered to Soviet Jews before their arrival in the country. The Zionists believe that genuine supporters of Zionism must emigrate to Israel.[13] Such an attitude was bound to compromise Jews in the Arab countries, who were in an even more difficult position than the Soviet Jews because of the state of war which has existed between Israel and the Arab countries.

A comparatively recent example of the problems caused to some Jews by Zionism was the situation which arose at the time of the upheavals in Iran during the winter of 1978. Commenting on the urgent calls of right-wing Knesset (Israeli parliament) members that Iran's eighty thousand Jews should be evacuated to Israel, and on a statement by a spokeswoman of the Knesset immigration committee that the views of Iranian Jewish communal leaders were not accepted, a columnist in the *Jewish*

Chronicle wrote: 'Who is she, or her committee, to accept or reject anything? Iranian Jewry is not a dependency of Israel. It has a life of its own. . . . Moreover, although the country is in trouble, it is not impossible that there are Jews sufficiently concerned for their homeland to wish to see it through its troubles.

'Iran, though a Moslem country, has never sided with the enemies of Israel . . . and none of the violence of recent weeks has been directed specifically against Jews. The difficulties the Jews face are precisely those faced by the rest of the country. . . . I feel it is a little soon . . . to call for its [the Iranian Jewish community's] dissolution in order to swell Israel's immigration figures.'[14]

Nevertheless, in spite of this plea, the *Jewish Chronicle* reported shortly afterwards that: 'The Jewish Agency [which is concerned with the immigration of Jews throughout the world to Israel] is planning a big operation to absorb a large number of Jewish immigrants from Iran. . . . Mr Raphael Kotlovitz, the chairman of the Jewish Agency's Immigration Department, has disclosed that a number of emissaries are seeking to convince Iranian Jews, particularly those of limited means in smaller communities, that it is in their interests to emigrate now. . . . Mr Moshe Katzav, the Mayor of the development town of Kiryat Malachi, near Ashkelon [non-European Jews are generally sent to 'development towns'] and a Knesset member, is flying to Tehran to persuade the Jewish leaders to support such moves for the entire community. . . . In addition, the Chief Rabbinate Council has issued a call to the Iranian community "to take immediately all necessary steps" to emigrate to Israel.'[15] Two weeks later, it was reported that: 'In Israel, attempts to persuade Iranian Jews, who arrived during the past two months, to remain have not been very successful. Of several thousand arrivals, only some five hundred decided to stay. Most of the remainder returned to Tehran.

'Meanwhile, the Israeli Foreign Ministry has urged the Jewish Agency to give less publicity to the attempts to encourage large-scale immigration from Iran. The Foreign Ministry is distressed that such publicity complicates the situation of the Iranian Jewish community, particularly as Israel has been the target of repeated attacks by the Shah's opponents on the alleged ground that Israel is helping to shore up his régime. . . .'[16]

In fact, Iran was the main supplier of oil to Israel; and Iranian army officers were trained in Israel while the Shah's dreaded SAVAK (secret police), who were notorious for their barbaric torture of political prisoners, had co-operated with (and were said to have been trained by) Mossad (the Israeli secret service) since the 1950's.[17]

As there was intense hatred, among the Iranian people, for the Shah, popular anger against his régime was naturally directed towards his friends and supporters too. By their insistence on 'representing' the Iranian Jews, the Israelis ensured that the Jews would be identified, along with the Israelis, as 'enemies', a situation which, to a somewhat lesser extent, echoed events in the Arab countries three decades previously.

However, despite the undeniable fact that some Jews are increasingly finding themselves in jeopardy in their own countries as a result of various Zionist actions, it is very difficult for the majority to repudiate Zionism because those who criticize this creed are maligned and reviled. Many critics are effectively silenced by being labelled 'anti-Semitic' even when they have the best interests of the Jews at heart, and if the critics happen to be Jewish, they are referred to as 'self-haters'. It was largely as a result of the Nazi extermination of the Jews that opposition to Zionist policies became muted because most people were, understandably, reluctant to be bracketed with Hitler. Before the rise of Nazism, however, there were no such inhibitions among world figures and many were outspoken in their condemnation of Zionism.

After the First World War, for example, Lord Beaverbrook wrote that, 'to be a friend of the Jews is not equivalent to believing in the Zionist movement. It is certainly not equivalent to favouring the establishment of the British protectorate in Palestine whereby the great Arab majority in that country is held down by the British bayonet, and placed in an inferior position to the Jewish minority, all at the risk and expense to the British taxpayer.

'In fact, a dislike of the Zionist programme is by no means confined to Christians. Many of the best and wisest Jews objected to the adventure. . . . At one time these anti-Zionist Jews, many of whom were to be found especially in England, used to express their opinions freely enough. Lately, they have been terrorized by the violent abuse of the Zionist Press and the accusations of treachery to their race, into an enforced silence. They think exactly as they did before, only they dare not speak. . . . I objected particularly to the Palestine adventure because it subjected an Arab majority to an unjust domination by the Zionists . . . in the spring of 1923 I went to Palestine to form my own conclusions on the spot. I returned more than ever convinced that the setting up of a Zionist state by force of arms is unjust to the Arab majority who have, after all, lived there in history quite as long as the Jews. . . . I am amazed at the ferocity —for I can use no other terms—with which the Zionists criticized the anti-Zionists in their press [and] the extraordinary susceptibility to such criticism displayed by the victims, even when they were men of established position, wealth or even eminence.'[18]

Gandhi wrote, in 1938: 'My sympathies are all with the Jews. . . . But my sympathy does not blind me to the requirements of justice. The cry for the national home for the Jews does not make much appeal to me. . . . Palestine belongs to the Arabs in the same sense that England belongs to the English or France to the French. It is wrong and inhuman to impose the Jews on the Arabs. What is going on in Palestine today cannot be justified by any moral code or conduct. . . . If the Jews have no home but Palestine, will they relish the idea of being forced to leave the other parts of the world in which they are settled? Or do they want a double home where they can remain at will? This cry for the national home affords a colourable justification for the German expulsion of the Jews. . . . The Palestine of the Biblical conception is not a geographical tract. It is in their hearts. But if they must look to the Palestine of geography as their national home, it is wrong to enter it under the shadow of the British gun. . . . They can settle in Palestine only by the goodwill of the Arabs. . . .'[19]

Although the Nazi persecution of Jews was utilized to the full by the Zionists in order to stifle criticism of their actions, there seemed no doubt that Hitler's anti-Jewish measures assisted their political aims. Germany's notoriously racist Nuremberg Laws of 15 September 1935, stated that: 'If the Jews had a state of their own in which the bulk of their people were at home, the Jewish question could already be considered solved today, even for the Jews themselves. The ardent Zionists of all people have objected least of all to the basic ideas of the Nuremberg Laws, because they know that these laws are the only correct solution for the Jewish people too. . . .'[20]

Ironically, certain laws in Israel are identical to the Nuremberg Laws and, in Israel, wrote Dr Hannah Arendt, these laws 'forbid Jews to marry non-Jews, where children of mixed marriages are legally bastards, although children of Jewish parentage born out of wedlock are considered legitimate, and where a person with a non-Jewish mother can neither be married nor buried.'[21]

Moshe Machover and Mario Offenberg, two anti-Zionist Israelis, wrote that: '. . . . in Eastern Europe, and especially in Poland, the Yiddish-speaking workers who considered themselves Jews without reservation were the most resolute enemies of Zionism. They were determined opponents of emigration to Palestine. These anti-Zionists thought the idea of an evacuation, an exodus from the countries they called home, where their ancestors had lived for centuries, amounted to abdicating their rights, yielding to hostile pressure, betraying their struggle and surrendering to anti-semitism. For them, Zionism seemed to be the triumph of anti-semitism, legitimizing and validating the old cry "Jews out". . . . Zionism was indeed a *reaction* to anti-semitism; the basic assumption, however, on which Zionist ideology is based *agrees with that of anti-semitism.*'[22] According to the Israeli historian, Y. Elam, the Zionists took no interest in the situation of the Jews except in cases where the Jews were assisting Zionism and, after the Nazis came to power in Germany, 'when the demonstrations and protest actions against the Nazi régime of terror reached their climax, the voice of Zionism was not to be heard.'[23]

Unlike many of the survivors of Nazism who settled in Western countries, the majority of Jews from Arab countries had no choice but to go to Israel when they left their own countries. In order to explain and justify the mass exodus which took place and without which the State of Israel could not have been satisfactorily established, a number of myths have been perpetrated. It was said that a Jewish State was necessary in order to provide a refuge for the Jews who were 'expelled' from Arab countries although, in fact, no evidence has ever been produced to substantiate the story of such 'expulsions'. It has also been said that the Jews of Arab countries were savagely persecuted throughout history although a number of eminent Israeli, and Zionist, historians have described how, on the whole, the situation of Jews in Arab countries was a great deal better than it was in Europe. It has also been claimed that the Jews of Arab countries were oppressed and destitute, while, on the other hand, we are told that they lost property 'worth thousands of millions of pounds' when they left the Arab countries. Another frequently recurring complaint is that these Jews were 'segregated in ghettos', but the Jewish National Fund, which owns most of the non-urban land of Israel and large tracts of the occupied territories (much of this is expropriated Arab land) states, in its Constitution, that non-Jews are not allowed to live nor to work on this land. There are, in fact, areas in Israel, such as the town of Carmiel, which are designated for Jews only, and the apartheid system is identical to that of South Africa in some places where non-Jews may work but not reside.

The double standards which exist become apparent when one reads of an interview with Mr Teddy Kollek, the mayor of Jerusalem and a leading member of the Zionist establishment. He 'has supported the expropriation of Arab land for Jewish housing. He acknowledges ordering the destruction of the Moghrabi quarter in front of the Wailing Wall, in June 1967. He favours the exclusion of Arab residents from the reconstructed Jewish quarter of the Old City, even if they have lived there for generations. Communal separatism, he argues, is a Middle Eastern tradition.'[24]

The recognition by the United Nations of the Palestine Liberation Organization was a serious blow to the Zionists who had, for years, maintained that the PLO 'did not represent the Palestinians' and, anyway, the Palestinians 'did not exist'. They had adopted this stance because, once it was recognized that there was a Palestinian people, the entire world would immediately grasp the fact that they had undeniable rights (which had been usurped by the Zionists) to statehood. When it was no longer possible to maintain the fiction of Palestinian nonexistence, it was said that the unhappy situation in the Middle East had arisen because of 'the tragic conflict between two "rights" '. However, despite this acknowledgement of the Palestinian right to self-determination, the Zionists continued to insist on a Palestinian mini-state on the West Bank 'ruled by Jordan' or an 'autonomy' under Israeli military rule. This also explains why Mr Menachem Begin, who became Prime Minister of Israel in 1977 and who, as a former Irgun Zvai Leumi Zionist terrorist leader, proudly claimed 'credit' for some of the worst Zionist atrocities of the 1940s, repeatedly refused to negotiate with the Palestinians on the grounds that they were 'terrorists'.

The Jews from Arab countries are now increasingly beginning to realize that they, just as much as the Palestinians, have been the pawns of Zionism and its supporters. They bitterly condemn the few Jews of Arab origin who have lent their names to the numerous Zionist organizations which have been formed for the 'salvation' of Middle Eastern Jews, and they contemptuously refer to them as 'Uncle Toms'. The Zionist creed, they say, is one born of the reaction to persecution of the Eastern European ghetto Jews and it has nothing in common with their own history or culture. In comparatively recent years, they point out, many formerly hidden facts about the Palestinians have been revealed. For example, the pretence that Israel was operating a 'benevolent occupation' has been shattered by reports of torture of political prisoners, arbitrary arrest and demolition of houses of the relatives of suspects who, in many cases, had not even been charged with any offence. One United Nations report stated that: 'Israeli authorities in the occupied territories have abused prisoners, deprived Arab civilians of their human rights, and fined or jailed parents of minors accused of security offences.'[25] Many of the Jews from Arab countries are now saying it is time that the world became aware of their sufferings too. It is hoped that the following description of how, whether they wished it or not, they became involved in the 'Zionist enterprise' may possibly cause other Jews to ponder on their own future safety and security. William Zukerman, an American Jew and publisher of *Jewish Newsletter*, who repeatedly warned Jews of the dangers of Zionism, wrote in an article entitled 'The Menace of Jewish Fascism' that Eastern European Jews 'come to Palestine not with the old idea of transforming their lives, but with the idea of transforming the country to fit their old economy; not to escape from the ghetto, but to transplant it; not to build a new home on entirely new social foundations, but to resurrect the old one—

the ideal of the middle-class fascist the world over. . . .' Comparing Zionism to Nazism, he added: 'The crime of Zionism will be even greater, for it has already the lesson of German nationalism before it, and there is no excuse for ignorance and blindness now. Zionism today is fighting a terrible battle. It fights not only for its own soul but for the soul and even the physical existence of the Jewish people.'[26]

As any non-Zionist journalist or author who writes on the Middle East will testify, much vital material has been suppressed because of the intimidation of editors and publishers faced with accusations of 'anti-Semitism'. Fortunately, the situation has changed dramatically in recent years and many facts which would never have seen the light of day a few years ago are now being published. However, material is still frequently labelled 'Arab propaganda' when it is critical of Zionism. If, as is the case with this work, the most significant material comes from Israeli sources, it is unfailingly said to have been 'taken out of context' although it is generally difficult—and often even impossible—to imagine in which context it could have any different meaning. Readers are, however, free to make their own judgements by consulting the sources listed.

Arabic words have been transliterated, as far as possible, as they are pronounced, except where they might be unrecognizable if not rendered in the popularly accepted spelling. In both Arabic and Hebrew names, the letter 'ayn' has been omitted as there is no acceptable substitute for it.

REFERENCES

1. Martin Gilbert, *The Jews of Arab Lands: Their History in Maps*, published in conjunction with the World Organization of Jews from Arab Countries and the Board of Deputies of British Jews, London, 1976.
2. Henry Cattan, *Palestine, the Arabs and Israel: The Search for Justice*, Longmans, London, 1969, pp. 3–4.
3. *Jewish Newsletter*, New York, 19 May 1959.
4. Arthur Koestler, *The Thirteenth Tribe: The Khazar Empire and its Heritage*, Hutchinson, London, 1976.
5. *Jewish Chronicle Colour Magazine*, 9 June 1978.

6. Doreen Ingrams, *Palestine Papers 1917–1922: Seeds of Conflict*, John Murray, London, 1972, p. 73.
7. Theodor Herzl, *Diaries*, Dial Press, New York, 1956, p. 391.
8. *Guardian*, 28 June 1976.
9. *Jewish Chronicle*, 9 July 1976.
10. *Ibid.*, 25 March 1977.
11. 20 July 1973.
12. Raphael Shapiro, 'Zionism and its Oriental Subjects' in *Khamsin*, 'Oriental Jewry, No. 5', Pluto Press, London, 1978, pp. 15–19.
13. *Ibid.*, pp. 19–20.
14. *Jewish Chronicle*, 17 November 1978.
15. *Ibid.*, 15 December 1978.
16. *Ibid.*, 29 December 1978.
17. Fred Halliday, *Iran: Dictatorship and Development*, Penguin Books, Harmondsworth, 1979, p. 279.
18. Lord Beaverbrook, *Politicians and the Press*, Hutchinson, London, n.d., pp. 99–103.
19. M. K. Gandhi, 'The Jews in Palestine 1938', from M. K. Gandhi, *My Non-Violence*, comp. and ed. by Sailesh Kumar Bandopadhaya, Navaijivan Publishing House, Ahmedabad, 1960, cited in Walid Khalidi (ed.) *From Haven to Conquest, Readings in Zionism and the Palestine Problem until 1948*, The Institute for Palestine Studies, Beirut, 1971, pp. 367–9.
20. Moshe Machover and Mario Offenberg, 'Zionism and its Scarecrows' in *Khamsin*, op. cit., No. 6, p. 38, citing *Die Nürnberger Gesetze*, 5, Auflage, Berlin, 1939, pp. 13–14.
21. Hannah Arendt, *Eichmann in Jerusalem: A Report on the Banality of Evil*, Faber and Faber, London, 1963, pp. 37–8.
22. *Khamsin*, No. 6, p. 38 (emphasis in text), citing Isaac Deutscher, *The Non-Jewish Jew*, London, 1969, p. 67.
23. *Khamsin*, No. 6, p. 39, citing Y. Elam, *Introduction to Zionist History*, Tel Aviv, 1972, pp. 113 and 122 (Hebrew).
24. Eric Silver, 'The Man who Built the New Jerusalem', in the *Observer*, 5 November 1978.
25. *The Times*, 21 November 1978.
26. William Zukerman, 'The Menace of Jewish Fascism (1934)' in *The Nation*, cited in Gary V. Smith (ed.) *Zionism: The Dream and the Reality*, David and Charles, Newton Abbot, 1974, pp. 93–6.

One

In the Beginning

THE CONQUEST OF PALESTINE

IN order to understand the enormity of the tragedy which engulfed the majority of Jews—innocent victims of a conflict which did not concern them—in the Arab countries in modern times, it is necessary to learn something of their early history, and of their ancestors who invaded the land of Palestine in the twelfth century B.C. The name 'Palestine' came from the Philistines who had inhabited the southern coastal part of the country which is referred to, in the Bible, as 'the land of Canaan' (Numbers 34:1, 35:10) because of the Canaanites who had settled in the plains and on the coast about the twentieth century B.C.[1] Abraham and his tribe, the ancestors of both Jews and Arabs, emigrated from Iraq and northern Syria to Palestine around the year 1500 B.C. and, later, some clans travelled to Arabia and settled there.[2]

It had been because of famine that seventy members of the Israelite tribe had left the land of Canaan and made their homes in Egypt. The Israelites prospered and multiplied until there were twelve tribes living in northern Egypt (the land of Goshen). Professor Graetz tells us that they would have remained there indefinitely and would gradually have become assimilated with the Egyptians if they had not been reduced to slavery by a king who feared that their increasing numbers might constitute a threat to Egypt. In Graetz's opinion, this condition of slavery would, in time, have resulted in 'a state of savagery' for the Israelites, had it not been for memories of their ancestors.

When, after the death of Moses, the Jews under the leadership of Joshua invaded and conquered the land of Canaan, the inhabitants of four cities, the Gibeonites, threw themselves on the mercies of the invaders who 'reduced them to a state of serfdom'. Although other inhabitants, such as the Jebusites, a powerful tribe whose territory was protected by 'the rocky and inaccessible Mount Zion', offered stiffer resistance, the conquest of most of the land took place so rapidly that the conquerors, believing there was something miraculous about their achievements, looked upon the territory as 'holy'.[3]

It is, however, more likely that the ruthlessness of the invaders was responsible for their success because, when they conquered Jericho, they 'utterly destroyed all that was in the city, both man and woman, young and old, and ox, and sheep, and ass, with the edge of the sword' (Joshua 6:21). Although the Philistines had retained control of the coastal plain along the Mediterranean, the remainder of the country was occupied by the Israelite settlers who established the kingdom of Israel in the north and the kingdom of Judah in the south.[4]

The Captivity

In the year 722 B.C., the inhabitants of Israel had been taken into captivity by the king of Assyria and, later, history was to repeat itself in Judah. Three months after Jehoiachin had succeeded his father Jehoiakim in 598, Nebuchadnezzar, the Babylonian king, arrived in order to supervise personally the siege of Jerusalem, whereupon Jehoiachin immediately surrendered and, along with the queen-mother, his haram and members of his court, he was taken as a captive to Babylon. The nobility went too, and so did many ordinary citizens, including seven thousand soldiers and one thousand craftsmen and their families. Some of the sacred vessels, and other treasures from the Temple and the palace, were also taken to Babylon in this, the first Babylonian deportation, in the year 597.

Zedekiah (597–587), who was the last king to reign on David's throne, had been placed there by Nebuchadnezzar because he was easy-going and pliable—he was then twenty-one years old. He swore an oath of allegiance to Nebuchadnezzar, who had allowed only those Judeans who supported him to remain in Jerusalem as he considered that the kingdom of Judah constituted a buffer against Egypt, a country which he wished to conquer. One of the reasons why he had sent the noble families into exile was because he wanted to prevent them from persuading the king to rebel against him.

Although the most outstanding citizens had been exiled, Judah soon became prosperous once more; there was a large olive crop from the hills between the Mount of Olives and Hebron, while so much wine was produced that large quantities of it were exported abroad. Sculpture was introduced from Assyria, and local artists fashioned stone, gold and silver statues. The houses of the rich were artistically decorated, and floors were inlaid with multi-coloured mosaic. Education was widespread and all classes were literate.

Women were active in the life of the community, and they had considerable power; some of them encouraged their husbands to indulge in unlawful activities because of their desire for luxury and, according to the Deuteronomic code, women had to be present at the reading of the Law and were required to take part in its study. (Later, the customs changed and women were excluded from Jewish religious rites.)

Because of the social conditions pertaining at that time, the population of Judah became divided into separate classes; the vast majority of the people, who lived in villages and earned their livelihood by agriculture and the breeding of cattle, were simple and ignorant; the ruling classes, who considered themselves cultured and refined, treated the peasants patronizingly and contemptuously but, nevertheless, managed to gain control over the masses by their eloquence; the kings amused themselves in their harams and surrounded themselves with black Ethiopian eunuchs who prevented ordinary citizens from approaching their masters. When the people in general had attained a state of monogamy, the kings still practised polygamy, and they occupied themselves with trivial matters and lived a life of luxury instead of attending to affairs of state. The royal princes became effeminate and spent their time in improving their appearance instead of ruling the country. Although Zedekiah meant well and, unlike the majority of the populace, did not indulge in idolatry, he was weak, and he listened to false prophets who spoke of the great future which would be Judah's if the country freed itself of its links with Babylon. Zedekiah, therefore, refused to pay tribute to Nebuchadnezzar in the year 590 and, eventually, Nebuchadnezzar attacked Jerusalem.

Jeremiah advised the king to save the city by surrendering, but the prophet's advice was ignored, and he was locked up in the guard house. Zedekiah began to flee in the direction of the Jordan river, but he was caught at Jericho and taken to Riblah where he was forced to witness his sons being killed, along with members of the Judean nobility. Then his eyes were put out and he was taken in chains to Babylon.

The following month, the Babylonian commander-in-chief arrived with orders to destroy Jerusalem. The remaining sacred vessels were removed and so was some of the bronze from the columns and basins, while the Temple, the royal palace and many of the mansions of the nobility were set on fire and burnt to the ground. The people were led off in captivity to Babylon, and thus began the second Babylonian deportation.

After discussions with Jeremiah and other friends of Babylon, the Babylonian commander-in-chief decided to set up an autonomous community; many Jews (a corruption of the word 'Judeans'), including several princes and princesses, who had fled to neighbouring countries, returned, but the Ammonite king, Baalis, arranged for the murder of Gedaliah, the ruler of the territory, by Ishmael, a member of the former royal family, because Baalis wanted the region for himself. The murderers escaped, and those who remained decided to set off for Egypt, against the advice of Jeremiah who was, none the less, carried off to exile with them.

The Jews who settled in Egypt were very poor, and they joined other Jews who had arrived in the country earlier and who worked as horse-traders or were in the army; these Jews retained their nationality and continued to practise the religion they had followed in Judea. Jeremiah had no success when he attempted to persuade them to abandon their idolatry which continued until Persian times.

There were, of course, Jews remaining in Palestine, but on the whole they were the poorest classes. Some deserted areas were soon occupied by other peoples such as the Edomites, but in spite of losing both their statehood and the Temple, the Jews adapted themselves to their new circumstances, after their initial lamentations.[5]

THE EXILE

Babylon, the place to which most of the inhabitants of Judah

were taken (2 Kings 25: 9–11), lay between the Tigris and
Euphrates rivers and it is, today, modern Iraq. The exiles were
treated tolerantly and were granted communal autonomy. In
fact, they flourished to such an extent that, after the Babylonian
Empire was conquered by the Persians and the Jews were given
permission in 538 to return to Jerusalem, 'only a minority chose
repatriation'.[6]

It has been said that the dispersal of the Jews dates from the
fall of Jerusalem, but even in the sixth century B.C. the Jews
were not confined to Palestine, and they were scattered through
Egypt, Mesopotamia and Syria. There were only about a million
of them in Palestine, during the year A.D. 70, compared with
three and a half million in other parts of the Middle East and in
Europe.[7]

The Resh Galutha, or exilarch, who was the leader of the
Jewish community in exile and had his seat in Iraq, was considered to be a descendant of the royal house of David and this
assumption was, according to Professor Goitein, probably correct. The exilarch was one of the foremost dignitaries of the court
and, in pre-Islamic times, he was accorded the title of 'king', as
were the provincial governors of the Persian Empire.

Jewish peasants occupied large areas of land, and the exilarch
was responsible for collecting taxes and supervising markets,
while criminal cases also came under his jurisdiction. The
daughter of one of these Jewish rulers, Shushan-Dukht, was
married to the Persian king, Yezdegerd I, who reigned from 399
until 420. She established the Jewish colonies of Isfahan and
Hamadan which achieved prominence in Islamic times.[8]

The relationship of the exilarch to the king resembled that of
a feudal prince, and the insignia of his office were a silken cloak
and a golden girdle. In general, the duties of the Jews towards
the sovereign consisted of the payment of poll and ground taxes.
There was a great deal of unclaimed land in the Euphrates
region, and anyone who was prepared to pay taxes on any specific
stretch of such territory was allowed to appropriate it. Thus the
Jews occupied large areas of land in a country which, because of
its great fertility, was said to look like an enormous garden with
vast date forests. The Jews were engaged in handicrafts of all
types, in agriculture, in digging and clearing canals—the country
depended to a large extent on irrigation—in raising cattle, in

commerce and shipping. Owing to their numbers, they possessed
a certain amount of political independence and they looked upon
themselves as living in their own state.[9]

The earliest accounts of the Jewish exiles to Iraq have been
provided by the Old Testament; other sources, which are not
considered reliable by historians, have attempted to fill in the
gaps by drawing on material which is often legendary in origin.
What is considered certain, however, is that members of the
royal house of David occupied an exalted position in Iraq.

During the reign of Antiochus III, a large number of Babylonian Jews were settled by the king in his western dominions in
order to curb certain revolutionary tendencies among the populace of those lands. One of the armies which fought in Babylonia
was led by a Jewish prince, and when the Syrian king, Antiochus
Sidetes, marched together with Hyrcanus I, his Jewish ally,
against the Parthians in 129 B.C., the king ordered a halt of two
days because of the Jewish Sabbath and the Feast of Weeks.[10]

There was also a considerable Jewish presence in Kurdistan,
in northern Iraq. It was believed that the Jews had arrived there
at the time of Ezra although, according to the Jews themselves,
many members of the ten tribes had been settled in the area by
the Assyrian conquerors three centuries earlier. It was said that
as they did not return to Palestine or move anywhere else, the
Jews of Kurdistan must have been the descendants of the
ten tribes.[11]

Jewish influence in Iraq was so widespread that, around the
year A.D. 20, the entire royal family of the principality of Adiabene, on the Tigris, embraced Judaism. Rabbinical sources
provided amazing details of the orthodoxy with which Queen
Helena and her household carried out Jewish religious practices.
The queen and members of her family were buried outside the
walls of Jerusalem in what became known as the Tomb of the
Kings and, when the war against Rome took place, the king of
Adiabene and his brother fought valiantly on the side of the
Jews.[12] Jewish proselytism increased greatly at the beginning
of the Christian era, and as early as 139 B.C. the Jews were
banished from Rome for recruiting proselytes. At Antioch, the
larger part of the Jewish community consisted of converts.[13]

YEARS OF STRIFE

Jewish expansion reached a peak during the rule of John Hyrcanus, a high priest and prince of the Hasmonean family (135–104 B.C.) and, following the occupation of Jerusalem by Judah the Maccabee, assistance was given to Jews in areas in which they had been engaged in struggle against their non-Jewish neighbours.

Other Jewish rulers attempted to expand the territories under their jurisdiction and they set about a harsh and systematic campaign of conquest. They showed little humanitarianism towards those whom they conquered and, frequently, these people were expelled or forcibly converted to Judaism. John Hyrcanus seized territories beyond the limits of the state in all directions; eventually the feud between the Jews and the Edomites, which had been kept alive by the attacks of Judah the Maccabee, culminated in the conquest of the country, and its people were forced to embrace Judaism.

When John Hyrcanus died in 104 B.C., his eldest son, Judah or Aristobulus, succeeded him and proclaimed himself king. During his reign, which lasted for only one year, he conquered even more territory until his kingdom included the remainder of Galilee and some of the area around Mount Lebanon 'which he forcibly Judaized'.

Aristobulus was succeeded by his brother, Alexander Jannaeus or Jannai (Jonathan, King of Judea), who expanded his empire along the Philistine coast, towards the frontiers of Egypt, and also on the other side of the Jordan. The Jewish state was now as large as, if not larger than, it had been during the golden ages of David or of Solomon. It encompassed the whole of Palestine and the neighbouring territories, from the Lake of Merom to the frontiers of Egypt. To the east, it included large areas of Transjordan and on the west, it took in practically all of the coastal plain, with the exception of Ascalon, which the former kingdoms of Israel had never succeeded in conquering. Although they had been totally subjected, the Samaritans refused to become assimilated but, elsewhere, the process of Judaization was total, so that, a century after the Hasmonean revolt, the Jewish state had increased to ten times its previous size.[14]

B

Alexander's campaigns inflicted tremendous hardships on the people of Palestine. For example, he cultivated the Sadducees, the aristocrats, and, in order to demonstrate his affinity with them, he allowed the water to run on to his feet while offering the customary water libation on the Feast of Tabernacles, thus demonstrating his contempt for this Pharisaic custom. The people who were present were angry at this slight to the Pharisees to whom, on the whole, they gave their support, and so they pelted the king with the citrons which are customarily carried at the time of this festival. As a result, Alexander summoned his mercenaries who slaughtered six thousand Pharisees.[15]

Later, when Alexander returned from an unsuccessful foray against Obedas, the king of the Arabs, his people revolted against him; the war that followed cost fifty thousand Jewish lives. The people asked the Syrian king, Demetrius III, to help them fight against their own king and, after a bloody battle, Alexander lost almost his entire army and escaped into the mountains of Ephraim where a large band of the Pharisees who had fought with the Syrians, went over to his side.

Demetrius then withdrew from Judea and, instead of seizing the opportunity to conclude an honourable peace, Alexander continued to attack hostile Pharisees. He ordered eight hundred who had been captured to be nailed on crosses on one day alone and, according to legend, he also had the wives and children of the condemned men killed in front of him while he, 'surrounded by feasting courtiers and courtesans, enjoyed the bloody spectacle'. This savage act caused eight thousand Pharisees to flee to Syria and Egypt.[16]

Around the year 70 B.C., Ptolemy of Chalcis tried to capture the city of Damascus, which was described in the Babylonian Talmud (Er 19a) as 'a paradise'. Caravan routes, stretching from the Mediterranean, from Arabia, the Euphrates and from northern Syria, met in Damascus and made it an important trading centre (1 Kings 20:34). Aristobulus, son of the Jewish Queen Alexandra, marched to protect the city but, in the year 65 B.C., it was conquered by the Romans and was incorporated into the province of Syria.[17] During this period, about ten thousand Jews lived in Damascus and they were governed by an ethnarch (Acts 9:2, Cor. 11:32).

The pagans considered Judaism as a very desirable religion

and there were many converts, but, in the year A.D. 49, the disciple Paul persuaded a large number of Damascus Jews to embrace Christianity. When Paul announced publicly in the synagogues that Jesus was the Messiah, the Jews decided to kill him, but he learned of their plans. The Jews kept watch day and night on the city gates so that they could murder him when he passed until, one night, his converts lowered him over the wall to safety in a basket (Acts 9: 20–25).

FEAR OF EXTINCTION

From the time of their arrival in Babylon, the Jews had been obsessed with the problem of how to avoid extinction. When the northern kingdom, which consisted of the ten tribes, had been driven into exile by the Assyrians, the majority of the defeated Jews had become assimilated, and it was believed that if a similar destiny engulfed the people of Judah, Israel would soon entirely cease to exist. The Jews in Iraq, therefore, gave the matter a great deal of thought. Realizing that their unique qualities derived from their religion which had the Temple as its focus, they began to think of ways of preserving their faith, now that the Temple no longer existed.

The prophet Ezekiel spoke of three occasions when 'the elders of Judah' had assembled at his house and had decided on the compilation of the Torah, a Hebrew word often translated as 'law' but which, in fact, means 'teaching'. It was then that the synagogue (or house of assembly) was established. The Bible was read and discussed and, later, prayers were included so that the synagogue eventually became a place of worship. The people were instructed in the Torah by a group of teachers who were known as 'scribes'. One of these was Ezra who became aware that, to endure, Judaism must be a religion which would distinguish its practitioner from his neighbour 'not merely by a creed but by a mode of living; his home would be different; even in the common acts of daily life there would be distinguishing features which would constantly recall his Jewishness.'[18]

The fear of assimilation, which was born at that time, was to continue throughout history, and intermarriage was considered to be destructive of Judaism even when the non-Jewish partner became converted to Judaism.[19] 'We have trespassed against our

God,' declared Ezra, 'and have taken strange wives of the people of the land. . . . Now, therefore, let us make a covenant with our God to put away all the wives, and such as are born of them, according to the counsel of my lord. . . .' (Ezra 10: 2–3).

The exiles who returned were said to number more than forty thousand, and those who stayed behind in Iraq supported them financially. Most of them could trace their ancestry through several generations, and they often knew where their family property had been situated. About a tenth of the members of the expedition were priests and there were also some seventy thousand slaves of either sex.[20]

Certainly, four centuries later, the Jews had become extremely monotheistic, with a faith and a standard of life which set them apart from all other peoples. Their lives were governed by the Torah, and its teachings were obeyed to the letter so that Jews had become distinguished from other people by their strict observance of the required religious practices.[21]

While he was in Jerusalem the prophet Jeremiah carried on a correspondence with the Jews in Iraq. One of these letters remains and it is reproduced in the twenty-ninth chapter of the Book of Jeremiah, which revealed that God had said to the Jews who had been taken from Jerusalem to Babylon: 'Build ye houses and dwell in them, and plant gardens, and eat the fruit of them; take ye wives, and beget sons and daughters; and multiply ye there, and be not diminished. And seek the peace of the city whither I have caused you to be carried away captive, and pray unto the Lord for it; for in peace thereof shall ye have peace.'

The Lord then said, explained Jeremiah, that seventy years later, 'I will turn your captivity, and gather you from all the nations, and from all the places whither I have driven you . . . and I will bring you back unto the place whence I caused you to be carried away captive. For ye have said: "The Lord hath raised us up prophets in Babylon." For thus saith the Lord concerning the King that sitteth upon the throne of David and concerning all the people that dwell in this city, your brethren that are not gone forth with you into captivity.' He added that he would 'send upon them the sword, the famine, and the pestilence, and will make them like vile figs, that cannot be eaten, they are so bad . . . because they have wrought vile deeds in Israel, have committed adultery with their neighbours' wives, and have spoken words in My name falsely, which I commanded them not. . . .'

This passage was interpreted by Franz Kobler thus: 'Visualizing the connection of the Jewish national existence with the fate of the outer world, linking the hopes for Israel's redemption with the duties towards the living generations, Jeremiah revealed the very law of Jewish history. . . . Lands of exile could turn into homelands, and a new return to Zion could emerge from a community of exiles, if the people should search for God with all their hearts. . . . Thus, Jeremiah's letter contained a message to all later generations, a Great Charter for a wandering people which, after the loss of its homeland, started its life among the nations.'[22] In other words, 'Zion' need not necessarily mean a physical homeland but, rather, a state of mind, a 'Nirvana' for those who had found 'new homelands'.

REFERENCES

1. Cattan, *op. cit.*, p. 3.
2. S. D. Goitein, *Jews and Arabs: Their Contacts Through the Ages*, Schocken Books, New York, 1974, p. 246.
3. H. Graetz, *Popular History of the Jews*, trans. Rabbi A. B. Rhine, Hebrew Publishing Co., New York, 1930, Vol. I, pp. 2–8.
4. Cattan, *op. cit.*, p. 3.
5. Max L. Margolis and Alexander Marx, *A History of the Jewish People*, The Jewish Publication Society of America, Philadelphia, 1945, p. 109. *See also* Graetz, *op. cit.*, pp. 190–6.
6. Harold P. Luks, 'Iraqi Jews During World War Two', *The Wiener Library Bulletin*, London, 1977, Vol. XXX, p. 30.
7. Arthur Ruppin, *The Jews in the Modern World*, Macmillan, London, 1934, p. 22.
8. Goitein, *op. cit.*, p. 120.
9. Graetz, *op. cit.*, Vol. II, pp. 370–1.
10. *The Jewish Encyclopedia*, Funk and Wagnalls Co., New York, 1925, Vol. II, pp. 406–7.
11. Sidney Mendelssohn, *The Jews of Asia: Especially in the Sixteenth and Seventeenth Centuries*, Kegan, Paul, Trench, Trubner, London, 1920, pp. 181–2.
12. Cecil Roth, *A Short History of the Jewish People*, East and West Library, London, 1953, p. 120.
13. Abram Leon, *The Jewish Question: A Marxist Interpretation*, Pathfinder Press, New York, 1970, p. 114.
14. Roth, *op. cit.*, pp. 77–9.
15. *The Jewish Encyclopedia*, *op. cit.* Vol. I, pp. 352–3.

16. *Ibid.*, Vol. I, pp. 352–3.
17. *Ibid.*, Vol. IV, p. 416.
18. A. Cohen, *Everyman's Talmud,* J. M. Dent, London, 1971, pp. xv-xvii.
19. Ruppin, *op. cit.*, p. 318.
20. Roth, *op. cit.*, p. 53.
21. *Ibid.*, p. 62.
22. Franz Kobler (ed.), *Letters of Jews Through the Ages: From Biblical Times to the Middle of the Eighteenth Century*, Vol. I. Ararat Publishing Co., in conjunction with East and West Library, London, 1953, pp. 6–8.

Two

Jews and Arabs in Early Times

ISLAM AND THE JEWS

AT the present time, many Westerners make the mistake of comparing countries in the Middle East with those in the West and expecting identical social conditions, in spite of the fact that there is no logical basis of comparison between the two areas as the rate of progress and standards are entirely different. Similarly, the same criteria are applied to the past, although the history of the Jews of the Middle East and North Africa has been basically different from that of Western Jews; the Western Jew fails to realize this because he is inclined to interpret the problems of Eastern Jewry in the light of his own quite different historical experience and see them through the eyes of a Westerner. Until the end of the ghetto era, Western Jews belonged to self-contained groups with their own customs and traditions, quite separate from the local non-Jews. In the Middle East, however, the Jews have always belonged to the ethnic society. Jewish myths, legends, rites and superstitions were all part of Eastern tradition and were familiar to non-Jews. As people in the West became more and more conscious that they were members of nation-states, so they increasingly resented the 'communal sense of identity of the Jews' who lived among them, but this outlook was totally absent in the East until nationalism spread in modern times.[1]

Professor André Chouraqui, an Algerian Jew who emigrated to Israel, wrote that occasional outbreaks of violence against Jews in North Africa were caused not only by the attitude towards non-Muslims but also by 'the abject misery in which feudalism had plunged the entire population of the region'. He added that there was, however, never at any time a philosophy and tradition of anti-Semitism such as that which existed in Europe, and that claims made by European writers that there was, in fact, a similar attitude towards Jews as the European one, demonstrated the prejudices of these writers as well as their ignorance of conditions in North Africa. During most periods in history, he wrote, the Jews in North Africa were happier than the Jews in most parts of Europe; and the scorn that members of different religious groups displayed towards each other in this area did not hide the strong bonds which existed between them of a way of life which was intimately shared. Even the haughtiest Muslim nobleman did not hesitate to acknowledge that he was the brother of the humblest Jewish pedlar.[2]

David Corcos, another North African Jew, who was a member of a very ancient and distinguished Moroccan family, held the opinion that the attitude of Muslims towards Jews was basically tolerant, although this tolerance differed from that of West Europeans. He considered outbreaks of fanaticism to be, on the whole, exceptional phenomena which were not characteristic of Muslim-Jewish relations. The Jews were looked upon as true brethren, and he opposed the widely held belief that Jews in Morocco had been a greatly oppressed minority for many centuries, living in narrow and dirty ghettos which he referred to as 'the so-called mellahs'. He also expressed the belief that, although Almohad rule was made out in all standard works to be one of the blackest periods in the history of North African Jews, there was never any systematic persecution. For a long time there were no official decrees against Judaism, but there was a gradual deterioration of the status of the Jews, although there was no forced conversion from the beginning of Almohad rule.[3]

Dr Landshut emphasized that, on the whole, the tolerance of Muslims towards Jews and other non-Muslims compared favourably with that of other religious groups, and he suggested that the Western reader, in trying to picture their conditions of life, should remember that he was examining a period in history during which the high standards of the present day did not exist, and, what was even more important, a part of the world where, even in modern times, people were used to a much harsher mode of life than that which was commonplace in the West.[4]

Jewish settlement in Arabia had taken place long before the birth of Muhammad[5] and, in those days, the Jews were so totally assimilated with those among whom they lived that they could be distinguished from other Arabs only by their religion, while inter-marriage caused the links to become even stronger.[6]

In the year 622, Muhammad inaugurated the third of the world's great monotheistic religions, and he considered the Jews to be the most likely converts to the new faith because, like Judaism, Islam also insisted on monotheism and, in addition, practised circumcision and had similar dietary laws to the Jewish ones. Besides all this, the Muslims, too, revered the Holy City of Jerusalem. The words of Muhammad, which later became in-corporated in the Quran, described a great deal of Jewish history and legend with which the prophet had been familiar from his youth.[7]

The Jews, however, refused to co-operate. Muhammad at-tacked the inhabitants of Mecca and conquered them; he also expelled two of the Jewish tribes from Madina and had the third tribe massacred because he suspected its members of collusion with his opponents in Mecca. In 630, practically all the people of Mecca adopted Islam, the idols were destroyed and the Jews and Christians of the Hijaz recognized Muhammad's supremacy, as did Arabs from such distant spots as Oman, Bahrein and Southern Arabia.[8] Muhammad did not, however, emerge from his battles without some reminder of them. When his forces attacked the rich Jewish settlement of Khaibar, Zainab, a Jewess whose brother, Marhab, had been killed, put poison in Muham-mad's food. The prophet suffered from the effects of the poison for the remainder of his life.

When the Jews had been vanquished, Muhammad proclaimed Mecca as the Holy City of Islam and, after his death in 632, the khalif Umar expelled all Jews and Christians from the peninsula, although hundreds of years later prosperous Jewish communities could still be found in Taima and Wadi-l-Qura.[9] Professor Goitein considers it 'most remarkable' that, even when Christian-ity began to disappear in the Arab Empire, Jewish communities continued to survive and to flourish and, although this phe-nomenon arose because of certain historical factors, these did, however, demonstrate that 'under Arab Islam Jews were not treated differently from members of other non-Muslim re-ligions.'[10]

It was unfortunate that the struggle which had been forced on the Jews and on Muhammad by specific historical factors came to be recorded in the Holy Book of Islam. Although the prophet rejected Christianity with much more vigour than Judaism, his wars with the Jews caused him to say some unfavourable things about them, especially where he commented that they were more hostile to Islam than the Christians. It was, therefore, all the more worthy of note that Islamic law made no difference whatever between Jews and Christians with regard to their legal status under Islam, although the Arabs found that the Jews suffered from severe discrimination in the Christian countries which they conquered and they could, if they had wished, have found a basis for similar discrimination in the Quran.[11]

The Jews, of course, were not without their own prejudices. Because of its fear of assimilation and its opposition to intermarriage, the Jewish community considered itself to be superior to non-Jews. Although the ancient ritual laws, which referred to 'idolaters', were said not to include Christians and Muslims, the dietary laws prevented Jews from mixing socially with non-Jews. Even so, this obstacle could have been overcome, but the knowledge that wine produced by a Gentile might not be drunk and food cooked by a Gentile might not be eaten, while the evidence of a Gentile was not admissible in a court of Jewish law, all tended to shape Jewish attitudes. Thus because non-Jews were also considered to be on a lower moral level than Jews, these Talmudic rules which had been applied to idolaters were misinterpreted by uneducated, uncultured Jews who considered all non-Jews to be inferior and consequently treated them with a lack of respect.[12]

The Quran clearly distinguishes between Believers and Infidels and there is a third group, Ahl al-Kitab—the 'People of the Book'—which includes both Jews and Christians who had received a Scripture which had been accepted by Islam.[13] Even before the birth of Islam in Arabia, Jews were treated with tolerance and, at a time when they were being fanatically persecuted in Christendom, they were enjoying a life of peace and tranquillity in the Arabian Peninsula. They were free to achieve eminence and to play a full part in the life of a vigorous and talented population and they could, if they wished, take up arms against their enemies. They also became teachers of the Arab people and they engaged in agriculture. In fact, the Jews of Arabia were often the leaders of Arab tribes, and their history in the centuries before Muhammad and also during his time formed a splendid page in Jewish history as a whole.[14]

Nowadays, it is understood that it is erroneous to believe that the Muslim conquerors gave the subjugated Jews and Christians the choice either of conversion to Islam or death by the sword,[15] but there is still much ignorance on the subject.

In fact, during the reign of Umar, the Arab Empire spread until it encompassed Egypt, Palestine, Syria, Iraq and Persia. As there were large Christian and Jewish populations in these areas, it became impossible to continue the harsh treatment accorded to non-Muslims in Arabia. In order to avoid a mass exodus it was necessary to be more tolerant, and so the official policy of Islam towards the adherents of other faiths underwent a complete change. However, they were still subjected to a number of restrictions, mostly taken over from the legislation in force against the Jews in those provinces hitherto under Christian rule.[16]

In all the Islamic countries, Jews and Christians were allowed to live under Muslim rule on payment of a poll-tax, the amount of which varied from one area to another. Rich Jews and Christians had to pay a specific sum annually, while those who were not so rich paid half the amount, and the poor a quarter. Generally the non-Muslims themselves were responsible for collecting the tax which remained in operation in Yemen until modern times but was abolished in Egypt, Iraq, Syria and the Lebanon in the nineteenth century. Sometimes royal decrees required Christians and Jews to wear patches on their clothes and forbade them to ride horses or to build tall houses (so that they would not look down on Muslims).

These restrictions were, however, rarely enforced in Egypt, Iraq, Syria and the Lebanon and, in the capitals of these countries, Jews held positions of authority as medical and financial advisers at the courts of the khalifs.[17] The regulations frequently fell into disuse[18] and, when they were occasionally revived, they would only last for a year or two before being abandoned.[19]

Although the People of the Book were treated with tolerance and protected by Islamic rulers, they were, in effect, not subject to the jurisdiction of the State which was a theocracy, in principle at any rate. In addition to paying the poll-tax, they were also forbidden to carry arms, to give evidence against Muslims in a court of law and to marry Muslim women. They were, however,

permitted to run their own communal organizations, places of
worship and religious institutions, and also to retain their
personal status. While there were periods of persecution there
has on the whole been no attempt to exterminate them nor,
except in Abbasid times, to convert them forcibly (although very
many of them did become Muslim).[20]

In spite of the irksome regulations spasmodically imposed on
non-Muslims, Dr Roth stated that '. . . the essential tolerance of
Islam, in practice more than in theory, was to remain one of the
important factors in Jewish history for many centuries to come',[21]
while Dr Landshut wrote:

> Throughout the reign of the Ummayad dynasty in Damascus
> (661–750) and the Abbasids in Baghdad (approximately 750–
> 1258) there is no record of Jewish complaints of persecution or
> harsh treatment. . . .[22]

During the five centuries when the Abbasid khalifs ruled, the
position of the Jews was different from what it had been under
the Ummayads as the Abbasids were not worried by the possibility that the spread of Islam could be impeded by Jewish
influence. The Jews did not, however, have a totally carefree
existence since they suffered occasionally—as did, presumably,
the rest of the population—'from the incessant civil wars and
revolutions', while Haroon ar-Rasheed resurrected the Law of
Umar (which decreed that non-Muslims should wear distinguishing marks on their clothing, etc.). These regulations
were abandoned by succeeding khalifs, but they were revived by
the reactionary Al-Mutawakkil (850), although Al-Mutadhid,
who came to power in 892, employed many Jews in the service of
the state.[23]

Special sites had been allocated to both Christians and Jews
for their places of worship, and Jews were prominent in economic
life. After Jerusalem had surrendered to the Khalif Umar in 638,
a treaty was signed stipulating that no Jews should live in the
city, but this clause was ignored and immediately after its
occupation by the Arabs, the Holy City became accessible to
Jews. The Jewish community was given its own area on the
Mount of Olives and festival services were held there. Two
years later, the Jewish centre of learning in Palestine moved
from Tiberias to Jerusalem while, in Alexandria, the Jewish

community remained unmolested after the surrender of the city to the Arabs in 641. When the Arabs built a new capital in Fustat, which Landshut described, as many writers have done, as 'old Cairo', a large Jewish community was established which later became an important centre of Jewish learning and the seat of the Egyptian exilarch.[24] Professor Goitein wrote that the ancient capital of Islamic Egypt, (al) Fustat, which was sometimes inaccurately referred to as Old Cairo, was about two-and-a-half miles south of the city of Cairo which was founded by a Fatimid Khalif in the year 969 when his troops conquered Egypt; Fustat remained the economic centre of the country throughout the eleventh and during the first half of the twelfth century.[25]

THE GAONIC PERIOD

Jewish scholarship flourished in Iraq, and it was there that the famous Babylonian Talmud was produced as well as some of the most outstanding Jewish literary works. Learned rabbis presided over the great Jewish academies of Sura and Pumbaditha, and the exilarchs resided in those centres. Jewish history refers to the first five centuries of Islam as 'the Gaonic period' because the heads of the two academies (originally there had been only one) were known as Gaons who were considered, by Jews throughout the world, as the ultimate authority on all matters pertaining to religion which, of course, also included civil law in those days. Questions asked by Jewish communities everywhere were answered, in writing, by the Gaons, and these documents— thousands of which are still in existence—were known as responsa.

After the conquest of Iraq by the Arab armies, the situation of the exilarch had altered under Islam. The Jews had given up agriculture and settled in the towns so that they could safeguard their religion. Nevertheless, in Islamic times, the Resh Galutha— the head of the Jewish community—was treated with great respect and, according to a Christian source, he was given precedence over the Christian dignitaries at the court of the khalif. The Muslims addressed him as 'Our lord, the son of David', and as the Quran considers David to be one of the greatest prophets, the exilarch was naturally accorded the highest esteem. The khalif installed him in his office (one document of installation is still in existence) and, in the year 918, one of two competing exilarchs was appointed after reciting an acceptable Arabic poem before the khalif.

Although the exilarch had little real power, and his income was mainly derived from revenues obtained from his own lands and from money donated to his coffers, he was in good company, for Al-Biruni, a leading Muslim scholar who lived about the year 1000, explained that the position of the khalif—who had, more or less, become a figurehead in the Islamic world—was similar to that of the exilarch.[26]

In spite of the already mentioned restrictions on Christians and Jews, which had been imposed by the second khalif, Umar ibn al-Khattab (who ruled from 634 until 644), the khalif bestowed certain privileges on the Jews who had rendered much valuable assistance to the Muslims in their campaign, and, despite Muslim intolerance, the Jews of Iraq achieved a considerable degree of freedom as a result of the Muslim victories. Bustani, a descendant of the exilarchs, was recognized as head of the Babylonian Jewish communities and, around the year 642, the khalif chose as a wife for Bustani, Izdundad, the captive daughter of Khosrau II, the king of Persia. (According to some historians, however, Bustani married the daughter of King Yezdegerd.)

After the exilarch's death, quarrels broke out among his progeny. He had left several sons, the offspring of different wives, and one of these was the son of the Persian princess who, possibly because of his royal blood, was said to be his father's favourite and for this reason may have been Bustani's chosen successor. The other sons, born of Bustani's Jewish wives, were jealous and, considering him to be the offspring of a Gentile captive, attempted to sell him as a slave; although Haninai, the chief judge, obtained a letter of manumission for him, his descendants nevertheless bore the taint of illegitimacy for many years.[27] In early times, the only restriction on marriage between Jews and non-Jews was to be found in one passage of the Old Testament which excluded Moabites and Ammonites from the community for 'even to their tenth generation, [they] shall not enter into the congregation of the Lord for ever' (Deuteronomy 23:4). This prohibition, based as it was on nationality, constituted something exceptional in ancient Hebrew law, as the most common objection to inter-marriage was based on religious grounds.[28] Religion, as an obstacle to marriage among the Hebrews, was a consequence of a tremendous anxiety to eliminate paganism and, similarly, while the early Arabs did not consider difference of faith to be an obstacle to marriage, the Quran later forbade marriage with pagans, although there was no restriction on marriage with those who believed in one God. Muhammad would not allow marriage with 'idolatresses until they believe' (Quran 2:221) and the purpose of this was to prevent the spread of paganism.[29]

If Bustani's marriage had been adulterous, the offspring would be looked upon as mamzerim (bastards) and would not be allowed to marry 'until the tenth generation' (Deuteronomy 23:3); and it is interesting to find that this edict operates in present-day Israel. In 1973, a woman applied to the rabbinical court in Beersheba for a certificate to make her divorce decree absolute as she was pregnant by her lover and wished to marry him before the birth, but the rabbis declared that her unborn child was 'a bastard' and they referred her to Deuteronomy.

Two years later, the woman applied to Israel's Supreme Court which challenged the rabbinical ruling and thus triggered off a political crisis. The religious parties which held the balance of power in the Knesset (Israeli parliament) were incensed, and, supported by the Religious Affairs Minister and the two chief rabbis (one for the Ashkenazi, or European, Jews and one for the 'others'), the rabbinical court refused to accept the Supreme Court's decision that the ruling should be rescinded which meant, according to a newspaper report, that 'no descendant of the child could be accepted as a Jew till A.D. 2225'.

Although the husband and wife had separated two years before the woman became pregnant, the religious court said she had deceived her husband because divorce proceedings were still pending at the time. When the divorce was granted, the woman received a certificate stipulating that she could never marry her lover and also prohibiting her from remarrying her husband, which meant that the child could not be legitimized.[30] The important factor about all this is, of course, that such a child, and its descendants, would not only be considered 'bastards' but would also be outcasts from Judaism, which is a very severe disability in a Jewish State where, for example, they

would never be allowed to marry Jews. (There have been a
number of such cases in Israel in recent years.)

Much of the information which is today available about the lives
of Jews in the Middle East in medieval times is due to the
travels of Benjamin of Tudela, a rabbi from Tudela in Navarre
who compiled an account of his journeys in 1173: this consisted
of notes he had made during his wanderings, which had lasted
for thirteen years and were called *The Travels of Rabbi Benjamin*.
He described how, when the exilarch was received in audience
by the khalif, he drove through the streets of Baghdad, arrayed
in embroidered silk and wearing a white turban encrusted with
jewels, and flanked by an escort of horsemen. A herald marched
in front of the procession crying: 'Make way, make way, before
our lord, the son of David.'[31] When the exilarch appeared at
court, the khalif would rise and, after greeting him, would seat
him on a throne opposite his own, while the other princes present
would also rise to honour him.[32] Considerable influence was also
wielded by other Jewish leaders, such as the heads of the two
Jewish seats of learning at Nehardea, the main Jewish settlement
on the Euphrates, and at Pumbaditha, for these men were as
powerful as the Archbishops of Canterbury and of York in
medieval England.[33]

Benjamin, who visited Baghdad about 1170, also wrote of a
Gaon called Samuel ben Ali, who was known as Ibn ed-Dastur
and who could trace his ancestry back to the prophet Samuel. He
had no sons, but his daughter was extremely well versed in the
Bible and the Talmud. She gave scripture lessons through a
window of her house, and this arrangement allowed her to remain
modestly out of sight of the male students who gathered outside,
below the window, in order to receive her tuition. Samuel, who
ruled over the Jewish communities of the whole of Iraq and of
Damascus, was said by another Jewish traveller, Rabbi Petachia
of Ratisbon, to own about sixty slaves, but an Iraqi Jewish
historian who was himself descended from the exilarchs, thought
that this number may have been exaggerated and he described
how Rabbi Petachia had also written that Samuel lived in a
large mansion 'which is covered with tapestry; he, himself, is
clothed in garments adorned with gold.'[34]

The situation of the Jews remained excellent, and even after the siege of Baghdad, when the last Abbasid was captured and executed, the Jews did not come to any harm at the hands of the Mongols who had invaded Iraq in 1258 under the leadership of Hulaju Khan, a grandson of Jenghis Khan. The Mongol Khans employed members of a Jewish family as their physicians and wazeers, and a member of this family, Saad ed-Dawlah, whose father, grandfather and great-grandfather had all been attached to the Mongol court, was sent to Baghdad in 1284 by Arghun Khan, the grandson of the conqueror of the Abbasids, to assume the governorship of Baghdad. Subsequently, this Jewish ruler became chancellor of the empire and, in spite of the havoc created by the Mongols, he seems, by all accounts, to have been a capable administrator. In working to protect the interests of his master, however, he made many enemies among the people, who had no love for the Mongols.

Arghun Khan became ill, but although Saad, who was a physician, attempted to cure him, his efforts failed and the Mongol leader died. The downtrodden people of Baghdad then killed Saad and also avenged themselves on the other unfortunate Jews in the city, resulting in a great deal of bloodshed. Although subsequent Mongol rulers appointed Jews to high office, it appears that the Jewish community of Baghdad disintegrated in the fourteenth century, but Jews continued to prosper in other parts of Iraq.[35]

THE SO-CALLED GHETTOS

As we have seen, Judaism began, after the destruction of the First Temple, to segregate its adherents—this tendency became more marked in medieval times—because of the desire that Judaism should endure. Thus it was only natural that Jews should congregate in certain areas, especially as it was—and still is—forbidden for practising Jews to use any form of transport on the Sabbath so that, traditionally, Jewish congregations have always lived within walking distance of the synagogue.

The word 'ghetto', which is frequently used today to describe the Jewish quarters of Arab cities, in early times creates an entirely inaccurate impression because in Yemen, for example, the Jews lived in separate villages or quarters, and this separation, which has a long history, cannot be compared in any way with the ghetto of the European Jews. When the Arabs founded their cities, each tribe was given a quarter to itself, and the other sections of the population were also accommodated in accordance with their religion or nationality, in the same way as they had been in the cities of the East which were occupied by the Arabs at the time of their conquest. Therefore, as Professor Goitein emphasized: 'The fact of the existence of special Jewish or Christian quarters all over the Arab Muslim world had nothing humiliating in it.'[36]

The position was different in Yemen, however, because the Jewish quarters situated on the outskirts of Muslim towns were established as the result of religious persecution. The ancient Hebrew manuscripts which were written centuries ago in the Jewish villages, prove the antiquity of those villages.

At one time, the Jews lived in the towns but, in 1679, the Jews of central Yemen, which included the town of Sanaa, were expelled from the country although they had been living there for centuries. This was, wrote Goitein, 'an occurrence very common in Christian Europe but absolutely unheard of in Arab Islam.' A year or so later, however, the Jews were invited to return because their services as artisans and craftsmen were indispensable, but they were not permitted to go back to their former homes and they had to live outside the cities. Yet in spite of the reasons for their establishment, the Jewish quarters in Yemen were occupied by a contented Jewish population which was allowed to exercise autonomy in its own areas.

A large number of visitors to Yemen in the past have praised the cleanliness and beauty of the interiors of Jewish houses in the towns, although they have also mentioned that these dwellings appeared very modest from the outside. On the Sabbath, the Jews wore white garments and broad belts of various colours, and the women would bedeck themselves with their exquisite jewellery which the Jews designed and made and which was renowned throughout the Arab world for its intricacy and beauty. The Jews would gather in the courtyard of the synagogue to enjoy their day of leisure and to relax completely in congenial company.[37]

The so-called 'ghettos' of North Africa were inaugurated at the time of the Spanish Inquisition when the Jews had to flee from Christian Spain and were offered asylum in the Maghreb.

('Maghreb' is an Arabic word meaning 'Occident' and is traditionally used to describe all the countries to the west of the Nile
valley.) When the Spanish Jewish refugees arrived in Algeria,
Morocco and Tunisia, they were usually allocated living quarters
by the sultans, and these were generally situated near the royal
palaces. From these areas, the *mellahs* (Jewish quarters) gradually
evolved and within them were established the foundations of
Jewish life and community organizations which continued until
the arrival of the French in the nineteenth century. The Jews
were left in complete control of their *mellahs* in which they lived
as in miniature republics, enjoying a great deal of internal
autonomy, and they practised their religion, ran their communities and organized their judicial systems without interference from any outside source. Muslim law, wrote Professor
Chouraqui, 'was more explicit and more generous towards the
Jews in this respect than the legislation of Christian countries'.[38]

In an article entitled 'Distortions of a Textbook', which appeared in the right-wing Israeli newspaper *Yediot Aharonot*,[39]
Baruch Nadel, an Israeli journalist, has written that: 'A school
textbook by Dr S. Kirschenbaum, *Recent Jewish History*, has
lately caused a public uproar and contributed to emigration from
the country. The book has already been used for several years as
the main text on the subject by fifth and sixth form secondary
school students.'

The claims made by Dr Kirschenbaum that the Jews of Arab
countries were forced to live in ghettos in indescribably bad
conditions were vehemently contested by Jews from the Arab
countries, wrote Baruch Nadel who quoted Kirschenbaum's
statement that:

> The Jews lived in ghetto-like quarters in poor housing that did
> not meet hygienic requirements. They suffered from various
> diseases and plagues. In Morocco and Persia, these ghettos were
> known as 'Millah' and in Tunisia as 'Hara'. They earned their
> livelihood from primitive crafts and very small-scale retail
> trading (p. 162). The Jew [in Morocco] was forbidden to give his
> children any sort of general education. . . . The fate of the Jews
> in Syria and Iraq was similar [to that of their Moroccan breth-
> ren]. . . . There were no suitable conditions for independent
> Jewish development in Muslim countries. Political repression
> denied them any opportunity for economic activity and they

lived in poverty and misery. This is the reason why the Jews in
Muslim countries played no active role in Jewish history, and
were not allowed to participate in either Jewish social movements
or the Jewish renaissance movement. . . . [p. 165]

Quoting from a book entitled *Jewish Life in Morocco*, published by the Israel Museum, Mr Nadel wrote that in Morocco,
each town, each Jewish group and community had in its leadership members of the Jewish élite who were both educated and
influential and that, often, the rulers were served by Jewish advisers, physicians, translators, secretaries, diplomats and bankers.
Rich Jewish merchants benefited Morocco because of the way
in which they developed economic life, and many of them would
pay the levies for the poorer Jews.

Jews were not only outstanding poets and philosophers but
many were at the same time financial and shipping magnates or
diplomats. Massacres of Jews were rare in Morocco, and Muslims
worked in Jewish establishments, just as Jews worked in Muslim
institutions, while Muslim servants could be found in Jewish
houses.

The Jews were in charge of the royal mint and two Jews,
Mastra Mussa and, later, Joseph Valensa, were the most famous
of the king's personal doctors, while another Jew, Shmuel
Halash, signed the first treaty of friendship between Morocco
and a Christian country, Holland, and was appointed ambassador
to Amsterdam. He was the 'foreign minister' and personal adviser to four successive sultans. Mulay Rasheed, the first ruler of
the Alawi dynasty, had a Jewish confidant and treasurer, and the
Sultan Sidi Ben Abdallah liked the Jews to take part in every
commercial arrangement and, indeed, in all negotiations to be
conducted with European royal courts.

Baruch Nadel added that this situation differed greatly from
that portrayed by Dr Kirschenbaum who claimed that Jews 'had
to walk barefoot with their heads bent and step aside whenever
they encountered a Muslim, while the latter would insult and
beat them [Kirschenbaum, p. 162].' He also described how the
Israel Museum book made it clear that the situation from the
sixteenth to the nineteenth centuries, with the exception of
brief periods of power changes, was similar to that of the early
sixteenth century when the kings of the Saadi dynasty surrounded themselves with many Jews.

Nadel explained that 'Elharah' (and not 'Harah' as Dr Kirschenbaum had claimed), was not a 'Jewish ghetto' but the name of a normal Jewish quarter which had synagogues, spacious houses and workshops in addition to slum areas. Professor Ashtor wrote that it was the major aim of David Corcos to refute the widely held view that Moroccan Jewry had been suppressed and living in narrow ghettos for centuries and he emphasized that, in fact, the Jewish quarters of Morocco had been clean and spacious for centuries but had altered in character and became overcrowded and dirty at a relatively late period when, as a result of anarchy and insecurity, many Jews left their villages in the countryside and settled in the towns.[40] Nevertheless, this did not mean that the Jews were in any way being singled out because the general population—with the exception of the ruling élite—lived in appalling conditions.

Elsewhere, the situation of the Jews was excellent, even when they confined themselves to their own areas, such as the Harat al-Yahud (Quarter of the Jews) in Damascus. Menahem Hayyim, a Jewish visitor from Volterra, who travelled to Damascus in 1481, wrote that the city's four hundred Jewish families were 'all rich, honoured and merchants', and he added that the head of the community was a physician. Fifty years later another Jewish traveller, Obadiah of Bertinoro, wrote of the riches of the Jews of Damascus and of their beautiful houses and gardens.[41]

Jewish quarters in medieval times grew up around the synagogues which were the main centres of Jewish religion and culture, but there were no restrictions on Jewish social life in the Middle East, and the ghetto as 'a legalized institution' was totally unknown until the beginning of the fourteenth century in Europe. In fact, when Pope Paul IV established the ghetto in Rome in 1555, the Jews were already congregated in one particular area. In Spain, before the Inquisition, the ghetto was originally more of a privilege than a disability and the Jews sometimes insisted on it as a right when threats were made to demolish it.[42]

In 1412 all Jews and Moors (Muslims) had to live in separate enclosures and the ghetto, afterwards common all over Europe, was established, but it constituted no hardship for the Jews because it protected them. The gates of all ghettos were closed overnight in order to safeguard the Jews and they 'never complained of it.' Modern writers have misread history by imagining that there were grounds for complaint in what was a customary and commonplace factor of medieval life. According to Paragraph Seventy-six of the decisions of the Cortes of Toledo in 1480: 'As great injury and inconvenience results from the constant society of Jews and Moors being intermixed with Christians, we ordain and command that all Jews and Moors of every city, town and place in these our kingdoms . . . shall have their distinct Jewries and Moories by themselves, and not reside intermixed with Christians, nor have enclosures together with them.'

Thus the theory and practice of social ostracism began,[43] but the ghetto was an entirely European Christian innovation, and the Jewish quarters of Arab cities, irrespective of whether they were palatial or squalid, were certainly not ghettos in the European sense.

YEMEN AND ITS JEWISH KING

While legend has obscured the facts concerning Jewish settlement in Yemen, it appears to have taken place around the beginning of the second century, and it is said that the Jews were prosperous until the sixth century.[44] One story goes that a Jewish colony had been established in northern Arabia under the leadership of King David, while another declares that Jews had fled to northern Arabia after the destruction of the first Temple by Nebuchadnezzar. It was also claimed that the powerful kings of Judah had set sail, with their followers, across the Red Sea in order to establish centres in Yemen for trade with India,[45] and some Jews of Yemen maintained that their ancestors had arrived during the time of Solomon, while, according to the Jews of Sanaa, Jewish settlement there had begun forty-two years before the destruction of the first Temple. It was said that seventy-five thousand Jews had gone to Yemen with the prophet Jeremiah, and when Ezra instructed the Jews to return to Jerusalem and they refused to obey, he pronounced a ban on them which was to last for all time. According to legend the Jews then declined to bury Ezra in Palestine in order to punish him for his action, and for this reason, it is said, no Yemeni Jew ever called his child Ezra.[46]

When Abu-Kariba Asad-Toban, a king of Yemen who was

reputed to be valorous, intelligent and an accomplished poet,[47] became converted to Judaism, his new religion spread throughout the country, and the large number of foreign traders who travelled in Arabia brought the news to Jews everywhere that a Jewish kingdom had been established 'in the most beautiful and fertile region'.

Abu Kariba's younger son or grandson, Zurah Dhu-Nawas (520–30), took the Hebrew name of Yusef in addition to his Arabic name, and he was so committed to Judaism that he decided to avenge the discrimination suffered by Jews in the Byzantine Empire by ordering the arrest and execution of some Byzantine merchants who were travelling through Himyara on business. His action caused repercussions among the Christian traders in the area and, as a result, they stopped exporting spices. This led to a war, and Dhu-Nawas besieged the city of Najran which was inhabited by Christians. The king captured the city, and although some accounts say he behaved with great cruelty towards the vanquished Christians, others maintain that, while he did not show any great humanitarianism, his ruthlessness was greatly exaggerated by rumour-mongers who persuaded the Christians, including the king of Ethiopia, to attack Dhu-Nawas.

The king's capital, Zafora, his queen and his treasure were subsequently captured and the king threw himself, on his horse, from a cliff into the sea and was drowned in the year 530.[48]

THE JEWISH MOUNTAIN QUEEN

Kahena (or Kahiya) was a warrior-priestess who was chief of the Jerawara tribe in the eastern Aures mountains and, according to Arab historians, the members of this tribe adopted Judaism in the seventh century although later historians, while unanimously agreeing that the tribespeople were Jews, did not agree about their origins. Kahena became leader of the tribal resistance to the Arab forces in A.D. 687. Hassan ibn al Numan al-Ghassani, the Arab governor of Egypt, was leader of the Arab armies and, after he had destroyed Carthage, he asked who was the most powerful chieftain in Ifrikiya. He was told about Kahena, the Jewish woman who could foretell the future—it was said that all that she predicted unfailingly came to pass—and who ruled over the Berbers and lived in the Aures mountains.

Hassan was told that if she were killed, he would encounter no further resistance. He therefore marched against her forces and, according to the Arab historian Ibn Khaldun, he took up a position to the north of the Aures, on the banks of Al Meskyana River, in the year sixty-nine of the Hejira (A.D. 688). Kahena, at the head of her Berber troops, her strong camel-mounted forces and the remains of the Byzantine army, attacked and conquered the Arabs and expelled them from the Aures and Gabes areas so that they had to seek asylum in Tripolitania. Thus Kahena became queen of the Maghreb, but her kingdom lasted no more than five years for, as Ibn Khaldun pointed out: 'The Berbers deserted Kahena to make their submission to Hassan. The General took advantage of this fortunate occurrence and having succeeded in sowing dissension among the supporters of Kahena, he marched against those Berbers who still obeyed this woman, and put them to full flight. . . .'.

On the eve of the battle, Kahena had told her two sons that she had had a vision in which she had seen her severed head offered to the great Arab prince who was Hassan's ruler, and that she looked upon herself as already dead. Khaled, a young Arab warrior whom Kahena had adopted after he had attracted her attention at the battle on the Meskyana river, suggested that she should relinquish the country to the invaders, but she refused to countenance such capitulation. She was killed in the Aures mountains at a place which is still called Bir-el-Kahena (Kahena's Well), but there is no agreement among Arab historians as to the exact date of her death, some putting it at 693 or 698 and others at 701 or 703.

The Arab historians believe that Kahena's Berber kingdom may have collapsed because of the great cruelty of her reign. Among the folklore of the Constantine Jews is a ballad which seems to bear out this belief for it says:

> O! Sons of Yeshurun!
> Do not forget your persecutors
> The Chaldeans, Caesar, Hadrian and Kahiya—
> That accursed woman, more cruel than all the others together.
> She gave our virgins to her warriors,
> She washed her feet in the blood of our children.
> God created her to make us atone for our sins,
> But God hates those who make his people suffer.

Give me back my children
So that they can mourn me.
I left them
In the hands of Kahiya.[49]

Before she died, Kahena instructed her sons to yield to
Hassan and, after she had been conquered and killed, other
Berber tribes surrendered. The victorious Arabs treated them
honourably and invited them to join the Arab forces. According
to the account of Ibn Khaldun, Kahena's sons were put in charge
of the Jerawara and they controlled the Aures mountains. The
conscription of twelve thousand Berber horsemen took place,
wrote Al Bayan, another Arab historian, and they were commanded by Kahena's sons and instructed to conquer the remainder
of the country and to convert its inhabitants to Islam.

Another tribe which had adopted Judaism, the Nefusa, was
also conquered and converted to Islam, following a dispute in
695 when the Arab forces, travelling from Kairouan to Tripoli,
asked the Nefusa if they could use a narrow path, 'the width of a
turban', along the seashore, but the Nefusa refused and so a
battle took place and, while many Berbers were killed, the remainder became Muslims. This was the beginning of the practice
of the conquered becoming converts to Islam and it might not
have taken place so readily if the Berbers had not already become familiar with monotheism centuries before owing to the
influence of Judaism and of Christianity. However, although the
last Christian communities of the Berbers survived only to the
twelfth century, Judaism in North Africa retained the loyalty of
its proselytes until the present day.[50]

REFERENCES

1. S. Landshut, *Jewish Communities in the Muslim Countries of the
   Middle East: A Survey*, The Jewish Chronicle Ltd, London, 1950,
   p. 3.
2. André N. Chouraqui, *Between East and West: A History of the Jews
   of North Africa*, trans. Michael M. Bernet, The Jewish Publication
   Society of America, Philadelphia, 1968, p. 53.
3. E. Ashtor, Introduction in David Corcos, *Studies in the History of the
   Jews of Morocco*, Rubin Mass, Jerusalem, 1976, p. xv.
4. Landshut, *op. cit.*, pp. 1–5.

5. Roth, *op. cit.*, p. 149.
6. Graetz, *op. cit.*, Vol. II, p. 491.
7. Roth, *op. cit.*, p. 149.
8. George, E. Kirk, *A Short History of the Middle East: From the Rise of Islam to Modern Times*, Methuen, London, 1966, pp. 14–15.
9. Max L. Margolis and Alexander Marx, *A History of the Jewish People*, The Jewish Publication Society of America, Philadelphia, 1945, pp. 253–4.
10. Goitein, *op. cit.*, p. 65.
11. *Ibid.*, pp. 64–5.
12. Israel Abrahams, *Jewish Life in the Middle Ages*, ed. Cecil Roth, Edward Goldston, London, 1932, pp. 435–6.
13. Chouraqui, *op. cit.*, p. 44.
14. Graetz, *op. cit.*, Vol. II, pp. 488–9.
15. Landshut, *op. cit.*, pp. 1–5.
16. Roth, *op. cit.*, p. 150.
17. Hayyim J. Cohen, *The Jews of the Middle East: 1860–1972*, Halstead Press, John Wiley, New York, 1973, pp. 1–2.
18. Margolis and Marx, *op. cit.*, p. 254.
19. John Bagot Glubb, *Haroon al Rasheed and the Great Abbasids*, Hodder and Stoughton, London, 1976, p. 314.
20. A. H. Hourani, *Minorities in the Arab World*, Oxford University Press, London, 1947, pp. 17–18.
21. Roth, *op. cit.*, p. 150.
22. Landshut, *op. cit.*, p. 8.
23. *The Jewish Encyclopedia*, *op. cit.*, Vol. I, p. 39.
24. Landshut, *op. cit.*, pp. 8–9.
25. S. D. Goitein, *Letters of Medieval Jewish Traders*, Princeton University Press, Princeton, 1973, p. 4.
26. Goitein, *Jews and Arabs*, *op. cit.*, pp. 120–1.
27. Graetz, *op. cit.*, Vol. III, pp. 3–5.
28. *Maimonides Mishneh Torah, Hilkhoth Melakhim VIII 5*, cited by E. Neufeld, *Ancient Hebrew Marriage Laws: With Special Reference to General Semitic Laws and Customs*, Longmans Green, London, 1944, p. 216.
29. *Ibid.*, pp. 217–19.
30. *Sunday Times*, 15 June 1975.
31. Landshut, *op. cit.*, p. 9.
32. Roth, *op. cit.*, p. 151.
33. *Ibid.*, p. 129.
34. David Solomon Sassoon, *A History of the Jews in Baghdad*, Solomon D. Sassoon, Letchworth, 1949, pp. 63–4.
35. *Ibid.*, pp. 91–3.
36. Goitein, *Jews and Arabs*, *op. cit.*, p. 74.
37. *Ibid.*, pp. 74–6.
38. Chouraqui, *op. cit.*, pp. 95–6.
39. 23 July 1976.
40. Ashtor in Corcos, *op. cit.*, p. xvii.

41. *The Jewish Encyclopedia, op. cit.,* Vol. IV, pp. 417–18.
42. Abrahams, *op. cit.,* pp. 13–17.
43. *Ibid.,* pp. 79–82.
44. *The Jewish Encyclopedia, op. cit.,* Vol. XII, p. 592.
45. Graetz, *op. cit.,* Vol. II, p. 489.
46. *The Jewish Encyclopedia, op. cit.,* Vol. XII, p. 592.
47. Graetz, *op. cit.,* Vol. II, p. 489.
48. *Ibid.,* Vol. II, pp. 495–8.
49. Chouraqui, *op. cit.,* pp. 34–6.
50. *Ibid.,* pp. 36–7.

Three

The Spanish Jews

A GOLDEN AGE

BY the time the Arabs had conquered Spain in the eighth century, the most important Jewish communities had become Arabized; they spoke Arabic, their literature was in the Arabic language, and they adopted Arab names and Muslim customs and habits. The Jews gradually became prominent and successful in all spheres in Muslim Spain; they were powerful and influential figures at court and they were often astrologers and physicians.[1] One of the most outstanding of Spanish Jews was Hasdai, son of Isaac ibn-Shaprut of Jaen, who served under Abd ar-Rahman III (912–61) and his successor, Hakeem II (961–76), as both physician and inspector-general of customs.[2] He was entrusted with many secret and important negotiations, and it was in order to repay him for his services that the khalif had appointed him to the customs post in Cordova. He had become the khalif's confidant and adviser and he also acted as foreign minister. When the Holy Roman Emperor Otto I sent an embassy to Cordova in 956, Hasdai was entrusted with the task of negotiating with it, and the imperial ambassador, Abbot John of Gorz, said that in all his travels he had never come across an intellect to equal that of Hasdai.[3]

The khalifate was bordered on the north by several Christian kingdoms which frequently attacked the Arab territory. Ramiro II who was king of Leon (930–50) had subdued the Arab forces, but, after his death, civil war broke out in his kingdom concerning the succession. Hasdai and a Muslim colleague came to an agreement with Ordoño III, who was at loggerheads with his brother Sancho (955) and when, two years later, Ordoño died and Sancho succeeded him, he was overthrown by a plot against him.

The Byzantine emperor Romanus II (959–63) attempted to

ingratiate himself with the western khalif by lavish gifts which included a copy of a medical text in Greek by Dioscorides. At the request of his master, Hasdai asked Romanus to send a monk who had a knowledge of Greek and Latin to the khalif's court. While the monk read the Latin translation, Hasdai, assisted by Muslim scholars, prepared an Arabic text, to the delight of the court.

Hasdai's contacts with the Byzantine court caused him to begin a correspondence, of his own volition, with a Jewish monarch who was reigning in the land of the Khazars. Hasdai sent a reliable messenger, Isaac, son of Nathan, to Constantinople, on the first stage of his journey to the Khazar capital. The Byzantine officials, however, being unsure about the motives behind Hasdai's eagerness to communicate with the Khazar king, gave the emissary no assistance, and eventually he returned to Spain without having succeeded in his mission.

There were, however, two Jews in the embassy sent by Emperor Otto. Their names were Saul and Joseph and, when they learned of Hasdai's disappointment over his failure to establish contact with the Khazar monarch, they suggested that the letter should be taken through Germany to Hungary by Jews travelling in that area, and it could then be forwarded through Russia and Bulgaria to its destination. As it happened, the letter was delivered to the Khazar king by a German Jew called Isaac, son of Eliazar. The missive told of a change in the status of the Spanish Jews brought about by the coming of the Muslims, of the magnificence of the western khalif, and of Hasdai's position at court and his anxiety to learn as much as he could about the circumstances concerning the Jewish kingdom.[4]

The Khazars were people of Turkish origin, and their kingdom occupied most of South Russia.[5] The ruler had decided to adopt Judaism for political reasons, for if the Khazars had embraced Islam they would have become vassals of the khalifs, while if they had adopted Christianity the Roman Empire would have had some say over their spiritual destiny. Judaism, however, was a religion which was respected by both Christians and Muslims. Nevertheless, although the king's conversion to Judaism made him superior to the pagans and independent of both Christians and Muslims, he did not adopt Jewish intolerance and he allowed his people to continue to worship their idols.[6]

The letter which Hasdai wrote to Joseph, king of the Khazars, was sent from Cordova about the year 960; it sought news of the Khazar kingdom and also informed the king of the situation of the Jews in Spain. Hasdai ibn-Shaprut wrote in glowing terms about Abd ar-Rahman and his wise and enlightened rule, and he explained that kings of various countries who were aware of the magnificence and power of his ruler bestowed costly gifts on him in order to win his favour, and that all these gifts passed through the hands of Hasdai who was charged with the task of presenting gifts in return.[7]

Joseph's reply, written about the year 965, expressed his pleasure at having received Hasdai's letter, and he described how his ancestor, King Bulan (Bulan means 'the wise' in Turkish) was a wise man who had expelled all wizards and idolaters from the country and worshipped God alone. He had had a dream in which an angel appeared to him and told him that he should worship one God and, in return, he would be blessed and would multiply (Deuteronomy 7:13) and his kingdom would be established for ever.

According to the legendary account related by Joseph, the Byzantine and Muslim rulers sent envoys laden with many costly gifts, and, in addition, some wise men accompanied the delegations in order that they might convert the king, but he, being a wise man, sent for a learned Jew who brought representatives of the various religious groups together in order that they might have a discussion about the respective merits of their different creeds. However, each of them refuted the arguments of his opponents, so that they could not agree. The king therefore told them to go home.

Later, he assembled all his princes and ministers and his people, and he said: 'I ask you to choose for me the best and truest religion.' He asked the Christian priest: 'Of the religions of the Israelites and the Mohammedans, which is to be preferred?' The Christian priest answered: 'The religion of the Israelites.' He then asked the Mohammedan Qadi whether Christianity or Judaism was preferable and received the reply: 'The religion of the Israelites is preferable.' Thus the king chose to become converted to Judaism, and, according to Joseph's letter, 'Almighty God was his helper, and strengthened him, and he was circumcized, and all his servants.'[8]

Talmudic studies assumed a new importance in Spain under the patronage of Hasdai, and he sent to Babylon for a leading Talmudist, Moses, son of Enoch, to instruct the Jews of Spain. Unfortunately, the ship on which Moses and his wife and young son sailed was captured by Abd ar-Rahman's admiral, Ibn Rumahis. Fearing that she might be dishonoured, Moses' wife threw herself into the sea and was drowned; Moses and his son were captured and taken to Cordova where the Jewish community paid a ransom for them.

Moses began to preside over the first college of higher Jewish learning in Spain and his fame spread so widely that he attracted students from all over Spain and North Africa. There were considerable funds available to maintain Moses and his students in great style because the Jewish community included many rich families which attempted to outdo the Muslims in the opulence of their attire. Rich Jews wearing magnificent silk garments with turbans encrusted with precious stones on their heads could be seen riding in beautiful carriages or mounted on horseback in lordly fashion. The main source of their wealth was the trade in slaves, and they supplied the harams with inmates and also with eunuchs to guard them, while they also provided the army with recruits.[9]

When the Ummayad khalifate of Cordova collapsed and was divided up into various petty amirates, Arab civilization started to decline. Jewish culture, however, began at that time to enter a period of considerable glory and to expand. During the period from the beginning of the eleventh to the beginning of the thirteenth century, Jewish activities were immensely creative and invigorating. Although the academy at Pumbaditha in Iraq was still in existence and was presided over by its last head, the Gaon Hai, while the academy of Sura also existed, with the last Gaon, Samuel ben Hofni, in charge, Spain began to replace Iraq in terms of scholarship and Talmudic erudition.[10]

One of the most outstanding of Spanish Jews was Samuel ibn-Najdela, who was born in 993. He was a humble but well educated spice-seller whose little shop in Malaga was patronized by a favourite slave of the wazeer of King Habbus of Granada. The slave employed him to write her letters, as she was illiterate, and the scholarly tone of these so impressed the wazeer that he asked Samuel to become his secretary.

On his death-bed, the wazeer suggested to the king that
Samuel should succeed him. Soon, the Jew was ruling the kingdom.[11] His official title was 'Najid' (Prince), and he was the rabbi
of Granada and also head of the Jewish academy: he delivered
lectures on the Talmud to the students, pronounced on questions
of civil and ritual law and, as well as drawing up documents of
state, he also wrote dissertations and commentaries on the
Talmud.

He was in correspondence with all the great men of his
generation in Iraq, Syria, Egypt and Africa, and an Arab poet
sang of him (the Arabs called him Ishmael):

> If man could tell the true and false
> And could the difference understand,
> Instead of kissing Mecca's stone,
> They would, O Ishmael, kiss thy hand . . .[12]

Samuel had a large library and, each year, he supplied the
synagogues of Jerusalem with olive oil from his own plantations.
After the death of Habbus, Samuel continued to serve the king's
son, Badis, well and faithfully. On Samuel's death, he was
succeeded by his son, Joseph, both as the king's minister and as
head of the Jewish community. Joseph had been brought up like
a prince and had received an excellent Jewish education, but he
was ostenatious and overbearing. He lived in a marble palace and
when he rode beside Badis, he rivalled the king in magnificent
apparel. His arrogance and his tendency to advance his own
relatives or other co-religionists to public positions aroused the
envy of Berbers and Arabs.[13]

The people, goaded by a jealous poet, spread false rumours
about Joseph, and they accused him of many crimes in order to
rid themselves of him, for he completely dominated the king. On
a Sabbath, Joseph's palace was attacked; the minister hid himself
in a charcoal cellar where he blackened his face in an attempt at
disguise, but he was found, killed and fastened to a cross. The
people of Granada then began to massacre other Jews and loot
their property. The date was 30 December 1066, and nearly
four thousand Jews were killed.[14]

Jews remained unharmed in the rest of Spain, however, and
they continued to prosper and to produce scholarly works.
Gradually, the Christians began to advance into Muslim Spain—

Toledo surrendered in 1085 and was made the capital of Christian
Spain—but the Jews continued to enjoy all the advantages they
had received under Muslim rule. The last Muslim king was allowed to retire to Valencia; his closest companion was a Jew,
who remained faithful to him until his death although his own
tribesmen betrayed him. Nowhere in the world did Jews then
enjoy such equality as they did in the kingdom of Granada;
they occupied offices of state and also served in the army.[15]

The Muslim princes of Andalusia were dismayed by the fall of
Toledo and so they sought the assistance of Yusef ibn-Tashufin,
king of the Almoravids, a Berber tribe of North Africa which had
recently been converted to Islam and had established a vast
empire stretching from Senegal to Algiers. The Christians were
temporarily subdued and Jews fought in both armies, the
Christian and the Muslim.[16]

Judah (Abu al-Hassan), who was the son of Samuel ha-Levi,
was born in Toledo about 1086; he was a physician by profession and a poet by vocation. He was a great lover of the
Torah and he composed hundreds of hymns for the synagogue
as well as writing stirring, romantic, tender and religious poetry.
His most famous work is 'The Kuzari' which takes the form of
a dialogue between the king of the Khazars and a Jewish teacher
concerning the superiority of Judaism over other religions.[17]
Written in Arabic, the epic poem, like much of Judah's work,
described the superiority of the Jews over other peoples because
'The preservation of the Israelites in Egypt and in the wilderness,
the delivery to them of the Law on Mount Sinai, and their later
history are to him so many evident proofs of their superiority. . . .'[18]

Although Judah's beliefs were not typical of Jewish thought at
that period nor, indeed, during other eras, much emphasis is
based on his teachings at the present time. Thus we have the
complaint of a student, taking part in a discussion in Israel
about the contemporary education of university and high-school
students, who said: 'The most absurd thing is the study of "The
Kuzari". In the last year of school, they teach us, with the
utmost seriousness, this theological essay which speaks of the
superiority of the Jewish race and collective martyrdom.'[19]

At length, Judah decided to pay a visit to Palestine and set off
about 1141; his journey through Spain was like a triumphal pro-

C

cession. Cordova and Granada vied with each other to offer him presents and laudatory poems.[20] With a large supply of cash for the journey and accompanied by a band of close friends, he set sail for Egypt and, after a stormy passage, he arrived in Alexandria where he had planned to stay for a short time. At the insistence of the chief rabbi, Aaron Benzion ibn-Alamani, who was also a physician, a man of wealth and a poet, he stayed for three months, enjoying lavish hospitality. He then went to Fustat to visit the Jewish najid, Samuel, son of Hananiah Abu Manzur, and he also became friendly with Nathan, son of Samuel, the principal of the Jewish college at Fustat.

There are conflicting accounts of Judah's eventual end. According to *The Jewish Encyclopedia*, authentic records cease with a description of the poet, 'worn out, with broken heart and whitened hair, in Tyre and Damascus'. It was said that, as he approached Jerusalem, 'overpowered by the sight of the Holy City', he broke into song and intoned 'his most beautiful elegy, the celebrated "Zionide" '. At that instant, however, he was knocked down by an Arab on horseback who had dashed forth from a gate.[21] Another account has it that the poet was not only trodden under foot by the horseman but was also stabbed to death. The story which includes this legend relates that Judah was buried in Palestine and adds that the 'Zionide' is recited by Jews on the ninth of Ab, the day which commemorates the destruction of the Temple.[22]

Another outstanding Spanish Jew was Moses ben Maimon (usually referred to as Maimonides) who had been born in Cordova in 1135 and, after the city was captured by the Almohads, left with his family at the age of thirteen and went to Morocco, although he was eventually to settle in Egypt. His writings on medicine were of the utmost wisdom, but it was for his commentaries on Jewish theological works that he became renowned. Even before his arrival in Egypt, he had begun writing a brilliant Arabic exposition on certain aspects of Jewish teaching; but his greatest work, however, was a philosophical treatise on Judaism entitled 'Guide to the Perplexed'.[23]

THE EGYPTIAN CALIGULA

Many Spanish Jews settled in Egypt where they lived in peace and tranquillity and were renowned for their scholarship. There had, however, been one turbulent period during the reign of Hakeem (996–1021), whom Professor Graetz described as 'the crazy Egyptian khalif, a Mohammedan Caligula'; at this time all those who refused to believe that he was the incarnation of the divinity, irrespective of whether they were Muslims, Jews or Christians, were persecuted.[24]

One amusing story concerns a historian who believed that the Fatimid khalif's madness could have been averted if some rose oil had been poured into his nostrils to moisten his dehydrated brain. Yet Hakeem had personally saved two hundred Jews from the attack of fanatics who were about to massacre them in January 1012, before the onset of his madness. The Fatimid reign was one of the most magnificent periods in Egypt's history while its military strength depended on Berber troops from North Africa—the very people who had been responsible for the outrages of the Almohads—although the Fatimids were considered to be the most liberal rulers of the Middle East.

There is a great deal of information available about the clothes worn by Jews of that time, and this shows that the degrading regulations concerning the attire of non-Muslims were either not applied at all or else operated most leniently. It appears that ancient discriminatory laws against Christian and Jewish merchants were not enforced, and the Fatimid khalifs even contributed funds for the upkeep of the Academy of Jewish religious learning in Jerusalem. Thus it was nothing to do with the deviation from orthodox Islam or racial elements which governed the Islamic attitude towards non-Muslims, but the actual beliefs held by the particular sect.[25]

So at first Hakeem was praised for his excellent rule, but, as time went on, both Jews and Christians received their share of unjustified and irrational persecution. They were forced to wear black robes and, in the baths, the naked Christians had to wear large and heavy crosses while the Jews were forced to wear bells or, in the streets, a wooden image of a calf in order to remind them of a Biblical episode which they would have preferred to forget.[26] When Hakeem learned that the Jews were evading his decree by wearing golden calves as ornaments around their necks, he ordered them to wear wooden blocks weighing six pounds instead, as well as bells on their garments: later, he ordered the destruction of churches and synagogues and expelled the Christians and Jews from the country in 1014.[27] A factor which may have contributed to this decree was the discovery that the Jews were in the habit of gathering together and singing defamatory songs about Islam, as a result of which Hakeem ordered one night that the gates of the Jewish quarter should be closed and the place set on fire.[28]

As the kingdom of the Fatimids was very extensive at that time —it included Egypt, North Africa, Palestine and Syria—and as Hakeem had many followers in the khalifate of Baghdad too, there were not many places to which his persecuted subjects could go. Many Jews therefore pretended to embrace Islam, but the persecutions continued until the Muslims became disgusted with the activities of the mad khalif and strangled him in 1020.[29]

After the demise of the mentally unbalanced ruler, the Jews were treated well by his successors who appointed them as administrators, while the court banker and purveyor, Abraham (Abu Said) ben Sahl, who was wazeer to the sultan's mother, virtually ruled the country.[30]

REFUGEES

The persecution of Jews in Christian Spain began in Seville on Ash Wednesday, 1391. The violence spread

> . . . from the Pyrenees to the Straits of Gibraltar. In place after place, the entire community was exterminated. The synagogues, which had been the pride of Spanish Jewry, were turned into churches. . . . In the former kingdom of Valencia, not a single professing Jew was left alive. . . . Outbreaks were avoided only in Granada, the last surviving outpost of Muslim rule, and (thanks to the energetic measures taken by the sovereign) in Portugal. The total number of victims amounted, it is said, to upwards of seventy thousand souls.[31]

Spanish Jews poured into the Maghreb, and so many of them arrived in Morocco that there was overcrowding in the cities; this resulted in hostility among the Muslims, who feared that the price of commodities would be increased, and among the indigenous Jews who, having a hard struggle to earn a living, feared competition from the refugees. When the Inquisition spread to Portugal, still more Jews arrived in Morocco and, in spite of what they had suffered at the hands of the Portuguese, the Jews assisted their oppressors in the conquest of the seaport town of Saffee which, with its large Jewish population, had become an important trading centre.

Two years later, in 1510, the city was attacked by a large Muslim army, and a Portuguese Jew, Isaac Bencemero, went to the assistance of the besieged Portuguese with two ships, manned by Jews and fitted out by Jews entirely at their own expense. When King Sebastian and practically his entire army met their deaths in 1578, the few surviving noblemen were taken captive and sold to the Jews.[32]

When the Jews were expelled from Spain, a large number sought refuge in Algeria. According to an old chronicler, so many arrived at Oran that the local Arabs, on catching sight of their vessels, thought that an enemy invasion had started and they killed a number of Jews before they learned what was happening. The Muslim prince of the region then took pity on the Jews and allowed them to land. He had wooden cabins built on the outskirts of the city for them and for the cattle which they had brought with them. Because of what they had suffered at the hands of the Spaniards, the Algerian Jews held public celebrations on a number of occasions following Turkish victories over the Spaniards. Nevertheless, in 1566, Emperor Charles V despatched Jacob Cansino, a Jew from Oran, to act as his representative at the court of the Moroccan emperor and also to supervise the interests of Spanish subjects in Morocco.[33]

During the fourteenth and fifteenth centuries, Jews were not treated well in Tunisia and so, while their co-religionists were pouring into Algeria and Morocco from Spain and Portugal, few settled in Tunisia. After the Spanish occupation of the Tunisian coastal regions from 1535 until 1574, the Jewish communities of the seaport towns suffered greatly at the hands of the conquerors although, later, under Turkish rule, the condition of the Jews improved enormously.[34] In the thirteenth and fourteenth centuries, Jewish merchants in Algeria traded with Catalonia and other places while Tlemcen, which was the gateway to the Mediterranean and one of the stations on the Sudanese gold route—it was known as 'the Jewish road'—had a small and energetic Jewish community that traded with the rich Jewish merchants of

Barcelona, Valencia and other Spanish cities. Most of these merchants were North African, and the kings of Aragon singled them out for especially favourable treatment because their activities ensured the prosperity of the monarchs.

At that time Muslims were leaving the Spanish Christian kingdoms and settling in North Africa, and they were helped by the Jews in Spain, some of whom, like the great Spanish-Jewish North African Alatzar family, made considerable profit out of this activity because the Jewish merchants of central North Africa were active in the slave trade, although their main activity was concerned with trading in Sudanese gold.[35]

The Jews who left Spain in 1391 and settled in Algeria brought prosperity to remote areas of the country, for they exported ostrich feathers from Mzab and African gold from Tuat as well as rugs, burnooses, wool, pelts and cereals to Europe; they also sold European products to Africa and, at that time, the Jews owned estates, slaves and livestock. There were, however, certain problems for although the large numbers of Jews who arrived from Catalonia and the Balearic Islands were favourably received by the Muslim authorities, in particular by the Ziyanid princes, their relationship with the local Jews became difficult. The Algerian Jews had at first welcomed their Spanish co-religionists warmly, but later they became worried because of competition from the newcomers in various trades and professions. Differences in religious observance, language and social customs increased the tension between the two communities and 'the Sephardi (Spanish) Jews asserted themselves by their intellectual superiority, financial means, and their skills. The older community resisted the attempt of the newcomers to dominate communal life. . . .'[36]

We are told that the Sephardim

> . . . did not mingle with the lower classes. With their social equals, they associated freely, without regard to creed, and in the presence of their superiors they displayed neither shyness nor servility. They were received at the courts of sultans, kings and princes, and often were employed as ambassadors, envoys or agents.[37]

There was, however, little mixing with other Jews either. The Ashkenazim (European Jews)

... do not marry the daughters of Sephardic Jews who are denied to them, anyhow, as if they were of another race. Sephardic and Ashkenazic Jews do not eat at the same table; the former do not eat the meals prepared by the latter and vice versa because they consider the others' meats impure and they would therefore be committing a sin in indulging. Customs, prayers, liturgy, everything differentiates them. The Sephardic Jew looks haughtily down upon this poor, small Jew from the North. ... In his turn, the Ashkenazic Jew looks upon the Sephardic Jew with suspicion. He does not question his superiority but regards him as a kind of non-believer. ... After ten centuries of separation, these brethren ... have stopped acknowledging each other. ...[38]

The separation of Jews from non-Jews was also increasingly advocated. Joseph Caro, the last great codifier of rabbinical Judaism, who had been born in Spain or Portugal at the end of the fifteenth century, drew up the Shulkhan Arukh (Code of Daily Laws and Rituals) which contained hundreds of rules governing daily life and the consumption of food and drink. One rule, for example, decrees that: 'It is prohibited to drink coffee, chocolate or tea at the house of a non-Jew if a regular practice be made thereof', while another law declares that: 'An article of food that is not eaten in its natural state ... if cooked or roasted by a non-Jew, even in the utensils of an Israelite and in the house of an Israelite, it is yet forbidden food inasmuch as it is the cooking of a non-Jew.'[39]

REFERENCES

1. Roth, *op. cit.*, pp. 158–9.
2. Margolis and Marx, *op. cit.*, p. 308.
3. Roth, *op. cit.*, pp. 158–9.
4. Margolis and Marx, *op. cit.*, pp. 308–10.
5. *The Jewish Encyclopedia*, *op. cit.*, Vol. IV, p. 1.
6. Arthur Koestler, *The Thirteenth Tribe: The Khazar Empire and its Heritage*, *op. cit.*, p. 59.
7. Kobler, *op. cit.*, Vol. 1, pp. 98–101.
8. *Ibid.*, pp. 106–11.
9. Margolis and Marx, *op. cit.*, pp. 313–14.
10. Graetz, *op. cit.*, Vol. III, p. 132.
11. Roth, *op. cit.*, pp. 160–1.
12. Graetz, *op. cit.*, Vol. III, pp. 138–9.

13. Margolis and Marx, *op. cit.*, pp. 317–21.
14. *Ibid.*, p. 321.
15. Graetz, *op. cit.*, Vol. III, p. 139.
16. *Ibid.*, pp. 321–4.
17. *Ibid.*, pp. 327–8.
18. *The Jewish Encyclopedia, op. cit.*, Vol. VII, p. 351.
19. *Haaretz*, 20 and 22 October 1972.
20. Margolis and Marx, *op. cit.*, p. 330.
21. *The Jewish Encyclopedia, op. cit.*, Vol. VII, p. 347.
22. Margolis and Marx, *op. cit.*, pp. 330–1.
23. Roth, *op. cit.*, pp. 178–180.
24. Graetz, *op. cit.*, Vol. III, p. 129.
25. Goitein, *Jews and Arabs, op. cit.*, pp. 82–3.
26. Jacob Mann, *The Jews in Egypt and in Palestine Under the Fatimid Caliphs: A Contribution to their Political and Communal History*, based chiefly on Genizah material hitherto unpublished, Oxford University Press, London, 1920, Vol. 1, pp. 32–3.
27. Graetz, *op. cit.*, Vol. III, p. 130.
28. Mann, *op. cit.*, p. 33.
29. Graetz, *op. cit.*, Vol. III, p. 266.
30. Roth, *op. cit.*, pp. 178.
31. *Ibid.*, p. 238.
32. *The Jewish Encyclopedia, op. cit.*, Vol. IX, pp. 18–21.
33. *Ibid.*, Vol. 1, p. 382.
34. *Ibid.*, Vol. XII, pp. 272–4.
35. *Encyclopedia Judaica*, Keter Publishing House, Jerusalem, 1971, Vol. II, col. 612.
36. *Ibid.*, Vol. II, col. 614.
37. *The Jewish Encyclopedia, op. cit.*, Vol. XI, p. 197.
38. Joseph Nehama, *Histoire des Israélites de Salonique, La Communauté Sefardite, Période d'Installation (1492–1536)*, Tome 11, pp. 39–41. Cited in Mair Jose Benardette, *Hispanic Culture and Character of the Sephardic Jews*, Hispanic Institute in the United States, New York, 1953, pp. 64–5.
39. *Laws and Customs of Israel: Compiled from the Codes Chayye Adam and Kizzur Shulkhan Arukh*, trans. Gerald Friedlander, P. Vallentine, London, 1915, Vol. 1, Rules 2 and 5, pp. 72–3.

Four

The Maghreb

TUNISIA

JEWISH settlement in North Africa had, of course, taken place long before the time of the Inquisition, and it was, in fact, said to have begun even earlier than the destruction of the Temple. The Berber Jews of the Atlas and Rif mountains claimed to be the descendants of settlers who had arrived at the time of Solomon.[1]

In the year 788, when the Imam Idrees proclaimed that Mauritania was independent of the khalifate of Baghdad, the Jews joined Idrees's army under the command of their leader, Benjamin ben Joshaphat ben Abiezer, but they soon abandoned the struggle because they were reluctant to fight their fellow-Jews from other parts of Mauritania, who had chosen to serve under the khalifate. They were also annoyed by some indignities committed by Idrees against Jewesses. The Jews in the cities were attacked by Idrees and defeated. According to the peace terms, the Jews were required to pay a capitation tax and also to provide a certain (unspecified) number of virgins annually for Idrees's haram. The Jewish tribe of Ubaid Allah left their homes rather than agree to the Imam's demands, and the story goes that the Jews of Djerba are the descendants of this tribe.

Idrees was poisoned in 793 on the instructions of Haroon ar-Rasheed, and it was believed that the murder was committed by the governor's physician, Shamma, who was said to be a Jew.

The Jews in Tunisia prospered until the end of the dynasty in 909. Bizerta had a Jewish governor and Jews played a leading role in the political life of the country, while in the twelfth century they were permitted to settle in a special quarter of Tunis which was known as the 'Hira', but in 1270, because of the defeat of St Louis of France, who had engaged in a crusade against Tunisia, the cities of Kairouan and Hammat were declared holy, and non-Muslims either had to become converted to Islam or to leave the cities. From then until the conquest of Tunisia by France in 1757, Jews and Christians were forbidden to pass a night in either of these cities, and they were only allowed to enter them during the day by special permission of the governor.[2]

The situation of the Tunisian Jews improved greatly from the beginning of the eighteenth century as a result of the efforts of the European powers which worked to alleviate the hardships of the Christian community and which therefore felt obliged to speak up on behalf of the Jews as well because, of course, according to Islamic legislation, they were classified along with Christians.[3] In 1814 M. Noah, the United States consul to Tunis, wrote an account of the position of Tunisian Jews, as follows:

> With all the apparent oppression, the Jews are the leading men; they are in Barbary the principal mechanics, they are at the head of the custom-house, they farm the revenues; the exportation of various articles, and the monopoly of various merchandise, are secured to them by purchase, they control the mint and regulate the coinage of money, they keep the Bey's jewels and valuable articles, and are his treasurers, secretaries and interpreters; the little known of arts, science and medicine is confined to the Jews. . . . If a Jew commits a crime, if the punishment affects his life, these people, so national, always purchase his pardon; the disgrace of one affects the whole community; they are ever in the presence of the Bey, every minister has two or three Jewish agents, and when they unite to attain an object, it cannot be prevented. These people, then, whatever may be said of their oppression, possess a very controlling influence, their friendship is worthy of being preserved by public functionaries, and their opposition to be dreaded.[4]

The Jews were extremely prosperous throughout the reign of Ahmad Bey; and his successor, Muhammad Bey, who came to power in 1855, abolished the restrictions which had been imposed on the Jews,[5] but he issued a decree on 15 November 1856, that a tribunal should be set up 'to promulgate the law and to regulate religious affairs'. Batto Sfaz, a Jew who had been accused of 'uttering blasphemies against Islam' was brought before the tribunal and condemned to death. In spite of cash given to the judges, representations to the Bey by foreign rulers and the pleas of the princesses and other dignitaries Batto Sfaz was executed. Jews and Christians in Tunisia sent a joint delegation to Napoleon III to ask him to protect non-Muslims living in Tunisia because they no longer had any feelings of security. Europeans who were living in the country sought the reimposition of the Edict of Gulhane—according to which Abdul Medjid the Sultan of Turkey, had 'in 1830 abolished all discrimination among his subjects and guaranteed their equality without distinction of race and religion'—but the Bey refused to agree. When a large French naval squadron arrived, however, the ruler changed his mind and reverted to his former liberal attitude.[6]

Muhammad Bey issued a Constitution which declared that all Tunisians, irrespective of creed, were to enjoy equal rights. Article Four further affirmed that: 'No manner of duress will be imposed upon our Jewish subjects forcing them to change their faith, and they will not be hindered in the free observance of their religious rites. Their synagogues will be respected, and protected from insult', while Article Six declared that: 'When a criminal court is to pronounce the penalty incurred by a Jew, Jewish assessors shall be attached to the said court.'[7]

In 1863, the Alliance Israelite Universelle, which had been established in Paris in 1861, set up a committee in Tunisia. The Alliance has done sterling work in North Africa and in the Middle East in the fields of Jewish rights and education, and it continues to operate in these spheres. In 1877, the committee succeeded in having the Governor of Tunis prohibited from administering the bastinado to Jews although it was applied indiscriminately to all inhabitants. When Tunisia was ravaged by epidemics and famine (which claimed a third of the Jewish community) in 1866, 1867 and 1868, the Alliance and the Board of Deputies of British Jews in London raised money for the victims.

Hundreds of Tunisian Jews were found, in 1897, to be under the protection of various European powers and, in 1898, the Bar Association of Tunis supported the demand of Jews to be placed under the jurisdiction of French courts where they would be judged, as they were in Algeria, according to Jewish law. The Tunisian Jews sent a petition to Paris which said: 'We beseech Parliament to make us subject to the jurisdiction of the French courts which alone can give us impartial justice. . . .' However, despite the requests of the Tunisian Jews that they should be given French nationality, not one Jew was granted French citizenship between 1891 and 1910[8] although, between 1911 and the end of the Protectorate, 7,311 Jews were granted French nationality in Tunisia and they, with their descendants, eventually comprised one-third of the Jewish population of Tunisia.[9]

MOROCCO

Morocco which, in antiquity, formed a considerable part of Mauritania, was said to have been settled by Jewish colonists even before the destruction of the first Temple. One account describes how Jews in the Atlas region claimed that their ancestors left Jerusalem before its destruction and that they never went as exiles to Babylon; this story is supported, to some extent, by Hebrew inscriptions in the province of Fez.[10]

The Jews of the Maghreb lived in peace during the Almoravid dynasty but, when it was overthrown by the Almohads in 1146, they were persecuted,[11] and, although they suffered considerably, they might be said to have been 'privileged' in one sense for the Jews were the only *dhimmis* (protected people) allowed to remain in the whole of North Africa, as the indigenous Christian inhabitants had been virtually eliminated by the middle of the twelfth century during the Almohad persecutions.[12]

Because of a fanciful belief of the first Almohad, which had absolutely no basis in Muslim teaching, he pretended that Muhammad had allowed the Jews to practise their religion freely for no more than five hundred years, and he claimed that if, at the end of that period, the Messiah had not arrived, it was ordained that the Jews must be forcibly converted to Islam. His successors took similar measures so that the Jews either emigrated to the east or became Muslims. As the Almohads were not sure of the sincerity of the converts, they ordered them to wear special clothes so that they could be identified among other Muslims. Later dynasties, however, which shared the Maghreb among themselves after the downfall of the Almohads, treated the Jews with much more tolerance.[13]

It should, however, be realized that the Almohads were not only non-orthodox Muslims but also mainly non-Arabs; they were largely Berbers, who comprised the indigenous population of North Africa, and, in fact, the Almohads attempted to use the

Berber language instead of Arabic to put forward their ideas. Thus the Almohad persecutions, although ostensibly Islamic, were typical of neither Islamic nor Arab practice.[14]

Later persecution of Jews in Morocco was not typical of the Arab countries either and, indeed, some of it took place at periods when Jews were especially favoured in certain spheres. For example, in 1610, Shmuel al-Farrashi, a Jew, was appointed as Morocco's ambassador to the Netherlands and, from that time until 1828, a number of Jews served as Moroccan ambassadors in various European countries. In the eighteenth century, however, a traveller described the Jews in the following terms:

> The Jews possess neither lands nor gardens, nor can they enjoy their fruits in tranquillity. They must wear only black, and are obliged when they pass near mosques, or through streets in which there are sanctuaries, to walk barefoot. The lowest among the Moors imagines he has a right to ill-treat a Jew, nor dares the latter defend himself, because the Quran and the judges are always in favour of the Mohammedan. Notwithstanding this state of oppression, the Jews have many advantages over the Moors; they better understand the spirit of trade; they act as agents and brokers, and they profit by their own cunning and by the ignorance of the Moors. In their commercial bargains many of them buy up the commodities of the country to sell again. . . . More industrious and artful, and better informed than the Moors, the Jews are employed by the emperor in receiving the customs, in coining money and in all affairs and intercourse which the monarch has with the European merchants, as well as in all his negotiations with the various European governments.[15]

The Jewish Encyclopedia has pointed out that, although the nineteenth century brought emancipation to the Jews of most countries, those in Morocco were affected by the war with France in 1844 and the conflict with Spain in 1853 when many Jewish houses in Tetuan were looted and, although most of the Jews escaped by flight, four hundred were killed.[16]

In 1863, Sir Moses Montefiore, President of the Board of Deputies of British Jews, received an urgent request for help from the Moroccan Jews because nine or ten Jews had been imprisoned in Saffee on suspicion of having killed a Spaniard. Two others had already been executed at the instigation of the Spanish consul although they were said to be innocent.[17]

In spite of the fact that he was seventy-nine years of age, Sir Moses made the journey to Morocco and succeeded in having the imprisoned Jews released. He was twice received with great pomp and ceremony by the sultan, from whom he managed to obtain a decree, dated 5 February 1864, which declared: 'Every man has, in our eyes, an equal right to demand justice', although, as Professor Chouraqui has written, 'which justice and from whom, it did not stipulate. . . .'[18]

In December 1862, fifty years before the French Protectorate was established, the Alliance Israelite Universelle opened its first school in Tetuan and, by 1901, the Alliance was running eight groups of schools in Morocco while, by the time the French arrived, there were almost four and a half thousand pupils in the schools. Morocco was so isolated, however, that conditions were much worse than in Algeria or Tunisia, and the reports of the directors of the schools described, in graphic detail, their battle against the misery, filth and poverty of the *mellahs*. Children had to be washed, clothed and encouraged to study, but the schools also had to deal with the contrasting phenomenon of the daughters of rich Jewish families in Marrakesh arriving at school arrayed in gaudy, brightly coloured clothes, bedecked with the family jewels and sporting enormous feather hats especially ordered from Tangiers.[19]

The Jewish Encyclopedia tells us that:

> A change of ruler in Morocco has always meant a time of great danger to the Jews. . . . Many wholesale murders and plunderings of the Jews have followed upon their support of an unsuccessful pretender to the throne or upon some other lack of political foresight. An equally decisive influence in the passive character of the history of the Moroccan Jews is exerted by the conflagrations, famines and epidemics which claim their numerous victims in every decade, and against which the inhabitants, waiting in fatalistic inactivity, have not yet thought of opposing organized preventive measures. In Fez alone, 65,000 persons succumbed during the latest visitation of the plague, in 1799.[20]

At these times of catastrophe, Jews and Muslims would march through the streets together, entreating God to spare their lives, while barren women of both religions would visit the sanctuary of a Jewish saint in the mountains of Ashron in order to pray that they might conceive.[21]

The reign of Mulay abd ar-Rahman (1822–59) and his successors saw an increased activity by the Jews in the economic and diplomatic spheres. Many Jews, including 'the families of Altaras, Benchimol and Abensur, played important roles in Moroccan affairs. Until 1875, consular representation in the Moroccan towns was almost entirely the province of Jewish merchants, and many of them held such posts until the twentieth century.'

The *Encyclopedia Judaica* goes on to explain that the European powers granted protection to a large number of Moroccan Jews in order to safeguard their economic interests and, by frequently exploiting the defence of their protégés as a pretext, they interfered with the internal affairs of Morocco. Thus a Jewish consular agent, Victor Darmon, was executed in 1844 on a trumped-up charge, and this became one of the causes of the war with Spain in 1860.[22]

Many of the troubles which beset the Jews, including that which had received the intervention of Sir Moses Montefiore, arose because the Moroccan people 'accused the Jews of being the agents of European influence in Morocco'. In some of the Berber areas, the situation of the Jews became quite precarious. Measures which even went beyond the restrictions of Muslim law were imposed against the Jewish masses of the interior, which were more vulnerable than those living on the coasts.[23]

During the reign of Mulay al-Hassan and at the commencement of the rule of Mulay Abd-al-Aziz (1894–1908) the Jews lived in peace and tranquillity because the former treated them well and the Jews, in their turn, deeply respected the ruler. When he died, the wazeer, Ba Ahmad, was kind and considerate to the Jews and, throughout the nineteenth century, there were many famous rabbis, poets, talmudical scholars and legal authorities. When Ba Ahmad died in 1900, however, there was a plague epidemic which ravaged the entire country and, in the *mellah* of Fez alone, there were more than three thousand victims. Morocco then embarked on a period of extreme turbulence and, from the middle to the end of the nineteenth century, large numbers of poverty-stricken Jews flooded into the Jewish quarters of large cities, so that the overcrowding became indescribable. Indeed, the misery which existed in the Jewish quarters and which was partly due to the inability of the exvillagers to adapt themselves to urban life, became one of the social stains of Morocco.[24]

When the French Protectorate was established in Morocco on 30 March 1912, it was followed by a dreadful massacre in Fez on 17 and 18 April when sixty Jews were killed, about fifty were seriously injured and women were raped before being murdered; the entire *mellah* was sacked and a third of it burnt to the ground, so that ten thousand people were left homeless.[25]

Theoretically, at least, the situation of the Moroccan Jews improved under French rule but, in fact, the Jewish community became a wedge between Europeans on the one hand, and Muslims on the other, while it did not actually belong to either group. In typical colonialist fashion, the French encouraged, right from the beginning, the different religious groups to develop separately instead of instituting a policy of integration, so that the accord between Jews and Muslims which had existed for twelve centuries was upset.[26] Although the Jews performed an important function as a link between the French and the Muslims, they discovered, at the end of fifty years, that they had become alienated from both groups.[27]

The Jewish community's committees were supervised by a Jewish government official who had been appointed because of his pro-French attitude, and, according to the *Encyclopedia Judaica*, this strict control demonstrated the lack of trust of the French authorities although, in fact, few Jews felt any political hostility to France.

The members of the Jewish committees were generally pro-French and belonged to a new middle class which had arisen in Morocco, but the upper-class Jews from the old families, had, on the whole, nothing to do with these committees, composed, as they were, of members of a class which was becoming superficially westernized. The children of the Jewish aristocracy were sent to French schools and they received religious instruction from private tutors, whereas the changes wrought in the new class by the Alliance Israelite Universelle caused many of them to abandon orthodox Judaism, but their complete integration among the colonizers was prevented by the anti-Jewish views of the middle-class Frenchmen of North Africa.[28]

ALGERIA

Under Arab rule, the situation of the Algerian Jews was what that of 'the People of the Book' (Ahl al Kitab) has always been in Islamic countries. Although the Jews had to pay the poll-tax (*jizyah*), the régime was relatively tolerant, and they freely practised their religion.[29]

While the situation of the Jews was miserable, it was worse under Turkish rule—which commenced in 1519—than during Arab domination, but it is necessary to distinguish between the Leghorn or Frankish Jews who had settled in Algeria and the native-born Jews, because the Turks treated the native Jews abominably. They were required to wear skullcaps, grey burnooses and shoes without heels, while the women had to don caftans and were forbidden to cover their faces with veils as the Muslim women did. The Jews were also forbidden to ride horses as these were reserved for Muslims only and yet, in spite of the discrimination shown by the Turkish rulers, the Jews and the Arabs among whom they lived got along well together and, in fact, certain illustrious rabbis were venerated by Muslim Arabs as well as by Jews, and members of both religious groups would make pilgrimages to the tombs of these rabbis who were looked upon as saints by Jews and Muslims alike.[30]

The rabbis were exempted from the poll-tax which was levied on all non-Muslims, and so were the foreign Jewish merchants because they paid customs dues on their imports: they were in a more privileged position than the native Jews in other ways, too, for they had their own quarter, synagogue and even a cemetery; they also dressed differently from the local Jews and wore berets or hoods instead of the turbans of the Algerian Jews. The system of administering the Jewish communities, which was established in the fourteenth century and lasted until 1830, included the appointment of heads of the Jewish communities by the Muslim authorities. Each of these dignitaries had a prison and police at his disposal for punishing wrong-doers, and he also appointed officers who collected charitable donations and administered the synagogues and charitable institutions. In spite of the presence of rabbinical courts, however, Algerian Jews increasingly chose to litigate in the Muslim civil courts and, in an attempt to discourage this practice, the rabbis threatened—and, in some cases, carried out their threat—to excommunicate those who had spurned the Jewish courts.[31]

Many Jews were appointed by the Christian kings of Spain as their ambassadors to the Muslim courts, and four Jewish ambassadors visited Tlemcen in 1286. Jewish-Muslim relations were generally good, although it had been said that the loss of Granada by the Muslims in 1492 had had repercussions on the Jews in Algeria. Nevertheless, when outbursts of fanaticism caused local persecutions, the mosques, though closed to non-Muslims, would be used as a refuge for the Jews, and the Islamic religious leaders sometimes helped the Jews. Once, for example, the Muslim holy man of Blida, south-west of Algiers, stopped an attack on the Jews and forced the perpetrators to return goods they had looted.[32]

On the whole, the position of the Jews in the south was better than that of Jews in the areas governed by Turkish rulers who had come to exploit the country, and who treated the natives, both Muslims and Jews, badly. Most Jews were at their mercy, but, on the other hand, the rulers favoured the upper-class Jews, from among whom they chose their counsellors, physicians, financiers and diplomats. These Jewish envoys were entrusted with the delicate task of maintaining diplomatic relations with the European powers, which could not have been easy as European ships were occasionally attacked by pirates whose actions were condoned by the Algerian rulers. The rich and powerful Jews from Leghorn were, in the main, those who were appointed to high office, but they sometimes suffered because of the jealousy of the janissaries (army units in the service of the Turkish régime), who resented the privileged position of the Jews. However, the assassination in 1805 of the Dey's chief aide, the powerful Naphtali Busnach, was followed by the only massacre of Jews to take place in Algiers.[33]

The Busnach family had, in 1723, established a company in Algiers and, in association with the Bakri family, ran a consortium which conducted the major portion of Algeria's foreign trade.[34] After Naphtali Busnach was shot by a janissary on the threshold of the Dey's palace, there followed a pillage of the Jewish quarter, and fourteen Jews who were praying in the Sarfaty synagogue were murdered and the synagogue was des-

ecrated: altogether, forty-two Jews were killed and a large
number injured during the massacre which followed. Two
hundred Jews sought refuge in the home of the French consul,
and later a hundred Jewish families fled to Tunis and two
hundred to Livorno.

The following year, three hundred Jews were killed by the
janissaries, and then, when the Dey of Oran was defeated by
Omar Agha in 1813, the Dey's Jewish mistress was murdered
along with her five sons, while in 1818 the Dey of Constantine,
a self-indulgent, licentious man who had surrounded himself
with a group of Jewish followers, was defeated by Ahmad al-
Mameluke. The victor decided to revenge himself on the Jewish
community because of their support for the Dey, Kara Mustafa,
so seventeen young Jewish girls were kidnapped in Constantine
and given to the Dey of Algiers. However, Hussein, the Dey's
successor, eventually released them.[35]

Although the Jews of Algeria had fought with the Muslims
against the Spaniards in 1541 and 1775, they fought against the
Muslims in 1830, and the pleasure of the Jews at the French invasion greatly annoyed the Turks.[36] It was, in fact, because of the
huge amounts of money owed by the French government to the
Bakri and Busnach family firm, which had been delivering grain
to the French since the end of the eighteenth century, that
incidents occurred which triggered off events leading to the
French conquest of Algiers in 1830.[37]

The Dey attempted to settle the debt of several million francs
and, on 30 April 1827, a meeting took place between the Dey and
the French consul who agreed that his government would pay the
debt on certain conditions which caused the Dey to fly into a
rage; he struck the consul with his fly whisk, and it was this
occurrence which originated events that led to the French occupation of Algeria. Bakri and Duran, another Jewish leader,
offered their services to the French forces, and the Jews in the
streets knelt down and kissed the hands and feet of the French
invaders; in 1833, when Oran was besieged, the Jews fought
alongside the French to defend the city.[38]

When the government of Louis-Philippe sent a commission of
enquiry to Algeria in 1833, Aaron Moatti, the head of the Jewish
community, explained that the Jews would gladly accept the
civil and economic laws of France provided that these did not

conflict with Jewish law, but the commission viewed the rabbinical courts with disfavour because they were considered to employ methods even more degrading than those used in Islamic courts. From 1834, the Jews were free to use the French courts for all civil and commercial litigation and, in 1857, the former way of life of Jews in Algeria ended, and Algerian Jewry became completely assimilated to French Jewry.[39] The Algerian Jews asked for full French citizenship after the fall of the French monarchy in 1848, and this idea had probably first occurred to Adolphe Cremieux, the republic's minister of justice and himself a Jew, in 1843 when he was a member of the commission which had been established in 1833. On 14 November 1858, the Jews became entitled to elect one Jewish councillor for each province. They also looked upon the compulsory military service for which they became eligible two years later as a signal honour and a mark of confidence and esteem on the part of the French authorities.

On 24 October 1870, after twenty-seven years, Cremieux achieved his goal because, according to Article Seven of the Cremieux Decree: 'The Jews indigenous to the departments of Algeria are declared citizens of France.'

Unhappily, however, as a result of the new status of the Jews who had, from the time of the French conquest, been adopting with great enthusiasm the language, habits and culture of the French colonizers, there was a wave of anti-Jewish manifestations because the different religious groups, instead of developing in harmony, became even more rigidly separated. Socialist voters fought to have the Cremieux Decree repealed because the Jews generally supported right-wing parties.

Like most colonists, the French adopted a 'divide and rule' policy for, by stirring up hatred and suspicion among various religious and ethnic groups, they greatly minimized the risk of a strong and united opposition to their régime. Political differences caused unbridgeable gulfs between Europeans, Muslims and Jews, although with time and goodwill these might so easily have been overcome. There were various manifestations of anti-Jewish feeling in the press, on the streets and elsewhere, and Jews were sometimes attacked.

Abraham Meyer, a leading Jew in the town of Ain-Temouchent, who had a great sense of humour, called together the many

Muslims who worked on his land and taught them the most vicious anti-Jewish slogans. He then marched at the head of a procession of them through the streets, yelling these insults.

The anti-Jewish party, which had been responsible for the acts against Jews, was defeated and disappeared in 1902 when conditions improved for the Jews because the Muslims of Algeria refused to support anti-Jewish actions, to the disappointment of the agitators. In the words of Chouraqui: 'This phenomenon is a telling proof that the assertions regarding the so-called axiomatic hatred of the Muslims for the Jews were utterly unfounded.'[40]

REFERENCES

1. *The Jewish Encyclopedia, op. cit.*, Vol. IX, p. 18.
2. *Ibid.*, Vol. XII, pp. 272–3.
3. *Ibid.*, Vol. XII, p. 274.
4. M. Noah, *Travels in Europe and Africa*, New York, 1819, p. 306.
5. *The Jewish Encyclopedia, op. cit.*, Vol. XII, p. 274.
6. Chouraqui, *op. cit.*, pp. 159–60.
7. *The Jewish Encyclopedia, op. cit.*, Vol. XII, p. 274.
8. Chouraqui, *op. cit.*, pp. 163–8.
9. *Ibid.*, p. 170.
10. *The Jewish Encyclopedia, op. cit.*, Vol. IX, p. 20.
11. *Ibid.*, Vol. I, pp. 381–2.
12. David Littman, 'Jews under Muslim Rule in the late Nineteenth Century', *The Wiener Library Bulletin*, Vol. XXVIII, Series 35/36, 1975, p. 65.
13. *The Jewish Encyclopedia, op. cit.*, Vol. I, p. 382.
14. Goitein, *Jews and Arabs, op. cit.*, p. 81.
15. *The Jewish Encyclopedia, op. cit.*, Vol. IX, pp. 23–4.
16. *Ibid.*, Vol. IX, p. 24.
17. *Ibid.*, Vol. IX, p. 24.
18. Chouraqui, *op. cit.*, p. 173.
19. *Bulletin de l'Alliance Israélite Universelle*, 1901, p. 78, cited in Chouraqui, *op. cit.*, p. 212.
20. *The Jewish Encyclopedia, op. cit.*, Vol. IX, p. 25.
21. *Ibid.*, Vol. IX, p. 25.
22. *Encyclopedia Judaica, op. cit.*, Vol. XII, col. 339.
23. *Ibid.*, Vol. XII, col. 339.
24. *Ibid.*, Vol. XII, col. 340.
25. Chouraqui, *op. cit.*, p. 173.
26. *Ibid.*, p. 174.
27. *Ibid.*, p. 178.
28. *Encyclopedia Judaica, op. cit.*, Vol. XII, col. 341.

29. *The Jewish Encyclopedia, op. cit.*, Vol. I, p. 381.
30. *Ibid.*, Vol. I, pp. 383–4.
31. *Encyclopedia Judaica, op. cit.*, Vol. II, col. 614.
32. *Ibid.*, Vol. II, cols. 612–15.
33. *Ibid.*, Vol. II, col. 615.
34. Chouraqui, *op. cit.*, p. 141.
35. *Ibid.*, pp. 115–16.
36. *Ibid.*, p. 141.
37. *Encyclopedia Judaica, op. cit.*, Vol. II, col. 615.
38. Chouraqui, *op. cit.*, pp. 141–3.
39. *Ibid.*, pp. 144–6.
40. *Ibid.*, pp. 152–3.

Five

The Ottoman Era

IRAQ

DURING the period when the Turks ruled over most Middle Eastern countries from 1517 until 1839, the Jews were, as has already been described, given the status of second-class citizens, along with other non-Muslims, and they were required to pay the poll-tax. In contemporary accounts the impression is invariably given that it was only non-Muslims who were taxed, but in fact Muslims paid *zakat*, the poor tax, as well as *sadaqa* which was voluntary alms-giving.

The Jews were not oppressed by either the rulers or the religious functionaries, and the sultans made sure that the local governors protected the Jews and saw that they came to no harm from occasional provocations and from robbery and injuries sometimes inflicted by the janissaries on both Jews and non-Jews. They were also protected by the rulers against the frequent blood-libels (see p. 93) of this period, in which groups of Armenians and Greek Christians were settled.

Jews were often found in positions of importance as, for example, when, at the end of the eighteenth century, there were Jewish bankers and advisers to the district governors of Baghdad and Basra, and members of the Farhi family were appointed ministers of finance to the district governors of Damascus and Aleppo at the beginning of the nineteenth century.[1]

The Jews of Basra, a beautiful city surrounded by date forests in the south of Iraq, used to tell the story of how Karim Khan, the wazeer of the Shah of Persia, besieged Basra with the Persian armies in the year 1774, at a time when the Wali of Basra was Sulaiman Pasha, a great friend of the Jews, and Jacob ben Aaron was the Nasi (leader of the Jewish community). Eventually the gates of the city were opened, and the Persian troops entered Basra and embarked upon an orgy of looting,

robbery and rape. Persian rule was established, and many of the
leading citizens were imprisoned and their money taken from
them. Sulaiman Pasha, his family and members of his household,
together with Jacob ben Aaron and his wife and children were all
sent as prisoners to the Shah in Shiraz. Many of the Jewish
women burnt themselves to death rather than fall into the hands
of the Persians. Meanwhile, the Arabs attacked Karim Khan's
forces and defeated them, and the wazeer returned to Basra
where he gathered another huge army and attacked the Arabs
once more, but he was again defeated and large numbers of his
men perished, some of them in the rivers in which they had been
fighting. The Persian leader wanted to attack for a third time,
but his troops poisoned him and he died in 1775.

When the Shah heard of his wazeer's death, he ordered the
remaining troops to return secretly to Persia, and there was soon
not one Persian remaining in the city. The Jews rejoiced and
made a pledge to commemorate this day, which they called Yom
Ha-Nes, each year for evermore. Their rabbi composed songs
for them and these were sung at the annual festival.

The city of Baghdad also had its Yom Ha-Nes, when it commemorated the downfall of the Persians in the year 1638, and one
of the songs composed for the occasion became a traditional
Baghdad wedding-song which was preserved in a book of Arabic
folk-songs.[2] In fact, the Jews were the musicians of Iraq and
through the ages they composed and performed the most popular
music of the country. The Baghdad song was sung by women
accompanied by women musicians and they would sing before
the bridal couple. The song commemorated the persecution of
the inhabitants of Baghdad by the Persians who caused famine,
injustice and ill-treatment to become widespread in the city.

No one had been prepared to make the journey to Constantinople to report the situation in Baghdad to the sultan until a Jew
volunteered to act as messenger. He disguised himself as a
Muslim and pretended to be lame; and when he arrived at
Yildiz he attempted to enter, but the gate-keepers turned him
away. After persisting for some time, he was shown into the
presence of Sultan Murad IV and his ministers who treated him
in a friendly fashion, whereupon he delivered the letter from
Baghdad and described the state of siege existing in the city.

The sultan summoned his army and marched on Baghdad and,

arriving at the gates of the city, he stopped at the house of a
Jewish woman where he asked for food and lodging. Looking for
an omen, he decided that if the woman brought whole bread he
would defeat his enemies, but if she brought broken bread he
would be defeated. The woman brought whole loaves of bread
and the sultan drove the Persians from Baghdad.[3]

A great deal of the information which has come down to us
about the lives of Jews in the Middle East in past centuries has
been gathered by intrepid Jewish travellers like Benjamin of
Tudela who could not have found their journeys particularly
easy or comfortable in the conditions of those times. One of the
most interesting accounts is that of Rabbi David D'Beth Hillel
whose tour lasted from 1824 until 1832. It seems that he was of
Eastern European origin because he was in the habit of comparing the climatic conditions with those of Poland or Russia.

He described Baghdad as a very large town, with an area containing the palace of the ruler, the custom-house and the most
important buildings, and in this district, he wrote, the nobility,
the Jews and the Christians lived. There were, he added, about
six thousand Jewish families who had five large synagogues, and
some of the Jews were powerful merchants and very rich, while
the ruler's chancellor was a Jew who ruled over the other Jews
and they referred to him as 'The King of Israel'. He was em-
powered to punish the other Jews by fining them or having them
caned, as he wished, 'even when not lawful'. A hundred years
previously this office, which had been passed from father to son
in ancient times, began to be won in competition with other
Jews, and this resulted in money being paid for the honour and
even in Jews having their competitors killed or discredited. Thus
while the rabbi was staying in Baghdad (he spent about a year
there) two Jewish leaders were murdered by their competitors
who then took office.[4]

The rabbi described his visit to the sepulchre of the prophet
Ezekiel, which was situated on the banks of a tributary of the
Euphrates and which had built over it 'a fine house surrounded
by many other houses for the benefit of the people who come to
visit the place'. In the room containing the sepulchre was an
intricately worked wooden box 'about three English yards' in
length, two yards in width and two yards in height, covered with
a woollen cloth and surmounted, at the corners, with standards

embellished with carved pomegranates. The people told the rabbi
that Ezekiel was buried in this box, and he learned that in
ancient times much land was given to the sheikh who had been
appointed by the Jews in Baghdad.

The place where Ezra was said to be buried was also visited
by Rabbi David who described how a very high tower, with its
top painted green, had been built over the tomb, and it was
situated in a large courtyard, 'having many houses for the
benefit of the people who come to visit there'. There was also a
large box which was said to contain Ezra's remains, and nearby
was the village called Qurnah which was bounded by the Tigris
one one side and the Euphrates on the other.[5]

From Baghdad, Rabbi David made his way to Sulaimaniya in
Kurdistan, a seven days' journey at that time, and he wrote that
there were about one hundred Jewish families there who had a
very fine synagogue, and that most of the Jews were merchants or
craftsmen. The ruler's chancellor was a Jew and he was also the
head of the Jewish community.

Another part of Kurdistan visited by the rabbi was Urfa which
he described as Ur of the Chaldees (Genesis 11:28); the town
was built in a valley beneath a huge mountain in which was a
very large cave that was said to have been the supreme court of
King Nimrod. In the middle of the town is the place where, it
was believed, Abraham had been born, and if anyone who had
been guilty of murder sought refuge there, he had to be pardoned
for not even the ruler himself could punish him. Nearby there
was a large tank built of white marble and containing many
fish; this was said to be the place into which King Nimrod
caused Abraham to be thrown so that he could be burnt and
which was changed by God into a tank, which was why the
Muslims would not permit anyone to fish in the tank as they said
that the fish belonged to Abraham and were holy. If anyone was
found fishing in the tank, he was put to death; but the Christians
would go to the tank at night to wash their clothes after they had
dyed them, and they would secretly catch the fish and hide them
in the clothes and carry them home.

Food in the town was plentiful and cheap, and the wine and
water were both good while the climate was 'cold and whole-
some'. There were about forty Jewish families, some of them
rich; they had two synagogues, and practically all their trade was

conducted with Bedouins who lived outside the town in tents.
In one village, there were about forty families of rich, native
Jews who spoke Arabic and had a small synagogue, and in
another, Rabbi David found a custom-house with a Jewish
collector who was also the chancellor of the village sheikh;
and in Sitiya, a large plain containing about twenty villages in
some of which were Jews and synagogues, he saw places with
Hebrew names, such as Tel Yakub, meaning Mount of Jacob,
but the Jews seemed to know little of the Hebrew language or
Jewish customs and, in fact, there was no discernible difference
between them and their Arab neighbours except that 'they are
separate by eating, customs, and marriage; therefore I conceive
that they must be some of the lost Ten Tribes.'

In Mosul, which the rabbi also described as 'Assyria', there
were about six hundred families of native Jews; some of them
very rich merchants although the majority were workmen, and
they had a beautiful synagogue; in a large village called Sandor
were found about a hundred Jewish families who were all
farmers and they had 'an abundance of cattle, and most of them
are very rich. . . . This place is indeed a land flowing with milk
and honey.' Another village, called Sukho, situated in a valley,
contained about thirty Jewish families and a synagogue although
it was a small village. Rabbi David wrote: 'They are all farmers
and rich, having abundance of flocks. They have also a multitude
of fine, white cedar trees, which are planted round the village,
and with these they supply Assyria and Baghdad. Indeed, it is a
very rich and pleasant place.'

In Amadiya, there were about two hundred Jews, some of
whom were rich merchants, some workmen and some owners of
cattle. They had two fine synagogues and they spoke the same
language and had the same customs as the Jews in Zakhou, a
town to which, claimed the rabbi, the Jews were carried at the
time of their first captivity. He found six hundred Jewish
families there and he discovered that the town chancellor was a
Jew who was the head of the Jewish community. Some of the
Jews were very rich and owned much cattle, while others were
'weavers, goldsmiths and other artificers'. We learn that:

They have a very ancient and large synagogue, built of large,
hewn stones situated on the banks of the river. There are many

ancient manuscripts, which I have examined and find they are not different [from] ours, except in the form of some of the letters. . . . They are ignorant both of the Hebrew language and customs. . . . Their marriage ceremonies and other customs are after the manner mentioned in the ancient histories; therefore, I conceive that they must be some of the lost Ten Tribes. . . . There are Nazarenes [Christians] who follow the same customs and have the same language.

As further proof of his theory that the Jews of Kurdistan were members of the lost Ten Tribes, Rabbi David described his visit to the village of Shush in which were Jewish inhabitants using the same language and customs as those at Amadiya, and he pointed out that in ancient histories it was said that at the time of the captivity of the Jews by the king of Assyria, they settled in a place called Shush because they considered it similar to Palestine. He went on to explain that in his opinion the Jews he had met must be the descendants of the exiles, for in addition to the name of the place, which he felt confirmed the fact, there was also the language which was known as Lishna Yahudiyah (Aramaic) and was very similar to Hebrew and was even spoken by the Christians in the countries to which the Jews had been taken as captives. In addition, they celebrated weddings, circumcisions and festivals according to the ancient rites.[6]

From 1839 onwards, the position of Jews in the Ottoman Empire—and this, of course, included Iraq—improved, and they were granted equal rights with other citizens and ceased to pay the poll-tax, paying instead, a collective tax which exempted them from military service, although this was abolished in 1909 when Jews became obliged, like all other citizens of the Empire, to serve in the army. The Chief Rabbi of Baghdad was appointed by the Sultan of Turkey and, in 1876, when the first parliament was convened, the Jews of Baghdad were represented by one member.

Some Jews received civil service appointments and others were chosen to serve on district and municipal councils and in the courts, but many young people who wanted to enter officers' training schools were unable to do so. Nevertheless, the Jews felt secure, and so some of them began leaving the Jewish quarters of Baghdad and moving to mixed neighbourhoods and even to cities and villages where no Jews had previously lived.

Until 1914, the only governor who had shown any hostility to the Jews had been Mustafa Asim, who ruled in 1889, the year that a plague broke out in Baghdad. In order to prevent the spread of infection, the governor forbade the Jews to leave Baghdad (but we are not told whether he also forbade non-Jews to leave the city), and when Rabbi Abdallah Somekh contracted the plague and died, the Jews decided to bury him near the grave of Joshua, who is said to be buried outside Baghdad. As a result of this action, the governor became angry and dismissed four Jewish judges from office and arrested a number of Jewish notables. He was, however, removed from office that year as a result of British intervention.

During this period and until 1914, there was only one case of an attack on Jews in Baghdad and this was in 1908 after the Young Turks had seized power. The Baghdad Jews openly proclaimed their joy and this provoked a reaction from a Muslim group opposing the revolution. On 15 October 1908, they attacked the Jews in the city for several hours until some Muslim notables intervened to stop them.[7]

SYRIA

During the sixteenth century, the Jewish populations of Damascus and Aleppo increased through the number of exiles from Spain who settled in those cities, and it was owing to the arrival of the Spanish Jews that many *yeshivas* (religious seminaries) were opened. At the beginning of the seventeenth century, Jews emigrated from Palestine to Syria in order to study the Torah with Rabbi Hayyim Vital. Both Damascus and Aleppo were important centres for European and Far Eastern trade, and some of the leading merchants were Jews who, like the rest of their coreligionists, lived a secure and peaceful existence. There were, it is said, robberies and murders, 'but these were carried out by gangs of thieves who used to attack city-dwellers, irrespective of whether they were Jews or non-Jews.'

In the eighteenth and nineteenth centuries, however, when Greek Christians began to settle in Syria, the Jews encountered difficulties because some of the Greeks not only competed with the Jews commercially but even succeeded in ousting them from their positions as well as spreading blood-libels against them.[8]

The most famous of these was known as the Damascus Affair which took place in 1840 when the Jews of Damascus were accused of ritual murder. At that time, Syria was ruled by Muhammad Ali, pasha of Egypt, who had rebelled against the authority of the sultan of Turkey, while the governor of Damascus was an Egyptian Arab, who was called Shareef Pasha.

On 5 February 1840 Father Thomas, a Sardinian who was the superior of a Franciscan convent in Damascus, disappeared, along with his servant. The monk, who was a physician, was well-known among the Christians, Jews and Muslims of Damascus, and a few days earlier he had had an argument with a Turkish muleteer who had allegedly heard him make a blasphemous remark about Muhammad. The Turk was reported to have said: 'That dog of a Christian shall die by my hand.'[9]

Ratti Menton, an Italian-born French subject, who was the French consul in Damascus, was asked by the monks to enquire into the disappearance of Father Thomas. Ratti Menton had a dreadful reputation for, besides being dishonest and a fortune-hunter, he was heartless and a Jew-hater. Because some Jews had innocently said that they had seen Thomas in the Jewish quarter (nearly twenty thousand Jews lived in Damascus at that time), Ratti Menton concentrated his investigations on the Jews and refused to make enquiries in any other areas, in spite of the evidence concerning the muleteer. Shareef Pasha, anxious not to offend the French consul, was quite prepared to agree with Ratti Menton's findings, and a man was found who was prepared to perjure himself by stating positively that Thomas and his servant had been murdered in a certain house in the Jewish quarter.

The Jews were said to have killed Thomas and his servant 'in order to use their blood for the Passover celebration'.[10] This 'blood-libel', which has occurred at intervals throughout history when jealous and unscrupulous individuals have sought a scapegoat for the evils arising from their own tyrannical and reactionary behaviour, testifies to nothing so much as the ignorance and stupidity of the accusers when they claimed that human blood was used in the baking of *matzos* (unleavened bread) for Passover.

Of all the calumnies against the Jews, this is the most wicked and patently untrue, for blood of any kind is prohibited in the Jewish diet while the thought of human sacrifice is too monstrous to contemplate. It is true that we are told that '. . . ye shall offer a burnt offering unto the Lord; two young bullocks, and one ram, seven he-lambs of the first year without blemish . . . and fine flour for a meal offering, mingled with oil . . .' (Numbers 28: 11–15), but 'The blood found in eggs is forbidden and occasionally it is prohibited to eat the entire egg on account thereof. . . .'[11] while we are also told that: 'If one bite a piece of bread (or anything else) and if blood from his gums should come upon the bread, he must cut off the part where the blood is and throw it away. . . .'[12] Another Jewish law instructs that: 'Before the meat is salted [meat is always salted to remove the blood], it must be thoroughly washed in water. All the meat should be soaked and entirely submerged in water for half an hour. Where-ever a particle of blood is visible, it should be thoroughly washed off. This applies also to fowls. . . .'[13] There are a further twenty-six rules explaining in the minutest detail how to remove blood from meat before it is cooked. One of these rules says: 'A God-fearing woman will personally supervise the washing of the meat, for her servant may sometimes stint with the water and thereby blood may be there contrary to the law. . . .'[14]

But, we must return to Damascus, where several Jews had been arrested and taken before Ratti Menton who had caused a poor Jewish barber to be tortured so severely that he implicated seven of the richest and most prominent Jews, one of whom was an old man of eighty. In spite of their protestations that they were innocent, the Jews were tortured; they were made to stand for thirty-six hours without food, drink or sleep, but they refused to make false confessions.

Then Shareef Pasha ordered that more than sixty children, be-tween the ages of three and ten, should be taken from their parents by force, locked in a room and deprived of food and drink so that their mothers would be forced, by their cries, to confess, but this had no effect either.

On 18 February Shareef Pasha and his soldiers went to the Harat al-Yahud and demolished the beautiful mansion of a rich Jew. A young Jew appeared before the pasha and testified that he had seen Father Thomas going into a Turkish shop shortly before he vanished, but the young man was beaten so ruthlessly that he died that night.

Ratti Menton then purported to find a piece of bone and a rag, and he maintained that these offered conclusive proof that the Jews had murdered the monk because, he said, the bone was a human one and the rag was part of a monk's cowl. The seven accused Jews were subjected to renewed tortures during which the elderly Joseph Laniado died. The others, finally seeking the relief of death, confessed, but the French consul then demanded the bottle containing the monk's blood and the Jews were tortured once more. They withdrew their confessions, and so other Jews, including three rabbis, were arrested and tortured. The Austrian consul, Merlato, protested against these barbarities, and the Christian mob yelled abuse at him while the Muslim population was skilfully incited against the Jews.

Ratti Menton arranged to have Lucio Ferrajo's anti-Jewish book (*Pompta Bibliotheca*) translated into Arabic, for it claimed that it had been proved by the Talmud that Jews used blood in their rituals and that they slaughtered Christian children. The Arabic translation was circulated among the Muslims, and the pasha then ordered the rabbis to translate into Arabic passages from the Talmud which imputed the doctrine of ritual murder with the threat of death if they were not accurate in their translations.

At the same time, a ten-year-old Greek boy hanged himself on the island of Rhodes, which also belonged to Turkey, and the Christians accused the Jews of murdering the child. As a result of the two cases, there was much anti-Jewish feeling in Syria and Turkey, while in Beirut the Jews were saved from physical harm by the intervention of the Dutch and Prussian consuls.

Graetz has written that it took a long time, in both Damascus and Rhodes, for the truth to come out, 'because fiendish European Christians wilfully spread such a network of lies on the subject that even fair-minded people were deceived.' Ratti Menton's own version of the Damascus Affair was published in French newspapers, which were controlled by the Catholic clergy, and by the liberal press also because they wanted to enhance the power of France in the Middle East.[15]

On the same day, Adolphe Cremieux approached King Louis-Philippe of France and a deputation of English Jews called on Lord Palmerston, the British Foreign Secretary, to ask France and Britain to intercede on behalf of the Jews of Damascus. Louise-Philippe was evasive, but Lord Palmerston offered protection in the name of Queen Victoria herself.

As a result of European intervention, the Jews in Rhodes were exonerated, but the Damascus matter was not settled so easily. It was eventually decided that Sir Moses Montefiore and Adolphe Cremieux, accompanied by a retinue of distinguished Jews, should go to see Muhammad Ali in Egypt. Queen Victoria received Sir Moses in audience before his departure, and she placed at his disposal a naval vessel to take him across the Channel.

Montefiore met Muhammad Ali in Cairo on 6 August and asked for permission to travel to Damascus, but the pasha procrastinated and the Jews had to wait for three weeks until Cremieux evolved a plan which entailed approaching all the European consuls and asking those who would agree to present a petition demanding the release of the Damascus Jews.

Nine consuls signed the document, but the French refused, and, in order to make it appear that he had not given way to foreign pressure, Muhammad Ali sent an order to Damascus for the release of the prisoners. Shareef Pasha then released the nine Jews who were still in prison, but seven of them had been maimed by the tortures they had undergone, while four others had died. In Damascus, 'It became evident on this occasion that prominent Muslims had from the very beginning conceived a horror of the Christianity represented by Ratti Menton and the monks, for they displayed a deep sympathy for the Jews.'[16]

The head of the Jewish community in Damascus, wrote Rabbi David, was Muallim Moses Farhi who was very rich, charitable and kind, and he 'ruled over' the whole of Damascus and the surrounding countries because, although there was a pasha in residence, Muallim Moses was in charge of the government. The rabbi described how, about six years before his visit to Damascus, a Greek called Iskandar, who was chief secretary to Muallim Moses Farhi, wrote 'evil reports' about his master to the ruler, Sultan Mahmoud, who had the Jew imprisoned but released him on payment of a fine of two and a half million piasters. Muallim Moses felt insecure in Damascus as a result of his imprisonment and so he left and settled in Baghdad, while Iskandar became converted to Islam, married the daughter of the Mufti and took the place of his former master, in the government.

Later, however, there was an uprising against the Greek

D

because he had not paid the expenses necessary for the caravan which went regularly from Damascus to Mecca and which had always previously been financed by Muallim Moses. After some months, the princes and population of Damascus, as well as the 'priests of the caravan' wrote to the sultan and begged him to recall Muallim Moses, which the sultan agreed to do.

The Jew returned to Damascus with his nephew and was reinstated in his post, 'more honoured than before', while Iskandar was executed.[17]

On his journey to Damascus, Rabbi David passed through Beirut where there were about fifteen families of 'native' Jews (he described the indigenous Jews thus throughout his travels in order to differentiate between them and the immigrant, foreign Jews), and he explained that they had 'a neat little synagogue' which had its own large garden containing lime and citron trees.[18] There were about two hundred Jewish families in Damascus who spoke Arabic and they had three beautiful synagogues; some of the Jews were wealthy merchants and others dyers and weavers of the silk fabric manufactured in Damascus. The rich people's houses had interiors which were painted in silver and gold, and almost every house had a fountain of spring water, while the courtyards were paved with large slabs of marble in different colours such as white, black, blue and yellow, and the houses were surrounded by flower-filled gardens.[19]

In *The Jewish Encyclopedia*, there is a photograph of an old Jewish mansion in Damascus. As is customary, the house is built around a central courtyard which has paved walks, lawns and trees, and the house is very large, beautifully kept and ornately decorated.[20] In fact, several of these old Jewish houses still exist in the Harat al Yahud in Damascus, where the local Muslims refer to them as 'the Jewish palaces': they all have central courtyards, generally with fountains, marble floors, beautifully wrought antique brass lamps, much delicate carving and an air of extreme luxury.

Although the situation of the Jews in Damascus was, on the whole, excellent—with the exception, of course, of outrages such as those which have been described—it appears that the ancient law which prohibited non-Muslims from riding horses was still enforced, for Rabbi David reported that no one who was not a Muslim 'dare appear mounted in the town. . . . Even

Muallim Moses, with all his authority, cannot be seen mounted in the town, nor can anyone pass in European dress. . . .'[21]

Non-Muslims were not allowed to appear on the streets on the day when the annual caravan left from Damascus to make the journey to Mecca and Madina. All the shops and markets were closed, and the camels in the caravan were draped 'with fine coloured silk garments and with cashmere shawls' and wore golden crowns. Music was played and the procession, which usually took place on a Friday, was watched from the windows of the houses by non-Muslims. The caravan passed through a place which the rabbi described as 'a wilderness' in which the Tribe of Dan dwelt in tents, although the residence of their king was surrounded by a wall. All the Muslims who passed the headquarters of this tribe had to pay a tribute of one sequin and, if they refused, the entire caravan was robbed. The Arabs called this tribe Yahud al-Khaibar ('Jews of Khaibar') and members of the tribe sometimes visited Cairo and Alexandria in disguise to acquaint themselves with Jewish customs. It was the rabbi's opinion that they had left Palestine one hundred and fifty years before the destruction of Jerusalem by Nebuchadnezzar and, he added, this was confirmed in a book which had been written by a member of this tribe who went to Egypt and from there to Spain about six hundred years previously and had published his book, which Rabbi David had read, in Hebrew.[22]

Rabbi David explained that he had been told by the Jews that the city of Aleppo got its name (Halab) 'because our forefather Abraham used to feed his flocks around it, and here he used to milk them, milk being called in Hebrew *halav*.'[23] This story is common among Arabs too, and, of course, the Arabic word for milk is *haleeb*.

We are told by the rabbi that European, Persian and Indian merchants imported goods from their own countries to Aleppo and that there were about six hundred families of both native and European Jews and that many of them were 'very learned and kind people', while a large number were 'rich and great merchants'. They had a huge synagogue which was said to have been built by King David, and it consisted of hewn stones of marble, with twenty-six white marble pillars and a pulpit of white marble. The synagogue was so large that prayers and manuscripts would be read in two opposite parts of it, and in the middle was a small cave which, according to the local Jews, was one of the places where the prophet Elias used to appear. In the synagogue courtyard there were the graves of many Jews who had lived in ancient times, and oil was always kept burning over their tombs.

The consuls of various European kings also resided in Aleppo and most of them were Italian Jewish members of the Picciotto family who each had a small synagogue in his house. The British agent, however, was a Christian.[24]

EGYPT

After the Turkish sultan, Saleem I, defeated the last of the Mamelukes on 22 January 1517, he changed the status of the Jews and abolished the office of *najid*, making each community independent; he appointed a Jew, Abraham de Castro, to be master of the mint.[25] Following the French conquest of Egypt in September 1798, Napoleon Bonaparte issued a decree which proclaimed that all citizens were to have equal rights. There were at that time between six and seven thousand Jews in Egypt and many of them worked for the French as translators and tax-collectors, as did many Copts as well; these non-Muslims were allowed to sell wine, an innovation which led to rioting against non-Muslim minorities in Cairo in October 1798. The contemporary Egyptian historian, Abd ar-Rahman al-Jabarti, described how the masses turned on the Christians and Jews because some of them were employed by the French and they had 'become insufferable' and carried weapons and rode on horses. If they had not sought refuge in the Cairo fortress they would have been massacred, but apart from this episode the situation of the Jews improved considerably that year, although it deteriorated when French rule ended in 1801, and the Jews suffered at the hands of the Muslims who oppressed them because they considered them to be collaborators with the French. They had to pay poll-tax, once more as did all the inhabitants of the Ottoman Empire in those days.

However, when Muhammad Ali, an officer from Albania, seized power in 1805, his efforts to improve the Egyptian economy were aided by local Jews and Copts as well as by experts from Europe, and several of the Jews and Copts became important bankers and industrialists. During the forty-four years of his rule, European immigrants, including some Jews, settled in Egypt, but the majority of Egyptian Jews were poor and illiterate although there were some rich members of the community. Muhammad Ali established civil courts, and he curbed the powers of the religious ones so that Jews could appear before civil courts where their testimony against Muslims would be accepted.[26]

Jewish travellers of the nineteenth century reported that in addition to the Jewish communities of cities like Cairo and Alexandria there were small Jewish communities in many towns and villages, and Alexandria had a special Sephardic synagogue for Italian Jews as well as another synagogue for the indigenous Jews and a third for Jews from Eastern Europe, who numbered about fifty. The Jews in Cairo lived in an area called Darb al Yahudi, and although the streets were narrow, the houses were large, and the Jews were rich and mainly involved in banking.[27]

The two main Jewish communities—those in Alexandria and Cairo—developed considerably in the nineteenth century. Many individual Jews became prosperous, and a large number of communal establishments were founded. Well-equipped hospitals, schools, charitable institutions, sports clubs and social centres sprang up. The Egyptian Jews belonged to three classes. The highest consisted of a considerable number of extremely rich Jewish families who played a prominent part in the life of the country because of their wealth, their status in society, their personal connections and their commercial links with powerful Muslim and Copt landowners and politicians. Among these Jews were some who had been given the title of 'Pasha'. Below this group was a large number of very rich businessmen who were bankers or involved in the stock exchange, import-export, the cotton trade, the press and other commercial activities. In addition there were, in every important Egyptian city, many Jewish lawyers, doctors and shopkeepers while, at the other end of the scale, were the poorer Jews who were mainly peddlars, small traders or craftsmen, such as silversmiths and coppersmiths. Most of these Jews were descendants of the original settlers in the country, and the majority of the upper- and middle-class Jews were of Spanish, Italian or other foreign origin. The poor

Jews spoke Arabic and the rich ones spoke French. The use of the French language was indicative of a trend towards the culture of France and of Western Europe generally among the Jewish and other non-Muslim inhabitants of Egypt; and it caused a change in their way of life which tended to be rather superficial, and also, consequently, in their attitude towards the country in which they lived and its people. This trend was accentuated by the influx of many European Jews which had its effect on the situation of the Egyptian Jews because about thirty thousand—almost half of the total number—were foreign nationals even though many of them had never visited the countries whose nationality they held.[28]

Occasionally, in the nineteenth century, there were ritual murder accusations made against the Jews in Egypt which, although they fortunately did not have such serious repercussions as the Damascus Affair of 1840, were unpleasant. In most cases, a Greek mob spread a rumour that a Christian child had been kidnapped and killed, generally at the time of Passover. In some cases, the authorities found that the accusers had hidden the child, and they were arrested.

A typical incident occurred on 15 March 1892 when riots took place in Port Said after a Greek child had been playing in a Jewish house and the door had accidentally closed. The little girl's mother immediately called to passers-by to rescue her child without waiting to find out what had happened, and the rumour spread that the Jews had kidnapped the child in order to use her for purposes of human sacrifice. A Greek mob stormed the house and found the child alive and well but, nevertheless, they beat up an elderly Jewish man who subsequently died of shock. The old man's son, who had run to his father's aid, was also attacked by the crowd and nearly killed. The Jew who died was a member of the Carmona family, and the crowd attacked his house and injured the servant and a number of Jews. Some newspaper reports actually stated that the Jews were using the blood of Christian children for the baking of *matzos*.[29]

The propaganda against the Jews in Egypt and other parts of the Ottoman Empire was mainly carried out by Greeks because, with their commercial skill, they were the chief business competitors of the Jews. They sought, therefore, to make the Jews scapegoats for the hatred of foreigners which existed at that time, and thus deflect anger away from themselves. This was also, no doubt, the reason why the Greek press in Alexandria publicized such matters. Anti-Jewish feeling was whipped up because the Jews kept themselves separate from their neighbours in Egypt, and because they preferred to hold foreign citizenship. Another factor was the presence in Egypt of Syrian Christians who had left their own country after being persecuted in 1860 and who sought to cause trouble for the Jews in 1890, although not all of them participated in the agitation. Their motives were probably similar to those of the Greeks because they were also a foreign minority which was attempting to transfer the local dislike of foreigners to the Jews. In addition, there were economic factors which were exacerbated because the Syrian Christians owed money to the Jews.[30]

In the middle of the nineteenth century, the vast majority of Egyptian Jews had been described as 'destitute', but compared with the poverty of the non-Jewish population, the Jews were better off and, although their number was comparatively small, there were, at that time, rich Jewish bankers and merchants; but it was only from the 1860s onwards that fairly large-scale Jewish immigration into Egypt began.[31]

PALESTINE

The most frequently perpetrated myth of the Zionist propagandists is that Palestine was a 'desert' before the State of Israel was established and that the Israelis 'made the desert bloom'. For example, when Levi Eshkol was Prime Minister of Israel, he was asked whether, if the Jews were entitled to a homeland in Palestine, the Palestinians were not similarly entitled to their own State, and he replied: 'Who are the Palestinians?' He added that when he had settled in Palestine there were two hundred and fifty thousand 'non-Jews' there (this figure is ridiculous) who were 'mainly Arabs and Bedouins', and it was only after the Zionists 'made the desert bloom' that the Palestinians 'became interested in taking it from us'.[32]

Referring to this 'old chestnut' about 'making the desert bloom', *Middle East International* cited the Israeli writer Boaz Evron who described bitterly how, in 1973, he had seen bulldozers shovel sand over flourishing farm plots while their Bedouin owners were driven out and the area fenced off for Jewish settlement. '*We* created the wilderness,' he wrote.[33] Dr Mehdi has written: 'The truth about Arab settlements which used to exist in the area of the State of Israel before 1948 is one of the most guarded secrets of Israeli life. No publication, book or pamphlet gives either their number or their location. This, of course, is intentional so that the accepted official myth of "an empty country" can be taught and accepted in the Israeli schools and told to visitors. . . . This falsification is especially grave as it is accepted almost universally outside the Middle East, and because the destroyed villages were—in almost all cases—destroyed *completely*, with their houses, garden-walls, and even cemeteries and tomb-stones, so that literally no stone remains standing, and visitors who pass are told that "it was all desert".'[34]

Writing of 'the enormity of the propaganda trick that has been played upon us', Dr A. C. Forrest, a Christian clergyman who had been a farmer, realized that he was being told lies when he visited Israel and was shown orchards which were supposed to have been planted by the Zionists, although they obviously dated from pre-Zionist times. He wrote that half the citrus orchards and practically all the olive groves, as well as ten thousand shops, businesses and stores in Israel in 1953, had been stolen from absentee Palestinian refugees.

Dr Forrest cited Sir Moses Montefiore who wrote in 1839 that the Jewish settlers were ensured of success in the Holy Land because they would find wells already dug, olives and vines already planted and a land so rich that it would require little manure. He also quoted Ellsworth Huntington, an eminent American geographer, who had visited Palestine in 1911 and described the numerous wells dug by the Palestinian peasants in order to irrigate their oranges, lemons and other crops.[35]

When Rabbi David D'Beth Hillel visited Palestine early in the nineteenth century, he found a fertile country with abundant produce, and his account makes it very clear that there has been a considerable amount of 're-writing of history' in order to convey the impression that Palestine was 'a barren desert'. His description speaks for itself, for in Jerusalem he found olives growing in such abundance that there were many factories producing soap made from olive oil and it was of especially fine quality with a fragrant smell and was exported to Egypt and all the neighbouring countries. Three kinds of pomegranates, 'sweet, sour and mixed' were grown, and they were so big that some of them weighed 'an English pound'. There were also grapes—'each berry as large as the top of a man's thumb, and one branch frequently weighing about eighteen or twenty English pounds', as well as vegetables, apples, figs, which were very sweet and cheap; wheat, barley, rice and 'two kinds of honey in abundance, one made by bees and the other extracted from grapes', as well as wines, spirits, milk, cheese and 'plenty of mutton and beef, of good quality and cheap'.

Jaffa, which was described as 'a very large and fine town, enclosed with a wall', had excellent fruit that included very cheap oranges and limes, each bigger than a man's fist. The watermelons were so large that some of them could not be carried by one person and they were 'as red and as sweet as sugar candy'. There were, he added, no Jews living in Jaffa. Tiberias produced abundant vegetables and cotton, and Safad was surrounded with many vineyards, fig trees and olive trees. In Safad were ten thousand Muslim families and two thousand Jewish families, some of whom were Sephardi and some Ashkenazi, and each community had three synagogues.

Safad was built of hewn stones with some very fine houses, and each house had a pit cut into the rock on which the house was built and this acted as a reservoir for water from the roof which was used for cooking and washing. The houses in Jerusalem possessed similar reservoirs, and there were about ten thousand good houses built of large, hewn stones, from one to three stories high. Each house, with the exception of those belonging to the ruling classes, was occupied by three or four families. The streets, markets and shops were described as 'very good' and well supplied with all kinds of merchandise. The traders were chiefly Muslims or Christians and few of them were Jews.[36]

There were more than three thousand families of Jews who were both 'native-born and collected together from all parts of the world'. They had five synagogues, three belonging to the indigenous Jews and those from Muslim countries, and two for the Ashkenazi Jews. There were also four thousand Greek Christian families, ten thousand Muslim families, and about three hundred European Christians from various countries.[37]

When he travelled from Safad to Nazareth, the rabbi came

upon a forest consisting entirely of olive trees and extending a distance of three-and-a-half hours' journey; he was told by the Arabs in the area that many of the olive trees dated from the time of Titus.

He also visited 'a town called Peqiin' which was situated in a valley, six hours' journey from Safad, and it had an 'abundance of limes, sweet oranges, and citrons, and also of milk, butter, cheese and honey', with which the whole of 'Judaea' and the Mediterranean coast near Damascus were supplied.[38]

Hebron was said to be an excellent town with 'very good water, fruits and grain', and there were about eighty Jewish families, both Sephardi and Ashkenazi, in the town, each community having its own synagogue.[39]

In Acco (Acre), there were twenty-five Jewish families who spoke Arabic and had a small synagogue, two hundred Christian families and twenty-five thousand Muslim families. Rabbi David adds that during the reign of Jazzar Pasha, who became a ruler at Acco, Muallim Hayyim Farhi (the brother of Muallim Moses Farhi, whom we have already met) 'was the ruler over all Palestine'. The pasha 'was a very brave man but of a barbarous character. He cleared Palestine of robbers and thieves by cutting off their hands and noses and putting out their eyes. This, too, he did to his best friend and beloved Muallim Hayyim Farhi, a man rich, charitable, and kind to people of all nations.' The unfortunate Muallim Hayyim was put into prison several times and deprived of his nose and one eye, but later he was exonerated and honoured more than ever before, and his accusers were executed because it was found that they had made false charges against him. Muallim Hayyim ran the kingdom after the pasha's death and during the reign of his successor, Sulaiman Pasha, and when this pasha died, the Jew 'raised to power the present pasha Abdallah, then a young man, the son of a friend who, at his death, had requested Muallim Hayyim to take him under his charge.'

Abdallah, however, forgot the many kindnesses of his bene-factor whose enemies persuaded the pasha to have the Jew murdered, and so he was strangled and his body thrown into the sea. 'The present Sultan Mahmoud' then sent his army to attack the pasha because of his action, and the sultan 'shut up the fort for ten months', but the pasha later gave a great deal of money to the sultan who, owing to the intervention of Muhammad Ali Pasha, the king of Egypt, forgave the pasha.[40]

Two hours' journey from Acco was Mount Carmel, 'on the foot of which is built a little town surrounded with a wall, called Haifa'. There were about fifteen indigenous Jewish families there, with a small synagogue, and about fifteen hundred Muslim families.[41]

Rabbi David's account praised the fine wines obtainable in Palestine. In Safad, for example, there were four kinds of wine, 'white, red, black, [and] cooking, or boiled wine'. He added that some of the rich people had wine which was fifteen or twenty years old in their cellars.[42] At the end of the century, sesame, which produced a sweet oil, was exported in large quantities to France, while cucumbers, watermelons and tomatoes were exported to Egypt. But 'the largest item of export is oranges from the groves at Jaffa. From October, 1898 to April, 1899, three hundred and thirty-eight thousand boxes (containing about fifty million oranges) were exported, of which England received two hundred and seventy-eight thousand boxes.'[43]

However, the main obstacles to the development of Palestinian commerce arose from the Turkish government, in local taxation, the indirect levies of the Turkish officials and neighbouring sheikhs, and the irades (decrees of the Sultan of Turkey) against all electrical appliances.[44]

In an article entitled 'Palestine Before the Zionists', which was to form the basis of the first chapter 'of a history of the Arab-Israeli conflict', David S. Landes, a professor at Harvard, whose commitment to Zionism is obvious, wrote that the Jewish quarter of Jerusalem in the nineteenth century was

> ... a labyrinth of narrow, filthy alleys and dark, fetid hovels. It was here that the city shambles was located—the place of slaughter—where wild dogs and rats fought battle over the foul, bloody mess of rotting carrion, a source of noxious odours and a breeding place for disease. The location was no accident. The Arabs found the shambles there when they captured the city in the seventh century; they also found the rock on top of Mount Moriah, the old site of the Temple, covered with tons of garbage, laboriously hauled up and dumped there by way of insult and desecration. The Arabs cleared the rock and built the beautiful mosque that we now know as the Dome of the Rock or Mosque

of Omar. But the shambles was maintained, a lasting plague to the Jews of Jerusalem.[45]

According to Rabbi David:

> When Umar was conquering Judaea, he came to a village on the spot where old Jerusalem stood, and there he pitched his tent against a mountain in the midst of it. During the time he remained, he observed every morning and evening, men and women bring dust and cast it on the mountain, at which he was very angry, because he conceived it to be done out of disrespect to him. Accordingly, he summoned into his presence the elders of the village and enquired of them the reason of this conduct. They answered that they did it by command of their forefathers and priests, in order to conceal completely from view the sight of the temple.

As the khalif was grieved by this account, he told the people to clear the mountain and, because they were slow to obey his orders, he threw money among the dust so that, by looking for the coins, they would find the foundations of the Temple. The rubbish was all eventually cleared away and 'modern Jerusalem' was built where the city had existed before.[46]

Professor Landes wrote that by the late 1850s 'the Jews were the largest group in the city. Father Bourasse, writing in the late 1850s gives their number as seven thousand out of a total of over fifteen thousand (five thousand Muslims, two thousand five hundred Christians).'[47] The number of Muslims given in this account is lower than in others, and another traveller, who visited Jerusalem at the end of the nineteenth century, wrote: 'The population of Jerusalem has been increasing rapidly of late years, especially outside the walls. It is said to number now about sixty thousand. The number of Jews in and about the city is estimated at about forty thousand.'[48] The Jews who settled in Palestine, and especially in Jerusalem, during this period were religious Jews or members of the Chovevei Zion (Lovers of Zion), a colonization movement sponsored by Baron Edmund de Rothschild and other rich Jews, which preceded political Zionism.[49]

Professor Landes reported the impressions of various European travellers, such as a French visitor who described Jaffa at the end of the nineteenth century in the following terms:

The narrow, smoky streets, overhung by the houses on either side, are connected by black, viscous, half-collapsing stone staircases. Rotten rags dry on the ogival balconies.

Such streets are nothing but vaulted passages, blocked up with garbage and filth. . . . The pretty Moorish houses that one saw from afar turn out to be no more than crumbling hovels, open to every breeze. . . .

We are told in a footnote, however, that: 'As bad as the town was, it had beautiful, fragrant orange orchards in its southern and eastern suburbs.'[50]

As was pointed out in Chapter Two, western observers—and this applies equally to those of the nineteenth as to those of the twentieth century—tend to judge the countries of the Middle East by their own standards, without taking into account the ravages wrought by wars, famines, plagues and centuries of feudalism and foreign occupation. Thus we have a British clergyman lamenting the fact that nineteenth-century Palestine had:

. . . few well-cultivated fields to be seen anywhere, while there are no well-appointed farmsteads, no handsome country seats, pretty wayside cottages, or clean and tidy villages, such as make up the charms of other countries.[51]

Professor Landes also wrote that:

. . . as a result of centuries of Turkish neglect and misrule, following on the earlier ravages of successive conquerors, the land had been given over to sand, marsh, the anopheles mosquito, clan feuds and Bedouin marauders.[52]

Yet in 1891, Asher Ginzberg, a Russian-born Jewish nationalist who wrote under the name of Ahad Ha'am (One of the People), wrote in an article called 'Truth from Palestine', at a time when prospective Jewish settlers were touring the country looking for land, that it was difficult to find untilled land anywhere except on sand dunes or stony hills. He added: 'We think that the Arabs are all savages who live like animals and do not understand what is happening around them. This is, however, a great error.'[53]

That same year, Ahad Ha'am warned the settlers not to antagonize the Arabs of Palestine by behaving badly towards them and he wrote:

Yet what do our brethren do in Palestine? Just the very opposite! Serfs they were in the lands of the diaspora and suddenly they find themselves in unrestricted freedom and this change has awakened in them an inclination to despotism. They treat the Arabs with hostility and cruelty, deprive them of their rights, offend them without cause and even boast of these deeds; and nobody among us opposes this despicable and dangerous inclination.[54]

Ill-feeling and strife were intensified in Palestine and other Arab countries on the issuing of the Balfour Declaration which announced that the British Government 'viewed with favour' the establishment of a Jewish national home in Palestine. Michael Adams referred to this as '. . . the injustice done to the Palestinians, whose dispossession from the land of their ancestors was the culmination of a course of events set in motion by the publication in 1917 of the Balfour Declaration, the document by which the British Government had offered Zionism a home in Palestine, a land over which it had no rights whatever.'[55]

REFERENCES

1. Cohen, *op. cit.*, pp. 8–9.
2. David S. Sassoon, 'History of the Jews in Basra', reprinted from *The Jewish Quarterly Review*, New Series, Vol. XVII, No. 4, The Dropsie College for Hebrew and Cognate Learning, Philadelphia, 1927, pp. 438–9.
3. *Ibid.*, pp. 43–5.
4. Walter J. Fischel (ed.), *Unknown Jews in Unknown Lands: The Travels of Rabbi David D'Beth Hillel (1824–1832)*, Ktav Publishing House, New York, 1973, pp. 82–3.
5. *Ibid.*, pp. 86–8.
6. *Ibid.*, pp. 72–80.
7. Hayyim Cohen, *op. cit.*, pp. 23–4.
8. *Ibid.*, pp. 23–4.
9. *The Jewish Encyclopedia, op. cit.*, Vol. IV, p. 420.
10. Graetz, *op. cit.*, Vol. V, pp. 505–7.
11. *Laws and Customs of Israel, op. cit.*, Vol. II, Rule 1, p. 95.
12. *Ibid.*, Vol. II, Rule 3, p. 95.
13. *Ibid.*, Vol. II, Rule 1, p. 95.
14. *Ibid.*, Vol. I, Rule 12, p. 69.
15. Graetz, *op. cit.*, Vol. V, pp. 507–11.
16. *Ibid.*, Vol. V, pp. 512–19.
17. Fischel, *op. cit.*, pp. 66–7.
18. *Ibid.*, p. 64.

19. *Ibid.*, pp. 65–6.
20. *The Jewish Encyclopedia, op. cit.*, Vol. IV, p. 419.
21. Fischel, *op. cit.*, p. 67.
22. *Ibid.*, pp. 67–8.
23. *Ibid.*, p. 69.
24. *Ibid.*, pp. 69–70.
25. *The Jewish Encyclopedia, op. cit.*, Vol. V, p. 66.
26. Hayyim Cohen, *op. cit.*, p. 10.
27. *The Jewish Encyclopedia, op. cit.*, Vol. V, pp. 66–7.
28. Landshut, *op. cit.*, pp. 27–9.
29. Jacob M. Landau, *Middle Eastern Themes: Papers in History and Politics*, Frank Cass, London, 1973, pp. 99–105.
30. *Ibid.*, pp. 106–8.
31. Hayyim Cohen, *op. cit.*, p. 87.
32. *Jerusalem Post*, 17 February 1969.
33. November 1978, citing *Yediot Aharonot*.
34. M. R. Mehdi, *A Palestine Chronicle: Being a Record of Injustice.* Alpha Associates, London, 1973, p. 3.
35. A. C. Forrest, *The Unholy Land*, McLelland and Stewart, Toronto/ Montreal, 1971, p. 78.
36. Fischel, *op. cit.*, pp. 51–7.
37. *Ibid.*, pp. 51–2.
38. *Ibid.*, pp. 59–60.
39. *Ibid.*, p. 54.
40. *Ibid.*, pp. 60–1.
41. *Ibid.*, pp. 61–2.
42. *Ibid.*, p. 59.
43. *The Jewish Encyclopedia, op. cit.*, Vol. IX, p. 500.
44. *Ibid.*, Vol. IX, p. 501.
45. David S. Landes, 'Palestine before the Zionists', in *Commentary*, Vol. 61, No. 2, February, 1976, p. 51.
46. Fischel, *op. cit.*, p. 49.
47. Landes, *op. cit.*, p. 51.
48. Archibald Sutherland, *Palestine: the Glory of all Lands*, Oliphant, Anderson and Ferrier, Edinburgh and London, 1896, p. 67.
49. *The Jewish Encyclopedia*, Vol. IV, pp. 46–7.
50. Landes, *op. cit.*, p. 49, citing Jules Hoche, *Le Pays des Croisades*, Paris (n.d.) p. 10.
51. Sutherland, *op. cit.*, p. 19.
52. Landes, *op. cit.*, p. 49.
53. Hans Kohn, 'Ahad Ha'am: Nationalist with a Difference', in *Zionism: the dream and the reality* (ed. Gary V. Smith), *op. cit.*, pp. 31–2.
54. *Ibid.*, p. 31.
55. Christopher Mayhew and Michael Adams, *Publish It Not . . . The Middle East Cover-up*, Longman Group, 1975, p. 9. For full details of the Balfour Declaration and other official British documents concerned with the decision to make Palestine into a Jewish State, see Doreen Ingrams, *Palestine Papers 1917–1922: Seeds of Conflict, op. cit.*

Six

Zionism

A EUROPEAN PHENOMENON

MICHAEL SELZER, a Jewish scholar, has written that 'Zionism is a complex phenomenon, adequately understood by only a small percentage of its critics and by an even smaller percentage of its supporters',[1] which is why some Arabs—especially among the ranks of the uneducated masses—believe that all Jews are Zionists. This belief is, of course, fostered in every way possible by the Zionists themselves, and, indeed, a majority of Jews have come to accept the Zionist teaching that modern, political Zionism is a necessary component of, or a substitute for, Judaism, without properly understanding the significance or the hazards of such a stance.

When Theodor Herzl formulated his plan for what he considered to be the solution to 'the Jewish problem', he had absolutely no knowledge or understanding of the social and economic conditions which cause the persecution of minorities: and his major error was that he took no account of two extremely important factors, namely, the existing population of the proposed Jewish State and the effect of their dispossession and the expropriation of their land and property on Jews in neighbouring countries. Herzl was solely preoccupied with the condition of Jews in Eastern Europe, and a study of his writings makes it obvious that he hardly knew—and cared even less—about the Arab inhabitants of Palestine, the country eventually chosen for Jewish colonization, although, at the time, they formed a majority of more than ninety per cent. This indigenous population appeared to Herzl to be invisible. He also appeared blithely unaware that there were Jews living in the Arab countries surrounding Palestine.

When he visited the country he passed through at least a dozen Arab villages but completely failed to notice any Arabs either in these places or in the city of Jaffa. The only reference he made to the indigenous inhabitants of Palestine in either his diary or any of his other written reports about his journey was once when he mentioned a 'mixed multitude of beggars, women and children'. Amos Elon, an Israeli writer, commented: 'The natives seemed to have vanished before his eyes . . . or else they assumed no political importance in his mind.'[2]

Moshe Menuhin, a Jew who was born in Russia in 1893 and whose family settled in Palestine, left Palestine and made his home in the United States after completing his higher education because he was disenchanted with the development of political Zionism which, he felt strongly, was causing the degeneration of Judaism. He wrote:

> Dr Herzl saw anti-Semites in all Gentiles, exactly as did the ghetto Jews of Russia and Poland. His yardstick, too, was exactly like theirs: *Is it good for the Jews?* The disabilities, injustices and exploitations that the common masses of the Gentile world lived through and revolted against escaped him completely. He could not and would not see the evolution of history, the struggle for emancipation of the entire world, the brotherhood of man that was evolving gradually and most painfully, but surely.[3]

In the early days of Zionism, the movement's hardest battle was fought with the Jews, and most especially with those who had become assimilated in the countries in which they lived.

Thus upper-class Jews in Britain were totally opposed to Zionism,[4] and the Jewish masses turned their backs on it too.[5]

The Jews in Eastern Europe had always been in the forefront of the struggle against reaction and feudalism and, in any case, as Dr James Parkes correctly explained:

> Political anti-Semitism had extremely little to do with the Jews as such. . . . The enemy was 'liberalism', 'industrialism', 'secularism'—anything the reactionaries disliked; and they found by experience that there was no better way of persuading their electors to dislike these things also than to label them 'Jewish'.[6]

Critics of Zionism complained that, instead of encouraging Jews to fight for emancipation in their own countries, the Zionist movement sought to remove them to a separate State and, to this end, it became necessary for the Zionists to collaborate with anti-Semites. Karl Kautsky pointed out that the Zionist belief was that:

> The Jew is secure against oppression only in a state in which he lives not as a foreigner, in a state, therefore, of his own nationality. Only in a real Jewish state will the emancipation of Judaism be possible.
>
> This is the guiding thought of Zionism. Even among the circles of Western European Judaism, this idea has in recent years been replacing the idea of assimilation, of equality of rights within the existing states, which had until recently been dominant among the Jews. Zionism is coming more and more in conflict with this thought, for as assimilation progresses, the national Jewry loses its strength. It is therefore necessary to segregate Jews as sharply as possible from non-Jews.
>
> Zionism meets anti-Semitism half-way in this effort, as well as in the fact that its goal is the removal of all Jews from the existing states. . . . In the civilized world all regions have been preempted; there is no more room for a Jewish state. It is only outside of the limits of the civilized world, and only under the tutelage and patronage of a non-Jewish national state that a Jewish community is still conceivable. . . . But, curiously enough, there had already been a Jewish state in Palestine, founded by Jews in exile, under the protection of a non-Jewish state; and even at that remote period—two thousand years ago—this state had not served as a very powerful attraction for the Jews living in the Diaspora. Most of the Jews chose to remain in Babylon, Damascus, Alexandria, Rome, and in other places of domicile, only a portion of them settling in Jerusalem. Most of them contented themselves with an occasional pilgrimage to the Holy City. They found that they prospered better when living as strangers among strangers.[7]

Herzl's attitude towards anti-Semitism was indeed strange, but he seemed oblivious to the contradictions which were bound to arise because of his beliefs. (Although the term anti-Semitism is factually incorrect when used to refer to anti-Jewishness—because, as Arabs frequently point out, they are more 'Semitic' than the majority of European Jews—it is now so widely used in this sense that it is employed here for want of a better term.) He actually welcomed anti-Semitism for he wrote that: 'Great exertions will hardly be necessary to spur on the movement. Anti-Semites provide the necessary impetus',[8] and he also wrote, in his diaries, that, 'anti-Semitism no doubt has within it something of the divine Will to Good, for it forces us to close ranks, unites us under pressure, and through our unity will bring us to freedom.'[9]

It is frequently claimed that one of the major purposes of Zionism was 'to restore the Jews to their ancient homeland', but, in fact, Herzl, a secular, non-practising Jew, had no particular preference regarding the location of the Jewish State until he and his followers began to realize that there was much to be gained from the decision to choose Palestine. Indeed, Herzl wrote: 'Shall we choose Palestine or Argentina? We shall take what is given us, and what is selected by Jewish public opinion.'[10]

In an article entitled 'Background to Zionism', George Edinger wrote that it was sometimes stressed that every Jew had a longing to 'return to Zion', and if that were the case then he, the writer of the article, would have to consider himself 'a biological freak'; but, he added, all the evidence pointed the other way, as Jews had never sought refuge in Palestine when they were persecuted. The refugees from fifteenth-century Spain settled in Poland and in the western part of the Turkish Empire where their descendants 'still speaking the Spanish of fifteenth century Castile' could still, at that time, be found, while the victims of the pogroms in nineteenth-century Russia flocked to London and New York where even the most committed Zionists had every intention of staying.

Michael Selzer pointed out that Zionism was

> ... frequently depicted by its supporters as a political means toward the realization of two thousand years of Jewish yearning for redemption. The extravagant, pseudo-Messianic mythology which has been created around this notion should be recognized for the propagandistic device which it is. It has served a useful purpose in enlisting the support of fundamentalist Christians, in particular, for the Zionist cause, and has legitimized Jewish attachment to the movement by establishing a vivid, albeit spurious, continuum between the aspirations of the World Zionist Organization and those of traditional Judaism.

He added that with the loss of their 'geographical fatherland' the Jews acquired 'a portable fatherland'; they became a spiritual people and, although powerless, made themselves even more vulnerable by maintaining their unique social and cultural attributes, and their powerlessness, in their view, would have no adequate meaning if it did not have the effect of exposing them to pain; this explained why the Zionists' renunciation of Jewish political powerlessness 'so often took the form of an assault on the socio-cultural uniqueness of the Jews'. As their sufferings would redeem the world and bring about the coming of the Messiah, the Jews understood and, indeed, even welcomed the powerlessness which 'exposed them to such awful harassment'.

He also believed that Zionism was a *counter*-revolutionary, rather than a revolutionary, movement because the latter seeks to change society from its previously 'normal' situation while a counter-revolution restores the *status quo* and, although the Zionists claimed that their movement was revolutionary because it set out to 'normalize' the Jews, in fact what they set out to do was to restore the *status quo* which had been repudiated two thousand years previously.[12]

In spite of the warning voices which were raised by many Jews, the Zionists continued with their pressures on the Western powers to facilitate the establishment of a Jewish State in Palestine. Edwin Montagu, Britain's Secretary of State for India, and a Jew, wrote in a secret memorandum:

> Zionism has always seemed to me to be a mischievous political creed, untenable by any patriotic citizen of the United Kingdom ... it seems to be inconceivable that Zionism should be officially recognized by the British Government, and that Mr Balfour should be authorized to say that Palestine was to be reconstituted as 'the national home of the Jewish people'. I do not know what this involves, but I assume that it means that Mohammedans and Christians are to make way for the Jews, and that the Jews should be put in all positions of preference. . . . Mohammedans in Palestine will be regarded as foreigners, just in the same way as Jews will hereafter be treated as foreigners in every country but Palestine. . . . When the Jews are told that Palestine is their national home, every country will immediately desire to get rid of its Jewish citizens, and you will find a population in Palestine driving out its present inhabitants, taking all the best in the country, drawn from all quarters of the globe. . . . I have always understood, by the Jews before Zionism was invented, that to bring the Jews back to form a nation in the country from which they were dispersed would require Divine leadership. I have never heard it suggested, even by their most

fervent admirers, that either Mr Balfour or Lord Rothschild
would prove to be the Messiah.[13]

Many orthodox Jews were equally opposed to Zionism. The
extremely devout Neturei Karta sect, which totally repudiates
Zionism, said that: 'All the Zionist propaganda about the miraculous way of the establishment of their state and the "liberation"
of the Jewish people is but one chain of falsehood and negation
of the true Jewish essence.'[14]

The Zionists obviously believed that they were acting in the
best interests of the Jews, but both they and their opponents
were entirely concerned with the problems of the European
Jews, and it did not ever seem to occur to either faction that
those who were bound to be most compromised would be the
unfortunate Jews of the Arab countries.

Neville Laski, the president of the Board of Deputies of
British Jews (an organization which is now totally committed
to Zionism) wrote in 1939 that:

> To Western Jewry, as represented by many prominent English
> and American Jews, the idea of a Jewish State is no less distasteful
> now than it was twenty years ago, and they hope that it has been
> finally discarded. What they want to see in Palestine is a system
> which will give both to the Jewish population, which is almost a
> third of the total, and to the Arab population complete political
> and civil security and self-government in matters that concern
> each community alone. They want to see in Palestine neither a
> Jewish nor an Arab state, but a Palestinian State. . . .[15]

Another Jew, Nathan Weinstock, pointed out that it is
necessary 'to refute the grotesque myth of the purported "historical rights" of the Jews in Palestine', because, even before the
Roman conquest of Judaea in A.D. 70, three-quarters of the Jewish population lived outside Palestine and, he added, because
there was so much inter-marriage at one time, today's Palestinians are descendants of the Hebrews. He also asked why, if
the Jews have claims on Palestine, the Arabs have no claims on
Spain or Sicily, which were once integral parts of the Islamic
Empire. He explained that Israel did not come into existence
because of the Nazi persecutions, as the foundations of Zionist
colonization were laid at the end of the nineteenth century when
the first wave of immigrants arrived in Palestine in 1882 and,

moreover, 'the Jewish community of Palestine was not saved from genocide because of its presence in the Holy Land, but—like American and British Jews—simply because of the fortunate fact that Hitler did not conquer the Middle East.' He blamed 'the western "democracies" [and he put the word in inverted commas] which systematically refused to open their borders to the victims of fascism', and he added that they are 'really responsible for the genocide', while 'As for the Zionist leaders, they never hesitated to deal with the most prominent anti-Semites to gain their objectives.'[16]

Critics of Zionism frequently claim that the blame for the failure of western countries to offer refuge to the persecuted Jews of Germany and its satellites must be put on the Zionists for their insistence that the oppressed Jews should go to Palestine, but, while it is true that the Zionists made no pretence about their political aims, there is evidence that, with the rise of Hitlerism, previously non-Zionist Jews began to support Jewish settlement in Palestine, simply in order to protect their own privileged positions by preventing an influx of destitute Jewish refugees into their countries.

The British Embassy in Washington revealed, for example, on 12 December 1942, that the Central Committee of the American-Jewish Committee, in a secret meeting, had made certain decisions which were described by the British Embassy as follows:

(1) A large post-war immigration of Central European Jews into Palestine is unanimously urged. This is naturally a proposal irresistible to all American Jews of whatever political colour, since it offers an alternative to an attempt at Jewish immigration into the USA which is viewed by most US Jews with apprehension.

A carefully qualified approval of the Zionist programme is expressed. We have been unable to ascertain the details of this. We suspect that it is a guarded approval of some sort of Jewish Commonwealth, possibly within a large federation *should* the Jews ever attain the majority in Palestine, without any overt hope that this situation will arise.

(2) The resolution [relating to the above proposals] is now to be circulated to the membership of the American-Jewish Committee before being published. But this is mere conjecture founded on not very reliable gossip. What is clear is that the

Committee, with its non-Zionist membership, is careful to dissociate itself from any common platform with the Zionist Organization, while being prepared to make a benevolent unilateral gesture. We are told that Mr Benjamin V. Cohen, now with the Byrnes office, who had a great deal to do with the drafting of the Palestine Mandate, was consulted about this latest step by the American Jewish Committee of which he is not a member.[17]

A Time of Tension

Ahad Ha'am issued a further warning twenty years after his previous one of 1891 when, on 9 July 1911, he wrote from London to a friend, Mr Eisenstadt in Jaffa: 'As to the war against the Jews in Palestine—I am a spectator from afar with an aching heart, particularly because of the want of insight and understanding shown on our side to an extreme degree. As a matter of fact, it was evident twenty years ago that the day would come when the Arabs would stand up against us.' He complained bitterly that the Jews had refused to learn the language of the country and had also declined to study the spirit of its people, and he found the same lack of understanding evident in the boycott of Arab labour proclaimed by the Zionists.

He also wrote from London on 18 November 1913, to Moshe Smilansky, an early Zionist settler in Rehovot in Palestine about this boycott: 'Apart from the political danger, I can't put up with the idea that our brethren are morally capable of behaving in such a way to humans of another people, and unwittingly the thought comes to my mind: if it is so now, what will be our relations to the others if in truth we shall achieve at the end of times power in Eretz Israel? And if this be the "Messiah", I do not wish to see his coming.'[18]

The tension and violence which had resulted from increased Jewish immigration into Palestine had their inevitable effect on the unfortunate Jews of the Arab countries, although the Palestinians were joined by the indigenous Jews in their resistance to the Zionist colonization of their country from the very beginning of the Zionist influx and especially from 1908 onwards.

This resistance was expressed in the harassment of the Jewish colonies by peasants who had been forced off their land and by

the uprisings of 1920 and 1921, which were part of the general
revolt of the Arabs in Syria, Iraq and Egypt against British and
French domination.[19]

The situation deteriorated still further as the years passed, and
the bloody events of 1929, which have been amply chronicled
elsewhere, appeared inevitable to some observers, one of whom
was Vincent Sheean, the American author and journalist who had
been pro-Zionist until he went to Palestine that year and saw for
himself what was happening. He wrote:

> It may be seen that in three weeks I had already acquired
> serious misgivings about the wisdom of the Zionist policy. I still
> knew nothing about the Arabs of Palestine, but I could see them
> all around me everywhere, and if my long experience in political
> journalism had taught me anything, it was that one people did
> not like being dominated or interfered with in its own home by
> another. . . . What I wanted to hear was what the Zionists were
> doing about it; and instead I was given a large number of
> irrelevant statements about standards of living, etc., etc. . . . I
> had arrived on June 25th with a genuine sympathy, however
> ignorant or romantic, for the Zionist effort. . . . I saw Jewish
> islands in an Arab sea. . . . And on the whole the Jewish dis-
> regard for the Arabs seemed to me (from their own point of
> view) perilous in the extreme.
>
> After July 17th, therefore, I made some attempt to find out
> what the Arabs of Palestine were like. I remained in touch with
> the Zionists, visited Tel Aviv, continued to read Zionist literature
> and talked to Zionist friends.
>
> But I no longer tried to ignore the fact that Palestine was, by
> an overwhelming majority of its population, an Arab country.[20]

In the years following, the violence continued, and with the
emergence of Nazism in Germany, many Jews who had previously
opposed Zionism, began to support it, especially after the full
horror of the Nazi atrocities became apparent. Although it is
not the purpose of this book to examine in any more detail than
has already been briefly undertaken the reasons why Jewish
refugees from Hitlerism were denied entry to many countries,
there is no doubt that the extermination of the Jews by the
Nazis played a decisive part in the eventual decision, by the
United Nations, to recommend the partition of Palestine.

Expulsion or Transfer?

Although Herzl had been hardly aware of the presence of Arabs in Palestine, he had intended, right from the beginning, to expel the indigenous inhabitants of whichever country the Jews should decide to colonize. Thus he suggested that the Zionist settlers should expropriate the property of the native population and attempt 'to spirit the penniless population across the border by procuring employment for it in the transit countries, while denying it any employment in our own country. The property-owners will come over to our side.'[21]

In 1937, David Ben Gurion, a Zionist leader who was to become Israel's first Prime Minister, commenting on the Peel Commission's visit to Palestine, said, at the Congress of the World Council of Poale Zion:

> The Commission itself did not overlook the meagreness of the territory that it offers to the Jewish State, and in the proposal to transfer Arab populations out of the area, if possible of their own free will, if not—by coercion, a possibility is offered to enlarge Jewish colonization. . . .
>
> The Commission does not suggest dispossessing the Arabs; it advocates their transfer and settlement in the Arab State. It seems to me unnecessary to explain the fundamental and deep difference between expulsion and transfer. Until now, also, we have achieved our settlement by way of transfer of population from place to place. . . . Only in very few places in our colonization were we not forced to transfer the earlier residents.[22]

He added that he did not look upon partition as the 'final solution' to the problem of Palestine as 'this country was not given for us to partition it—for it constitutes a single unit, not only historically, but also from the natural and economic standpoint.'[23]

Another delegate, Y. Idelson, spoke about the 'evacuation' of the Arabs and said that they would not agree to this, '. . . and we shall not be able—for they will not let us expel them by force; because we have hostages in all the world and in the neighbouring Arab states. Why should the Arabs want to abandon good lands, a quiet area with convenient marketing possiblities and lucrative side-jobs, and move to an unsure place, a place where a great chapter of suffering will start? And, aside from all that, for the *fellah*, his land is not such a casual factor. He has struck deep roots in it; what force will compel him to leave it?'[24]

A. Cizling, one of the leaders of Mapam (a 'socialist' Zionist party) said: 'I do not contest our moral right to advocate an exchange of populations. ... The possibility is more real and more sensible, to operate an actual exchange of populations between a united land of Israel, some time in the future, and Iraq and other Arab countries, by way of transfer of their Jews to Eretz Israel. And if this vision is also far remote, at least it coincides with interests that are quite compatible with it.'[25]

Another comment was made by A. Lulu who said that there were some 100,000 Jews at that time in Iraq, Syria, Arabia and Yemen. In exchange for the land he left behind, 'the Arab emigrant from the Land of Israel will acquire land parcels in Iraq . . . and even if it is implemented by coercion, we'll be right all along the way.'[26]

Mrs Golda Myerson (later Meir and later, also, Prime Minister of Israel) said: 'I would agree that the Arabs leave the country, and my conscience would be absolutely clear. But is there such a possibility? . . . Let us go to the Jewish masses and ask them: 'are you ready to save one and a half million Jews within ten years, without any possibility to change the borders afterwards? Only wars change borders. Maybe there will be a war in the near future, but how can we be sure that this war will change borders in our favour?'[27]

A question put by A. Tratakower was whether sufficient attention had been paid to the question of 'the transfer from the point of view of future Jewish settlement in the countries of the Middle East. Isn't there a danger that if we establish the principle of a national state clean of national minorities in its midst, then they will use this principle against us in the neighbouring Arab States, and will not let us set foot in them? Isn't this too heavy a price that we are paying, in order to get rid of a few dozens of thousands of Arabs in the Hebrew State (for we shall not be able to get rid of more than that)?'[28]

Berl Locker, who had been head of the Jewish Agency during the 1950s and 1960s, said that he had no qualms about the 'transfer', but he asked whether it would be possible 'to uproot and replant several thousands of peasant families against their will? Wouldn't it become, notwithstanding all the agreements, a source of continuous hatred, and a source of friction between the Jews and the Arabs who will remain inside the Jewish State, as well as between the Jews and the neighbours all around? And in a small state such as this one cannot afford such luxuries.'[29]

A Zionist labour leader, Berl Katznelson, said: 'I believed, and still believe, that they are destined to move to Syria and Iraq.'[30]

Many years later, Yeshayahu Ben Porat described how he had arrived in Palestine in 1945 and had belonged to a Zionist youth movement, and

> ... from the age of seven, I was trained to military action with the conquest of the country in view. As a child in Austria, I grew up with the feeling that there would come a day when we would have to conquer the country by force of arms. I was trained to despise the Arab population. They did not tell us explicitly that they were 'human dust', but this is the concept that has stuck to my conscience since then—that the Land of Israel is ours, and the Arabs that live in it will be authorized to continue living there, on condition they do not bother us. And if they bother— we shall expel them. . . . They did not train us to respect the Arab neighbour. They did not educate us in the perspective that there will be a Jewish State here where Arabs and Jews will live together. The hidden thought, and sometimes the overt thought, was: they shall go away and we shall stay. And after 1945, it was clear to all of us that there would be a war, not only to expel the British, but also because we needed a war with the Arabs. In the kibbutzim they looked at the Arab villages in the vicinity and they divided up their lands in their thoughts.[31]

Unfortunately, no attention was paid to those Jews who warned of the dangers of needlessly provoking and antagonizing the indigenous population of Palestine which, as Professor Rodinson wrote, were 'native in all senses of the word'. He added that '. . . ignorance, sometimes backed up by hypocritical propaganda, has spread a number of misconceptions on this subject, unfortunately very widely held.' He pointed out that it has been said that because the Arabs took the country by military conquest in the seventh century, they were occupiers like any others and it was asked why they should be regarded as any more native than the others, particularly the Jews who were native in ancient times. He wrote that, to a historian, the answer was obvious. A small body of Arabs did conquer the country in the seventh century, and the Palestinian population 'soon became Arabized under Arab domination, just as earlier it had been Hebraicized, Aramaicized, to some degree even Hellenized'. But, 'it became Arab in a way that it was never to become latinized or Ottomanized. The invaded melted with the invaders.' Similarly, it would be ridiculous to call English people of the present day 'invaders and occupiers, on the grounds that England was conquered by the Angles, Saxons and Jutes in the fifth and sixth centuries'.[32]

Jews such as Dr Judah Magnes, head of the Hebrew University of Jerusalem, and Professor Martin Buber, who advocated a bi-national state in which Jews and Arabs should have equal rights, vigorously opposed the Biltmore programme of 1942, at which an American Zionist Congress adopted a programme calling for a Jewish State in the whole of Palestine, but their objections were ignored.[33]

The American Zionists went even further at their annual convention held at Atlantic City in October 1944, for they not only adopted a resolution demanding a Jewish State in the whole of Palestine 'undivided and undiminished', but also, wrote Dr Hannah Arendt, made no reference at all to the Arabs of Palestine. The Biltmore programme, she continued, had stated that the Jewish minority would grant minority rights to the Palestinian majority, but: 'This time the Arabs were simply not mentioned in the resolution, which obviously leaves them the choice between voluntary emigration or second-class citizenship.'[34]

From then on, anti-Zionist feelings were intensified in Arab countries and the situation grew considerably worse after 15 May 1948, when the State of Israel was established, for, in the words of Professor Rodinson: 'As for the Arabs, a foreign colony had succeeded in seizing a part of their territory and driving out a number of its Arab inhabitants—and this with the support of the entire Western world, regardless of ideology, from the capitalist United States to the socialist USSR.'[35]

Joseph Weitz, who was from 1932 Director of the Jewish National Fund Land and Afforestation Division (the Jewish National Fund owns all the land acquired in Palestine, Israel and the occupied territories for Jewish settlement, and non-Jews are not permitted to live, nor work, on this land), made it clear that those who had been expelled were not to be allowed to return. He wrote in his diary that: '. . . it becomes clear that our views on the question of abandoned villages coincide: destruction, improvement and settlement [from 1948, 385 Arab villages were totally destroyed by the Israelis] . . . A conversation developed around the latest events, and the principal question was the return or non-return of the Arabs. One opinion now prevails in all circles. No! By no means. We must prevent their return, and at the same time fill up the void.'[36]

In another entry in his diary, Joseph Weitz wrote: 'I went to visit the village of Muar. Three tractors are completing its destruction. I was surprised; nothing in me moved at the sight of the destruction. No regret and no hate, as though this was the way our world goes . . .'[37] He also confided to his diary that: 'The session of the "Transfer Committee" took place today. . . . We decided to conduct propaganda in newspapers and broadcasts in Arab circles, so that they may know we do not intend to let them return.'[38] He explained that the President, Chaim Weizmann, had invited him for a conversation in Rehovoth and that Dr Weizmann had smiled and said: ' "Now, do you have enough land to be satisfied?" . . . he agreed with me on all points. The Arabs cannot and need not return. We shall pay for their property, so they can settle in Arab countries.'[39] To the time of writing, however, no payment has been made for the property of the refugees.[40]

Nathan Chofshi, another Israeli Jew, wrote:

> We came and turned the native Arabs into tragic refugees. And still we dare to slander and malign them, to besmirch their name; instead of being deeply ashamed of what we did, and trying to undo some of the evil we committed, we justify our terrible acts and even attempt to glorify them.[41]

Ner, the organ of Ihud, an organization founded by Dr Magnes and other supporters of the bi-national idea, commented:

> Only an international revolution can have the power to heal our people of their murderous sickness of causeless hatred [for the Arabs]. It is bound to bring eventual complete ruin upon us. Only then will the old and the young in our land realize how great was our responsibility to those miserable wronged Arab refugees in whose towns we have settled Jews who were brought

from afar; whose homes we have inherited, whose fields we now sow and harvest; the fruit of whose gardens, orchards and vineyards we gather; and in whose cities that we robbed, we put up houses of education, charity and prayer, while we babble and rave about our being the 'People of the Book' and the 'Light of the Nations'.[42]

It was believed, for many years, that the Palestinians had left of their own accord after being instructed to do so by their leaders, but this story was finally demolished in 1961 when Erskine Childers conducted a thorough investigation of the supposed 'broadcasts' which were said to have taken place, and confirmed the findings of Professor Walid Khalidi, who had also carried out some painstaking research into the subject two years previously.[43]

After an American rabbi repeated the false claims which had been made about the flight of the Palestinians, Nathan Chofshi wrote: 'If Rabbi Kaplan really wanted to know what happened, we old Jewish settlers in Palestine who witnessed the flight could tell him how and in what manner we, Jews, forced Arabs to leave cities and villages ... some of them were driven out by force of arms; others were made to leave by deceit, lying and false promises. It is enough to cite the cities of Jaffa, Lydda, Ramle, Beersheba, Acre from among numberless others.'[44]

THE RISE OF TENSION

The discrimination shown towards Jews in some Arab countries at certain periods in the past was not, as has been pointed out, specifically directed towards Jews *qua* Jews but towards all non-Muslims, yet some writers give the impression that it was only the Jews who were invariably singled out for persecution. Maurice M. Roumani, Head of the Research Division of the Department of Sephardic Communities of the World Zionist Organization in Jerusalem wrote:

Life for Jews in Arab countries was always circumscribed by anti-Jewish sentiment. Therefore, the position of Jews in these countries, throughout their two thousand years of settlement there, was always insecure and unstable. The inferiority of Jews was not only enforced by degrading civil codes, it was also legitimized by religious writings which officially decreed Jews as 'infidels'.[45] (According to Professor Chouraqi, however—see Chapter Two—Jews were not considered 'infidels'.)

Although Western political power and liberal ideas in the Middle East had created a climate which did not favour discrimination, they also tended to enhance the differences between the Jewish and Muslim communities, and even before the advent of Zionism, the growing Western viewpoint of the Jews, on the one hand, and the growing nationalism of the Muslims, on the other, were increasing the gulf which already existed between the two groups. Although the Palestinian Arab Revolt of 1936 (caused by large numbers of Arabs being thrown out of work because of massive Jewish immigration into Palestine) was regarded sympathetically by the general public in the neighbouring Arab countries, the Palestine issue was not, originally, looked upon as anything more than a local problem which mainly concerned the British, the Palestine Arabs and the Zionists; and, on the whole, the Jews in the Arab countries were not particularly sympathetic to the efforts of the Zionists to establish a Jewish State in Palestine. In fact, leading Jews in Iraq, Syria, the Lebanon and, to a lesser degree, Egypt, voiced their opposition to Zionism on a number of occasions because they looked upon the movement as a threat to the security of the Jews in the Arab countries.

What support there was for Zionism in the Arab Jewish communities was mainly to be found among the younger generation, particularly among those who had had a European education, and this was, in a large measure, due to the proselytizing work of Zionist emissaries from Palestine, but the leaders of the Jewish communities, as well as the Jewish masses in the Arab countries, did not look favourably upon Zionism.[46]

Long before the United Nations partition recommendation of November 1947, there was much anti-Zionist feeling in the Arab countries. In Syria, for example, there was anger, bewilderment and consternation when, in response to Zionist demands, Britain extended the frontiers of Palestine to take in both banks of the Upper Jordan River, the eastern shores of Lake Huleh and Lake Tiberias, and a portion of land connected with southern Lebanon which provided Palestine with control of one source of the Jordan, after the First World War.

Transjordan, under the British mandate, became a separate emirate, and France ceded to Turkey the Syrian cities of Aintab and Urfa as well as the fertile farmlands of Cilicia, the hill country of the north and the Baghdad Railway, which crossed northern Syria, so that the railway's southern edge became Syria's preposterous northern frontier. Thus the Turks were thirty miles from Aleppo; and Aleppo was deprived of its natural markets and its water supply because much of the water of the Quwaik River was diverted into Turkey. In addition, tens of thousands of Armenian refugees poured into Syria which was, at that time, suffering from severe unemployment.

Lebanon then became a separate state, which was three times the size of the district it had been previously, so that Greater Lebanon acquired the predominantly Muslim areas of Beirut, Tripoli, Sidon and Tyre, the fertile plains of the Biqa Valley and the Shia Muslim districts south of Mount Hermon, although the majority of the inhabitants of these regions had no wish to belong to Maronite-dominated Lebanon.

The inhabitants of Syria suffered greatly from the carving-up of their territory because where they had once been able to travel freely between one place and another, there were now barriers, and families were separated so that merchants in Damascus or Aleppo were cut off from their relatives in Jerusalem, Beirut, Tripoli or Jaffa. The deep bitterness and total disillusionment caused by the dismemberment had their effect on the political development of Syria and ensured instability in the area. This, in turn, affected wider Arab politics.[47]

The Arabs had not even been informed about the decisions taken by the British and the French concerning the administration of Syria and, after the fate of the country had been settled, there was disagreement between the two powers concerning the governing of internal Syria which was then in the hands of King Feisal, but which France wished to take over. In March 1919, President Wilson of the United States suggested that an international commission of enquiry should be held to determine the wishes of the population of the areas concerned, but both Britain and France refused to participate. The commission, therefore, became an exclusively American one, which was known as the King-Crane Commission as it was composed of Dr Henry Churchill King and Charles Crane. Their findings were ignored at the time and they were not published until 1922.

The commission had advised against partition because it found Syria's 'economic, geographic, racial and language unity too manifest', and urged that 'the unity of Syria be preserved in accordance with the earnest petition of the great majority of the people of Syria', warning against the danger 'of breaking Syria up into meaningless fragments'. Although the commission had, originally, been sympathetic towards Zionism, its members came to the conclusion that the Zionist programme of unlimited Jewish immigration which planned to make Palestine 'distinctly a Jewish State' required 'serious modification', because it involved 'a gross violation' of the principle of self-determination and 'of the people's rights' which could be imposed only by force.[48]

Feisal and other leaders made speeches calling for Christian, Muslim and Jewish unity in a common struggle, but, as Syrian or Arab nationalism reached the consciousness of the masses, it turned into Sunni Muslim nationalism and sometimes fanaticism which was intensified by French efforts to exploit sectarian divisions.[49]

There was much anti-Zionist sentiment in Iraq, as in all Arab countries, and there were demonstrations in the streets against the British Zionist, Sir Alfred Mond, when he visited Baghdad in February 1928, while demonstrations in the city and the mosques took place the following year, accompanied by a two-minute silence in parliament, newspapers with black borders and telegrams to London concerning Iraqi disapproval of Britain's pro-Zionist attitude; but the time when these emotions would turn to personal violence directed against the Jews of Baghdad who were anxious to dissociate themselves from Zionism, still lay some years ahead.[50]

Sir Francis Humphrys, who was British Ambassador in Baghdad at the end of 1934, described the situation of Iraqi Jews in a confidential memorandum to the Foreign Office in which he reported that:

> Before the war they probably enjoyed a more favourable position than any other minority in the country. Since 1920, however, Zionism has sown dissension between Jews and Arabs, and a bitterness has grown up between the two peoples which did not previously exist. ... The wiser and more experienced Jews, while probably sympathizing with the general aims of the Zionist

E

movement, openly deplore the unfortunate repercussions which
it has had on their position in Iraq.

They appreciate that feeling is only exacerbated by Zionist
propaganda, and they have no desire that it should be extended
in this country. . . . Jewish newspapers, both British and Palestinian, frequently contain scurrilous attacks on the Iraqi Government, and grossly misleading accounts of the situation of the
Jews in this country. . . . In these circumstances it is, I think,
understandable that the authorities should tend to strike at the
roots of the trouble by endeavouring to prevent the circulation of
publications containing provocative attacks on Iraq.

Indeed, there is much to be said for the banning of such
literature in the interests of the Jews themselves, since the
exacerbation of feeling which follows its entry into this country
seriously impairs their relations with the Arabs. . . .

In my view, there is no natural antagonism between Jew and
Arab in Iraq. . . . Normally, the two communities are friendly
towards each other. . . .[51]

Anti-Zionism increased rapidly in Iraq, where the Arab
strike in Palestine caused several days of mourning in Baghdad
while collections were made for the Palestinian martyrs, and
deputations called on the British ambassador (although Iraq had
gained 'independence' in 1932, it was not freed from colonialist
domination until the revolution of 1958). The strike ended,
following appeals by Iraq, Transjordan and Saudi Arabia, and
these same countries persuaded the Palestinian Arabs to state
their case to the Peel Commission of 1937 instead of boycotting
it, but the report, advocating partition, was issued, and it brought
forth further warnings from Iraq to the British ambassador and
to the League of Nations.[52]

'During the British occupation,' wrote Professor Cohen, the
Jews had 'gained confidence, some feeling themselves to be
British citizens', and they also had an active Zionist organization,
which was officially recognized in Baghdad in March 1921, but,
when Iraq came under British Mandatory control, the authorities refused to renew the licence of the Zionist organization in
July 1922, although the Jews were not attacked, either by the
government or the people, and even Zionist activity was allowed
to continue on a small scale until 1929, when it was forbidden.
From then until 1934 this activity was carried on almost underground. Jews were not, however, harmed as Jews, but contact

with Jews in Palestine was gradually restricted, until it was stopped in 1935.

After the riots which had taken place in Palestine in August 1929, and the large demonstration in Baghdad against Zionism and against British policy in Palestine, no Jews were harmed in Iraq although they began to feel uneasy, especially as regards Palestine and Zionism. They felt it wise to contribute to pro-Arab and anti-Zionist funds and some made anti-Zionist declarations. In July 1935 the president of the illegal Zionist organization was asked to leave the country.[53]

The Arabs became more and more disturbed by Jewish terrorism in Palestine, by evidence of European and American support for Zionism and, especially, by the universal Jewish approval of the Biltmore Programme which had, of course, called for a Jewish commonwealth in the whole of Palestine and for unrestricted Jewish immigration into Palestine. Newspapers in Iraq wrote anxiously against Zionism, and nervousness began to increase among the thousands of Baghdad Jews, to whom Zionism was distasteful and potentially ruinous. In 1945 the British Labour Party, which had achieved power, was known to be mainly pro-Zionist; President Truman of the United States, without waiting for any investigation into the subject, was pressing the British authorities to admit more Jews into Palestine, and the World Zionist Organization had endorsed the extreme Biltmore demands. Little optimism could be felt in Iraq or elsewhere in the Arab world that the rights of the Palestinian people whose homes, country and very lives were in jeopardy would be upheld. Iraq announced a boycott of all goods from Palestine, to take effect from 1 January 1946.[54]

At the same time as insisting on an independent Arab Palestine, the Arab League was also issuing assurances that, if such a State were established, the Jewish minority in it would have little to fear, but, by 1947, the tone had altered and Arab politicians began issuing warnings about the position of the Jews in the Arab countries. The entire Arabic press displayed a total opposition to Zionism, and the speeches of Arab politicians tended to rouse the masses to hysterical anger against the Zionists.

A statement made by Faris al-Khoury, the Syrian representative, was typical of the comments being made by Arab dele-

gates to the United Nations. In an interview which was reported
in the *New York Times* on 19 February 1947, he said: 'Unless
the Palestine problem is settled, we shall have difficulty in pro-
tecting and safeguarding the Jews in the Arab world.'

Haykal Pasha, the Egyptian delegate to the United Nations
Palestine Committee, said on 24 November: 'At present, we regard the million Jews in our countries as brothers ... your
decision might prompt some of our people to regard them as
enemies (*Manchester Guardian*, 25 November 1947).'[55]

At that time, too, as in previous eras when they had aligned
themselves with despotic rulers, the Jews caused feelings of
resentment among their fellow-citizens in certain Arab countries
because in Egypt, for example, most of the Jews, including the
local ones, considered themselves to be strangers and some of
them did not even learn to read and write Arabic. Most of them
attended foreign schools, and they felt superior to the local
Muslims while they showed no interest in Egypt's struggle for
independence.

When Britain granted independence to Egypt in 1922, the
political situation of the Jews did not change and, from 1924
until 1952, they were represented in the Egyptian Chamber of
Deputies and the Senate, and a Jew was appointed Minister of
Finance. A large number of Jews were in the civil service and,
until the rise of Zionism, there was no sign of anti-Jewish feelings in Egypt except on the part of the Christians who, as we have
already seen, occasionally spread blood-libels against them.

From 1938, there were incitements against the Jews, and
these were the result of nationalist activity. At that time, an
organization led by Ali Alluba Pasha became active in Egypt,
and it called for the imposition of a boycott against Egyptian
Jews because they were accused of raising money for the Zionists
in Palestine.[56]

The *Jewish Chronicle* described how Jews in Egypt had never
had such a good life because they were well-educated and well-
paid and, indeed, enjoying the best of what life had to offer.
Their prosperity was said to have come about through Egypt's
trade which was conducted by its Jewish citizens. Of these
Jews, only about twenty per cent had bothered to take out
Egyptian citizenship because they considered it more sensible to
have foreign nationality as those whom 'the British called Wogs

respected, they believed, people who were considered colonialists'.[57]

The Egyptian Nationality Law of 1929 had declared that every resident's application for Egyptian citizenship would be granted unless it was proved that he held the nationality of some other country, but, with few exceptions, the Jews of Egypt, including those born in the country, did not take the trouble to apply for Egyptian citizenship as they did not think the matter was very important.[58]

The Jews of Iraq were very much more assimilated than the Egyptian Jews and, at first, they had no problems because, from the time that the Iraqi authorities had begun, in August 1929, to prohibit Zionist activities and to attempt to cut off contacts between the Iraqi Jews and the Zionists in Palestine, the Jews were not persecuted as Jews.[59] The Jews knew little about Zionism and they were not interested in it. In the opinion of Professor Cohen, they may also have been afraid of the Arabs who had, he wrote, shown a lack of tolerance towards national minorities by the massacre of the Assyrians in the summer of 1933 and by the repeated attacks on the Kurds. He believed that it was possible that if it had not been for the policy adopted by the heads of the Jewish community in avoiding Zionist activity, the Jews of Iraq would also have been considered a national minority and they might have angered Arab nationalists, but, as long as they remained a religious minority, they remained unharmed, as other Iraqi religious minorities were unharmed.[60]

DUAL LOYALTIES?

Nathan Weinstock has written that: 'By improperly posing as the representatives of world Jewry—although six-sevenths of the Jews live outside Israel—and by spreading in international public opinion the notion of unconditional solidarity of the Jews with Israel, Zionist leaders in fact stimulate anti-Semitism. This is especially true in the Arab countries, where each Israeli military victory has allowed reactionaries to blame it on the indigenous Jewish communities which have, despite themselves, been compromised by the imperialist policies of the Jewish state.'[61]

We are told that:

The State of Israel regards itself as the creation of the entire Jewish people. . . . The State of Israel recognizes the World Zionist Organization as the authorized agency which will continue to operate in the State of Israel for the development and settlement of the country, the absorption of immigrants from the Diaspora and the co-ordination of the activities in Israel of Jewish institutions and organizations active in those fields. . . . The mission of gathering in the exiles, which is the central task of the State of Israel and the Zionist Movement in our days, requires constant efforts by the Jewish people in the Diaspora; the State of Israel, therefore, expects the co-operation of all Jews, as individuals and groups, in building up the State and assisting the immigration into it of the masses of the people, and regards the unity of all sections of Jewry as necessary for this purpose.[62]

It is obvious that such demands, made on loyal citizens (who, apparently, have no say in the matter) of countries which are on terms of friendship with Israel, such as those in Western Europe or the United States, are not likely to jeopardize (or have not jeopardized so far) the position of the Jewish populations of these places, but, in countries which considered themselves to be at war with Israel, such attitudes inevitably brought suspicion and anger down on the heads of the hapless indigenous Jews. Their situation was not helped at all by the frequently expressed pretence that—to quote Mr Yigal Allon, a former Foreign Minister of Israel—'Zionism is in reality a modern expression of Judaism',[63] while Jewish alarm could only be enhanced by the knowledge that: 'Strong appeals to world Jewry to settle in Israel and implied criticism of Jews who either remain in their own countries or settle outside Israel were made by Israeli leaders. . . .'[64]

Although fears had been expressed by many Jews concerning the problems which would be caused by Zionism to Jews in the West, it did not occur to them in the early days that the difficulties would be immensely magnified for Jews in the Arab countries. A month before the establishment of the Jewish State, George Edinger prophesied the contradictions which would eventually arise when he wrote:

There is no reason in Zionism. . . . Ethnically and historically, it is hard to see where the Zionist claim to Palestine lies. Economically, a Jewish Palestine, let alone a Jewish half of Palestine, could never absorb a fraction of the world's Jews. Far from ending race antagonisms as Zionists profess, it could only acerbate them, as it has already done, by branding the Jews as strangers in all the lands where they have painfully won the rights of full citizenship. . . . The Jews . . . were in Palestine as conquerors, and their conquest, according to the Old Testament, was achieved by distinctly Nazi methods. Nor were they any longer in the land than, for instance, the Romans. Compared with nine centuries of Arab rule, the period of Jewish domination, which covered four centuries between the final capture of Jerusalem by King David in 1048 B.C., and the storming of Jerusalem by the Babylonians in 605 B.C. is not impressive. Nor, in fact, is it by any means certain that there is such a thing as a Jewish race at all, or that any appreciable proportion of those who practise the Jewish faith ever came from Palestine. . . . The largest single block won for Judaism were the Khazars, a Black Sea tribe converted in the eighth century, from whom most Jews in the world of 1948 most probably spring.[65]

Unfortunately for all the inhabitants of the Middle East, however, the Zionists were determined to establish a solely Jewish State. For many years, the fiction was maintained that the Palestinians had forfeited their right to statehood by refusing to agree to the partition of their country and the refusal to hand over the major and most fertile part of it to a minority group of foreign settlers—a totally illogical argument, in any case. It is now abundantly clear, however, that the Zionist intention always was to make the whole of Palestine into a Jewish State.

Jewish allegiance to, and support for, this State was not only encouraged but was taken for granted; and the Arabs, not unnaturally, became more and more dubious about the affiliations of their Jewish neighbours who were subjected to much coercion from Zionist 'emissaries' who travelled throughout the Arab countries, attempting to persuade Jews to emigrate to Palestine.

The Zionist demands for Jewish loyalty have been voiced by even such 'moderate' Zionists as Dr Nahum Goldmann, a former president of the World Jewish Congress who, although often critical of Israel's policies, said: 'The real test of Jewish solidarity with Israel will come when we support Israel against the views of the states in which we live.' He also spoke of 'the absolute obligation of all Jews to stand by Israel in case of need even if they, themselves, disagree with Israel's policies. . . . This absolute obligation to support Israel will expose the Jews to charges of double loyalty.'[66]

It is not difficult to imagine the effect of such opinions, which have been voiced by Zionists for many years, on people in the Arab countries, but what is surprising is that the Arabs, at a time when they were struggling to free themselves from feudalism and foreign occupation, were expected to behave with far greater magnanimity, sophistication and wisdom than western countries at a totally different stage of development.

In 1946, a Jewish publication announced that, in general, the pages of Jewish history in the Islamic world made pleasant reading, but it was difficult to generalize on the situation of Jews in the Muslim countries at that time because conditions varied according to the state of development of the countries concerned. These were going through a transitional period in which the old order of Islam was breaking up, and, also, the war had caused a deterioration of ethics and morals similar to that which had occurred in the west. The growth of nationalist movements, economic chaos, the development of a middle class and the struggle of labourers and peasants for a better life were all factors which had to be considered.

It was therefore natural that Jews should feel insecure and should face the future with some dread, but many Moroccan, Algerian and Tunisian Jews were supporting the nationalist movements in their countries, although the supporters of both French assimilation and Zionism were trying their best to disturb the accord of Jews and their fellow-citizens. Zionism had also been responsible for a deterioration of the Jewish position in Egypt, Iraq, Syria and Lebanon, added the article, and, in these countries, it was considered a threat to Arab interests and a means of creating a British bridgehead which would split and control the Arab world.

The Zionist 'missionaries' had shown a complete disregard for the safety of their fellow-Jews who had, at that time, a large measure of autonomy with regard to personal status, taxation, etc. In all these countries, there were Jewish government officials, members of parliament, professional men and rich merchants who played an active part in the political and economic life of their countries and were keen supporters of Arab aspirations.[67]

The account added that modern nationalist Arab theory

considers all those who speak Arabic as Arabs, and prominent
Arab leaders of that time had often stressed the distinction between Jews and Zionists; it especially referred to one of these
leaders, Abdurrahman Pasha Azzam, the Secretary-General of
the Arab League.[68]

Maurice Roumani wrote, however, that: 'As early as 1950,
Ismat, an Arab author, had warned . . .' that the Jews in the
Arab countries were, like the rest of the Jews in the world,
Zionists who were 'nothing but a fifth column in every country'.[69]

Such views were hardly unexpected, considering the bitterness
and hatred with which Zionism was viewed in the Arab world,
and the insistence of the Zionists in claiming the allegiance of all
Jews. The Arabs were by no means unique in such an attitude,
for other countries at a more advanced stage of development also
treated with suspicion those who were thought to have connections, no matter how tenuous, with an enemy. Thus those unfortunate German Jews who had sought refuge in Britain were
treated in a disgraceful manner in 1940 although they were the
last people in the world to merit such treatment.

During the second half of April 1940, a campaign being conducted in Britain against 'the fifth column' which had been
started by some members of parliament who were concerned
about certain high-born British subjects with markedly pro-
Nazi sympathies, was whipped up by the 'popular' press into a
demand to intern all aliens, under the spurious pretext that
'popular opinion' demanded it. Those papers which were most
active in the agitation against refugees were those which, before
the war, were the keenest in their advocacy of appeasement and
of collaborating with dictators. By insinuation and downright
lying, the true 'fifth-columnists' succeeded in creating the
impression that the traitors in Britain were the unfortunate
Jewish refugees from Hitlerism. The irresponsible sections of
the press eventually managed to provoke public antagonism
towards the refugees, and so, eventually, Jews who had struggled
against Nazi tyranny in their own countries before escaping to the
'safety' of Britain were sent off to internment camps.[70]

Bearing in mind the different states of development of Great
Britain and the Arab countries at that time, one might also in-
clude the example of Prince Louis of Battenberg who was
Britain's First Sea Lord at the outbreak of the First World

War. He had received this appointment on merit after forty-six years of distinguished service in the British navy, and yet, less than three months after the outbreak of war, he was forced to resign from office because of a public outcry over the fact that he had been born in Germany—the same hysteria, against everything German which at that time made it unsafe even to be seen exercising one's pet dachshund in public.[71]

It should not be difficult, therefore, to imagine the Arab reaction to such statements as that made by David Ben Gurion when he said:

> Even those Jews who have rejected the choice of *aliya* [emigration to Israel, literally 'ascension' as if to heaven], which the Declaration of Independence [the creation of Israel as a Jewish State] offered them, view the State as a national possession of their own. When a Jew in America or South Africa speaks of 'our Government' to his fellow-Jews, he usually means the Government of Israel, while the Jewish public in various countries view the Israeli Ambassadors as their own representatives.[72]

Although the previously cited statement of Dr Nahum Goldmann was made in comparatively recent times, he had expressed similar opinions some twenty years ago and, although he was speaking mainly of American Jews, his views were noted in the Arab countries and they were used as justification of the harsh treatment of Jews who found themselves increasingly powerless to combat the accusations against them. Thus ill-feeling against the Jews mounted, irrespective of whether they supported Zionism or not, when Dr Goldmann said that Jews had 'to overcome the conscious or unconscious fear of so-called double loyalty',[73] and 'American Jews must have the courage to declare openly that they entertain a double loyalty, one to the land in which they live and one to Israel. Jews should not succumb to patriotic talk that they owe allegiance only to the land in which they live. . . . They should live not only as patriots of the country of their domicile, but also as patriots of Israel. . . .'[74]

But probably one of the most damaging declarations as far as the Jews of the Arab countries were concerned, and one which was made at a time when many of them had not yet been obliged to leave their countries, was that of Dr Goldmann (an American citizen): 'Israel's flag is our flag. We must see to it that the

Zionist flag which has begun to fly over the State of Israel is hoisted aloft over the entire Jewish people until we achieve the completion of the ingathering of the exiles.'[75]

'Emissaries'

Before the Jews of the Middle East came into contact with modern, political Zionism, their 'Zionism' took the form of a religious attachment to Palestine, and especially to Jerusalem, such as is shared by Christians and Muslims throughout the world. The dearth of information on the subject of 'oriental' Zionism has been attributed to the suddenness with which the exodus of Jews from Arab countries took place and to the fact that most of the archives of the various Jewish communities in the Arab world were destroyed or abandoned. In addition, the secretiveness with which the Zionist movement operated in these countries also contributed to the general failure to maintain adequate records.[76]

The Zionist movement had very little success or effect in the Arab countries, and this was mainly due to the fact that those who ran it were almost exclusively of Eastern European origin and had made hardly any effort to understand the outlook and customs of the Jews in these countries. The emissaries who were sent to North Africa, for example, further demonstrated the complete lack of understanding of the Zionist leadership because those who were chosen to present the Zionist case to the leaders of the Jewish communities had no method of communicating with these Jews; not only did they have no knowledge of Arabic but few of them could speak French and none of them knew anything about the psychology of the local Jews.[77]

Because they refused to acknowledge the causes of the Arab opposition to Zionism, the European Zionists had no other choice than to ignore or dismiss, for the time being, the basic difficulties of the Arab Jews. They therefore assured the Jews that there was no Arab antagonism towards them, on the one hand, and they urged them to leave their jobs and possessions, on the other, in order to emigrate *en masse* to a country where immigration was both restricted and selective. Zionist propaganda methods demonstrated a similar obtuseness.

Discussions centred exclusively on the problems of European

Jews and the history of Jews in Russia or Poland, as if the Arab Jews did not exist. In addition, the language and propaganda had no meaning for the Arab Jews and, in Egypt at any rate, it was not surprising that the activities of the Zionists had little effect.[78]

The Zionists had certainly tried to win over the Egyptian Jews by establishing Zionist organizations in Egypt as early as the beginning of the twentieth century,[79] but, even so, the basic aims of Zionism remained a mystery, and it was not understood that the movement was not a humanitarian one, devoted to the saving of Jewish lives. Thus in a description of how two Zionist emissaries had come to an arrangement with the Gestapo and the S.S., two Zionist writers, Jon and David Kimche, wrote:

> These two Jewish emissaries had not come to Nazi Germany to save German Jews: that was not their job. Their eyes were fixed entirely on Palestine and the British Mandatory. . . . Their interest in those German Jews who turned to Palestine as a haven of refuge as the next best after the United States, or the United Kingdom, was secondary to their main purpose. . . .[80]

In recent years, too, there have been many cases of Soviet Jews who left Israel and went to various European countries but were refused assistance by Jewish relief organizations which said that they were only prepared to help Jews making their way to Israel. In a report headed, 'Hundreds of Soviet Jews pour into Belgium', the *Jewish Chronicle* described how a Roman Catholic charity was providing accommodation for some thirty Jews who were arriving daily from Israel. The report added that, having left Israel, the Jews could no longer be considered 'refugees' and were therefore not entitled to any help.[81] In Italy, Soviet Jews who had left Israel and were in 'dire straits' were being 'ostracized' by Jewish relief organizations such as the Jewish Agency, the Joint Distribution Committee and others, but they were being given assistance by the orthodox Rav Tov[82] which is strongly anti-Zionist, and, even in Britain, a group of Soviet Jews who had left Israel appealed for help to Jewish relief and welfare organizations which refused to give them any assistance because they had left Israel.[83]

After the war, many victims of Nazism chose to settle in the United States or other Western countries in spite of efforts to persuade them to make their way to Palestine. At a meeting of the Israeli Cabinet on 15 August 1948, the Prime Minister, David Ben Gurion, said: 'Generations have not suffered and struggled in vain to see only eight hundred thousand Jews in this country. It is the duty of the present generation to redeem the Jews in the Arab and European countries.'[84]

Before the commencement of the Zionist campaign concerning them, very few Arab Jews settled in Palestine, with the exception of the Jews of Yemen, but they were a special case because Yemen, of all the Arab countries, was particularly intolerant towards non-Muslims as the majority of the population practised sectarian Islam. In the central part of the country, most of the inhabitants were Shiites, who were characterized by an especially legalistic attitude towards religion, and this led to great stress being attached to the study of religious law; nevertheless, the Jews of Yemen felt that they belonged to the country and they accepted, with equanimity, the discriminatory laws concerning them.[85]

In any event, the situation which existed in the past, and even until comparatively recent times, is entirely different from the current attitude towards minorities existing in modern South and North Yemen. Even in less enlightened days, however, the Jews were not singled out as Jews, although modern writers often claim that they were.

Because the Yemeni Jews were extremely pious and looked upon settlement in Palestine from a religious rather than a Zionist nationalist viewpoint, a few thousand of them arrived in the 1880s, but they became paupers because their jewellery-making skills were not required. In 1908 the Palestine office of the Zionist movement commissioned one of its specialists, Dr J. Thon, to prepare a report on methods of making Jewish labour more competitive with Arab labour. This report stressed the importance of employing Jewish instead of Arab labour as this was one of the primary objectives of the Zionist colonization. The Thon Report suggested that the previously unsuccessful attempts to turn the Yemenites into agricultural labourers should be renewed. The Yemenites were hard workers and, if they could be settled in the colonies, their women and girls would work as domestic servants for the Zionists instead of the Arab women and girls who were at that time employed by almost every family of colonists.

It was then decided to import more Yemenites for the menial tasks which eventually became scorned by the European Jews. In December 1910 an emissary was sent to Yemen to tell the Jews that the Messiah was coming and that riches would be bestowed upon the Jews in the land of their ancestors. As a result of his efforts, several hundred Jewish families emigrated from Yemen to Palestine in the year 1912 alone.

Once sufficient labourers for the Jewish farms had been obtained, the Zionists decided to stop further Yemeni immigration 'until further notice' or, presumably, until the Zionists required more hewers of wood and drawers of water.[86]

The first Zionist emissaries to be sent to Middle Eastern countries other than Yemen for the express purpose of arranging the emigration of Jews to Palestine arrived in Damascus, Aleppo, Beirut and other Arab cities in 1938. They were under the command of Davidka Nameri, a settler from Ashdot Yaakov in the Jordan valley, and, after the Allied invasion of Syria in June 1941, Zionist activities in the Arab countries were increased. Some of the emissaries organized the smuggling of Jews to Palestine and others were sent to accelerate the indoctrination of young Jews in Arab cities where active assistance was given to the Zionists by the two Palestinian units in the British army which were stationed in Syria. The 'operation' was directed by members of *Mossad* (*Mossad le Aliya Beth*—'the Committee for Illegal Immigration'), and, in addition to Nameri, who was in charge of the activities of the emissaries in Syria and Lebanon, there were Enzo Sereni and others in Iraq, and Ruth Klieger in Egypt.[87]

Lithuanian-born Bracha Habas, a delegate at several Zionist congresses and a biographer of David Ben Gurion, explained that from the very first young Syrian Jews were more actively engaged in helping the Zionist emissaries than young Iraqi Jews. A Zionist youth group was formed in Damascus as early as 1929, and two years later this group produced leaders for the *Hehalutz Hatzair* ('The Young Pioneer') which was the first of the *Hehalutz* organizations that were formed in the countries of the Middle East. Bracha Habas wrote: 'It was the *Hehalutz* youth movement in Damascus that educated its members towards *aliya*—emigration to Palestine—and a life of labour in the Homeland, and took upon itself the responsibility for organizing underground emigration even before the coming of the emissaries of the Bureau. The initiative of these pioneer youths and the help they gave the emissaries made possible the emigration of the majority of Syrian and Lebanese Jewry into Palestine in the period between the two World Wars.'[88]

The account adds that the aforementioned events had been made possible by Syria's proximity to Palestine and by the Palestinian 'refugees and deportees' who had, during the First World War, established the Zionist pioneer group in what was referred to as 'the Damascus ghetto' and had converted some young Syrian Jews to Zionism when Yehuda Kopilevitz (Almog), addressed a gathering which was the first meeting of the Syrian Jews with 'an emissary who preached the goals of *Hehalutz* and the Hebrew labour movement'. In the course of his talk, he emphasized the necessity of 'settling the Hauran area', and he explained that, as members of his audience were near this region, they could play a decisive role in Jewish settlement there. The young Jews, however, realizing that their movement would be faced with strong opposition from the general Jewish population, decided to carry out their activities in secret.[89]

Munya M. Mardor, a member of Haganah (the Jewish army in Palestine before the establishment of the State of Israel) and one of the emissaries, wrote in a book with a foreword by David Ben Gurion that:

> Our chief concern in Syria and Lebanon was, as I have said, to persuade the youth to settle in Palestine. For the most part, the middle-aged and older Jews had become reconciled to their lot, and it was next to impossible to wean them from the attitudes and habits of generations, and to fire them with zest for a new life in the land of their fathers. The idea of beginning life afresh was a little too much for them. We usually had to accept that attitude, but not the assumption that the young people were satisfied with their lot and with the prospect of going on in their parents' immutable ways. We were determined to get them to Palestine and to a life of freedom, and of work in the service of their natural homeland.[90]

The emissaries also met with Jewish opposition in Egypt where the community was well established and included many rich and influential persons who looked upon Zionism in Palestine with considerable trepidation lest it might affect their settled positions in Egypt. They were considered to be—as, indeed, they were—loyal Egyptians, and so when Ruth Klieger was sent to Egypt to establish an organization for illegal immigration to Palestine and to raise funds for this purpose from the rich Jews in the country, Katani Pasha, the wealthy head of the Jewish community in Cairo, warned her that he would set his dogs on her and, indeed, on any other Zionist emissary who visited Cairo.

Her efforts, nevertheless, met with more success in Alexandria where she managed to convert some rich Jews to the Zionist cause, and, a few months later, she had succeeded in amassing £80,000 for additional illegal immigration.[91]

One of those who was most active in the support of the work of the emissaries was Berl Katznelson.[92] As has already been described in this chapter, Katznelson had declared in 1937 that in his opinion the Palestinians were destined to move to Syria and Iraq.

Although it was an acknowledged fact that the Iraqi Jews knew nothing about Zionism and, initially, wanted to have no contact with it, Bracha Habas wrote:

> In every period when Jews lived in Iraq, the longing for Zion was the chief force in the lives of the oppressed Jewish merchants, peddlers and artisans, who prayed for the day when the Messiah would come and return them to their land. However, Jewish migration from Iraq to Palestine had always been minute—a family or small groups now and then—and there had never been an open, active, Zionist movement in the country.[93]

She also wrote, however, that:

> . . . in spite of all their [the emissaries'] efforts, they did not achieve their main goal at the beginning of their activity. Jews were in no hurry to go to Palestine. One of the principal obstacles that stood in the emissaries' way was the Iraqi Jews' fear that they would have to engage in physical labour in the Homeland. For them, 'work' meant trade or peddling, but not physical labour. . . . In addition, they were afraid of emigrating to Palestine illegally.[94]

She added that: '. . . no sooner did the wounds inflicted by the pogroms of June 1941 [which will be described in the next chapter] begin to heal over slightly, than the Jews began to sink roots anew in the hostile country. Jews invested large sums of money in the construction of the new Baghdad; they erected a Jewish neighbourhood which became the centre of the capital. Within two years' time Jewish capital had created an entire city', and she added that it soon became obvious to the emissaries that few Jews were prepared to accept Zionist ideology. 'Enzo Sereni tried to win converts from among the intelligentsia but failed.'[95]

On the page after that on which she had referred to the 'oppressed' Jews of Iraq who were constantly 'longing for Zion', Bracha Habas wrote that at that time there were one hundred and twenty thousand Jews in Iraq of whom about one hundred thousand lived in Baghdad and constituted one-third of the population of the capital, and that some of them were rich merchants but the majority were members of the middle class. She explained that, when Iraq achieved independence at the end of the First World War (as has already been explained, Iraq achieved nominal independence in 1932 and full independence in 1958), the Jews played an important role in the Iraqi economy and government. The network of schools operated by the Alliance Israelite Universelle taught European languages as well as providing a general education, and Zionist activity flourished openly. In 1930 there were ten Jewish schools in Baghdad with a total of seven thousand two hundred pupils, two thousand of whom were girls. These pupils were taught Hebrew by teachers from Palestine who also organized Zionist activities. Bracha Habas added that, when the first group of Zionist emissaries arrived in Baghdad in 1942: 'The Jewish population was very fearful, and the emissaries realized that they would first have to educate the people before they could even hope to achieve anything.' They decided therefore that their first task was to teach Hebrew, but, as it was difficult to cross the border illegally, the emissaries gave lessons themselves instead of bringing in teachers from Palestine. These lessons were conducted in complete secrecy, while the emissaries went to great lengths to form a group of students who had learned Hebrew years before under Zionist teachers such as Reuben Zaslani (Shiloah) who had been expelled from the country by the Iraqi Government. All these activities took place at a time when the study of the Hebrew language was outlawed, along with all Zionist activities.[96]

Enzo Sereni, the leader of the Zionist underground movement in Iraq, was of the opinion that a large Jewish State should be established and: 'We must declare that at the end of the war we aim to transfer the bulk of the Jewish people to Israel and to proclaim: we are liquidating the Diaspora. Now, while the war is still on, we must educate the Jewish people towards such a transfer.'[97] He did not, however, live to see the outcome of his ambition, for he was captured by the Germans after landing by parachute in Italy in 1943 in an effort to save the Jews there (he was Italian and was a member of an old Roman Jewish family), and he died in Dachau.[98]

Solel Boneh, the construction company of the Histadrut (the Zionist labour federation), had been given a contract by the British to build airfields and other security installations, and also to expand the oil refineries in Iraq. Solel Boneh employed about four hundred Jewish engineers and technicians in Iraq, and Enzo Sereni went to Iraq in the guise of an employee of the construction company although he wore a British uniform marked 'special' because the British had demanded that all Solel Boneh employees should wear uniform in order to conceal their identities.[99]

There were also two other Zionist emissaries in Iraq, Shmarya Gutman and Ezra Kaduri who was a native of Iraq and had settled in Palestine as a child. A Jewish family called Sehayek rented a house in their own name in order to serve the movement, and he moved into it to conceal the house's true purpose. Although Enzo Sereni found that there was sympathy for the Jewish community in Palestine among Iraq's Jews, there was no Zionist political awareness, and he attempted to stimulate an interest in Zionism among Iraqi Jews and also to persuade the rich members of the community to donate money to the Zionist cause in Palestine. On one occasion, in 1942, he went to the office of Ezra Haddad, the director of a Jewish school and a member of the Iraqi Academy, and said: 'It is time that you work for the national cause. Your place is with us.' He succeeded in enlisting Ezra Haddad's help, and then he went to Palestine where he reported on his activities in Iraq, and he had the Zionist classic, *Auto-emancipation*, translated into Arabic as well as organizing the study of Hebrew among Iraqi Jews.[100]

When the first three emissaries had arrived in Iraq, they had taken it for granted that, following the riots of 1941, a large number of Iraqi Jews would want to set off for Palestine immediately. But by the time they got there nine months had passed since the riots and there was no further opportunity for encouraging large-scale emigration. In a report to the Jewish Agency, Sereni wrote: 'In recent weeks there has occurred a noticeable change in the mood of the Jewish population in Iraq, which cancels the enthusiasm for Palestine that was brought about by the oppression and the riots of last year.' He added that there were various causes for this attitude, one of which was the Jewish talent for 'forgetting and adapting to new circumstances that characterizes Jews everywhere', and there was also the current prosperity, resulting from the war, which all classes, and especially the traders, were enjoying. In addition, there was the attitude of the Iraqi Government which had paid compensation to the victims of the riots.[101]

Some young Jews, however, were persuaded to emigrate to Palestine, but a group of six young Iraqis, dressed as Arab peasants, who attempted to reach Palestine by illegal methods raised suspicions when they sat in a café in Aleppo in Syria talking loudly in the Baghdad dialect. They were arrested but soon released by means of bribery, and the emissaries moved to new addresses and discontinued their contacts for a while.[102]

Late in August 1942, Moshe Dayan arrived in Baghdad with three suitcases full of weapons for 'the Haganah cell in Baghdad',[103] He wrote that: 'The arms consisted of grenades—the well-known Mills Bomb and another variety, called "Polish Bombs" and made in our own workshops, which, however, we were reluctant to send because if come upon by investigators they could so easily be traced back to their origin. All these, together with practice bombs and a number of revolvers as well as the necessary ammunition, had been supplied from a Haganah arsenal.' This first consignment, however, had been a comparatively small one, and a method had to be found for 'getting the main supplies on their way, together with the wireless equipment for receiving and transmitting messages'. An opportunity arose when one of the Jewish transport units of the RASC, commanded by Captain Sammy Neeman, was ordered to form a convoy and proceed to Baghdad. The convoy was led by Sergeant Disjatnick and, shortly before it set off, the Zionists learned that

it was going across the Allenby Bridge over the Jordan River and
from there to Amman and to Mafrak, the terminus, and that it
was not due to go to Baghdad at all. Sergeant Disjatnick then
offered to take the whole consignment of arms from Mafrak to
Baghdad in a truck which he would detach from the unit and
drive himself. On top of the contents of the truck was placed one
of Disjatnick's wolf-hounds, tied to the back flap of the truck.
This meant that anyone trying to examine the contents of the
vehicle would encounter the fierce visage of the huge dog and
would hesitate before continuing his examination. The truck
safely reached Baghdad, and the arms and wireless equipment
were handed over to the members of the Zionist underground
there.[104]

In 1947 weapons were still being smuggled into Iraq, as was
made clear by a letter written on 1 January 1947 by Yigal Allon,
a former Deputy Prime Minister of Israel, and at that time
commander of the Palmach (described as 'the striking arm' of
Haganah) to Dan Ram, who he referred to as 'commander of the
Jewish ghettos in Iraq', in which he said he would do his utmost
to increase the Zionist underground's arms supplies and wished
Dan Ram luck with his primitive production of explosives.

He added: 'You see, Ramadan [Dan Ram's code name], one
cannot escape "soap-box Zionism". . . . You are doing the right
thing by combining your educational-organizational work with
the efforts of the pioneer-youth movements there. We must encourage all forms of immigration and I am very satisfied with
your efforts in this field. The sooner we bring these Jews over
here, thereby assuring their existence and increasing our strength
here, the better.'[105]

The emissaries had, meanwhile, widened their sphere of
activities because, wrote Bracha Habas: '. . . the search for new
bases for the illegal immigration effort was an unending one.
Step by step, the young men of the Bureau combed every Jewish
centre of population that was accessible to them by land. As a
result, in the thick of the Second World War, they hit on the
idea of expanding the effort to include North Africa. . . . It was
to this unknown and distant Jewry that the Bureau turned in
1943 in its search for new bases of operation.'[106]

The first three emissaries to be sent to Tunisia were Efraim
Friedman, Yigael Cohen and Naftali Bar Giyora. They were

supplied with military uniforms and passes[107] and they found that at that time there were more than eighty thousand Jews in Tunisia, living in various parts of the country. The Jews provided a link between the people of the country and the French rulers. They ran the cooking-oil and spice trades, and they were the important land-owners. They also constituted the majority of the Tunisian intelligentsia for they were the doctors, the pharmacists and the lawyers. A mere six thousand were French citizens and the remainder were subjects of the Bey. In spite of the fact that the emissaries arrived in Tunisia only four months after it had been liberated from Nazi occupation, they found that the Jews had been virtually unharmed owing to the vigilance of the Bey.

He invited the heads of the Jewish communities to his residence and, in the presence of members of his court, he declared his loyalty to the Jews—and he kept to his word. After the withdrawal of the Germans, however, the French deposed the Bey and he was replaced by one of his more pliant relatives who carried out all the commands of the French.

Shortly after their arrival in Tunisia, the emissaries discovered a strange phenomenon which was that the Jews did not hate the Germans who had killed few people during their occupation of the country although they did cause a rift in the Jewish community by bestowing certain privileges upon one section. The Jews refused to believe what the emissaries related to them concerning the extermination of European Jewry. Those who conceded that their account was true maintained that the Germans might do such a thing to the 'insolent' Jews of Poland, but not to obedient Jews like themselves.[108]

The emissaries persuaded some of the young Tunisian Jews to form a group, similar to the secret Haganah cells in Palestine, and in what Bracha Habas called 'an impressive and moving ceremony' the young Tunisians were sworn in in a dark, candle-lit room before a table which held a pistol and a Bible. At that time, there was virtually no Zionist consciousness in Tunisia.[109] One of the first actions of the emissaries was the establishment of Zionist organizations, but all these activities were carried out secretly, as Zionist activities and institutions were outlawed by the Government.

The emissaries concentrated their major efforts on the young people and, when they considered that these had been sufficiently indoctrinated with Zionist ideas, they decided to send some of them to Palestine so that they could establish a kibbutz for North African immigrants who would draw their fellow-countrymen to Palestine.[110]

One of the major problems for the Zionists had always been arranging for girls who had led sheltered lives to leave their parents and make their way to Palestine,[111] and it was decided that one of the Tunisian girls who had been chosen as a 'pioneer' would play the part of the wife of one of the boys, but her parents would not agree to the scheme. They padlocked the girl into her room, but after a week they allowed her to resume her teacher's training studies, her mother accompanying her to and from her classes. Meanwhile, the emissaries had studied the laws of the country and had learned that a Jewish girl above the age of twelve and a half could be married according to Jewish tradition, and so, having succeded in escaping her mother's surveillance for a few minutes, the girl underwent the ceremony of convenience. Then the emissaries discovered that even a married woman could not leave the country without her parents' permission and for a week there were violent scenes as the parents threatened to inform the authorities about the movement. Eventually, however, they gave in on condition that they were permitted to see their daughter before she left, and, thus the emigration of the first *halutza* ('girl pioneer') to Palestine was organized.[112]

Writing of the half-million Jews of North Africa, Bracha Habas commented that, for purposes of building up the land, they would make excellent 'human material' (an expression often found in Zionist writings: Theodor Herzl wrote: 'What human material we have in our people. They catch on the wing an idea which you have to hammer into other people's heads. . . .')[113] She added that the Jews were only waiting to be roused, organized and provided with proper leadership.[114] The emissaries met with difficulties, however, because their activities had caused the hostility of local Jews and, one day, they were ordered to appear before the authorities and were shown letters from the Jews denouncing them. They were ordered to leave Tunisia, and returned to Palestine.[115]

Two of the last emissaries to serve in Iraq and one of the first to serve in Syria were elected to the Knesset (Israeli parliament) as a gesture of gratitude towards the young men and women whose tireless efforts had helped so much towards the creation of a Jewish State.[116]

REFERENCES

1. Michael Selzer (ed.) *Zionism Reconsidered*, Macmillan, New York, 1970, p. xi.
2. Amos Elon, *Herzl*, Weidenfeld and Nicolson, London, 1975, p. 290.
3. Moshe Menuhin, *The Decadence of Judaism in our Time*, The Institute for Palestine Studies, Beirut, 1969, p. 36.
4. See Doreen Ingrams, *op. cit.*, pp. 15–16.
5. See Barnet Litvinoff, *Weizmann: Last of the Patriarchs*, Hodder and Stoughton, London, 1976, p. 58.
6. James Parkes, *An Enemy of the People: Anti-Semitism*, Penguin Books, Harmondsworth, 1945, pp. 10–11.
7. Karl Kautsky, *Are the Jews a Race?* Jonathan Cape, London, 1926, pp. 183–4.
8. Theodor Herzl, *The Jewish State*, H. Pordes, London, 1967, p. 57.
9. Theodor Herzl, *Diaries, op. cit.*, p. 62.
10. Herzl, *The Jewish State, op. cit.*, p. 30.
11. George Edinger, 'Background to Zionism', *World Review*, London, April 1948.
12. Selzer, *op. cit.*, pp. xii–xvi.
13. PRO/CAB 24/24, 23 August 1917.
14. Yerachmiel Domb, 'Neturei Karta (1958)', in *Zionism Reconsidered, op. cit.*, p. 43.
15. Neville Laski, *Jewish Rights and Jewish Wrongs*, Soncino Press, London, 1939, pp. 149–50.
16. Nathan Weinstock, 'The Nature of Israel: The Propaganda and the Facts', in *The Truth about Israel and Zionism*, Pathfinder Press, New York, 1970, pp. 4–5. For details about Herzl's approaches to Von Plehve, the notorious anti-Semite who was responsible for the pogrom at Kishinev, see Elon, *op. cit.*, pp. 377–84.
17. PRO/FO, E213/169/42.
18. Kohn, *op. cit.*, p. 32.
19. Weinstock, *op. cit.*, p. 5.
20. Vincent Sheean, 'Holy Land, 1929', in *Personal History*, Doubleday, Doran, New York, 1935, cited in Walid Khalidi (ed.), *From Haven to Conquest*, Institute for Palestine Studies, Beirut, 1971, pp. 280–1.
21. Theodor Herzl, *The Complete Diaries*, Herzl Press and Thomas Yoseloff, New York, 1960, Vol. 1, p. 88.
22. *On the Ways of our Policy*, Report of the Congress of the World Council of Poale Zion, held in Zurich from 29 July to 7 August, 1937, pp. 73–4.

23. *Ibid.*, p. 78.
24. *Ibid.*, pp. 106–7.
25. *Ibid.*, pp. 116–17.
26. *Ibid.*, p. 122. (The figure of 100,000 is inaccurate as there were more Jews than this in Iraq alone.)
27. *Ibid.*, pp. 122–3.
28. *Ibid.*, p. 132.
29. *Ibid.*, pp. 133–4.
30. *Ibid.*, p. 180.
31. Symposium, 'Zionism; A Moral or a Violent Movement?' *Yediot Aharonot*, 8 September 1972.
32. Maxime Rodinson, *Israel and the Arabs*, trans. Michael Perl, Penguin Books, Harmondsworth, 1970, p. 216.
33. Menuhin, *op. cit.*, p. 94.
34. Hannah Arendt, 'Zionism Reconsidered (1945)', in *Zionism Reconsidered, op. cit.*, p. 213.
35. Rodinson, *op. cit.*, p. 40.
36. Joseph Weitz, *My Diary and Letters to the Children* (Hebrew), Massada Publishers, Tel Aviv, 1965, Vol. III, Haifa, 13 June 1948, pp. 301–2.
37. *Ibid.*, Vol. III, Tel Aviv, 15 June 1948, p. 302.
38. *Ibid.*, Vol. III, Tel Aviv, 3 October 1948, p. 346.
39. *Ibid.*, Vol. III, Tel Aviv, 9 December 1948, p. 363.
40. See Cattan, *op. cit.*, pp. 73–88.
41. Nathan Chofshi, *Jewish Newsletter*, New York, 9 February 1959.
42. *Ner* (Ihud Journal: Hebrew), January–February 1961.
43. Erskine Childers, 'The Other Exodus', in *The Spectator*, 12 May 1961. See also weekly correspondence in *The Spectator* from 26 May until 21 July 1961.
44. *Jewish Newsletter*, New York, 9 February 1959.
45. Maurice M. Roumani, 'The Case of the Jews from Arab Countries: A Neglected Issue', in *Case Studies on Human Rights and Fundamental Freedoms: A World Survey*, Willem A. Veenhoven (ed.), Foundation for the Study of Plural Societies, Martinus Nijhoff, The Hague, 1976, Vol. V, pp. 71–3. (This work, which was revealed some time after publication to have been sponsored by the South African Government, contains a contribution defending apartheid.)
46. Landshut, *op. cit.*, pp. 23–4.
47. Tabitha Petran, *Syria*, Ernest Benn, London, 1972, pp. 61–2.
48. *Ibid.*, p. 56.
49. *Ibid.*, p. 57.
50. Stephen Henry Longrigg, *Iraq 1900–1950: A Political, Social and Economic History*, Oxford University Press, London, 1953, pp. 192–3.
51. PRO/FO, E7707/6495/93.
52. Longrigg, *op. cit.*, p. 265.
53. Hayyim J. Cohen, 'The Anti-Jewish *Farhud* in Baghdad, 1941', *Middle Eastern Studies*, October 1966, pp. 4–5.

54. Longrigg, *op. cit.*, pp. 329–30.
55. Landshut, *op. cit.*, p. 26.
56. Hayyim J. Cohen, *The Jews of the Middle East, op. cit.*, p. 48.
57. 25 August 1978.
58. Hayyim J. Cohen, *The Jews of the Middle East, op. cit.*, p. 50.
59. Hayyim J. Cohen, *History of the Zionist Movement in Iraq* (Hebrew), Hasifriyah Hatsiyonit, Jerusalem, 1969, p. 49.
60. *Ibid.*, p. 124. (Albert Hourani, *op. cit.*, explains that the Assyrians 'regarded themselves as in a special way the protégés of the British Government: when the Anglo-Iraqi treaty of 1930 was signed, they thought themselves to have been abandoned by their protectors, and feared the worst. Their fears were intensified by the work among them of a small group of agitators' (p. 101).
61. Weinstock, *op. cit.*, p. 4.
62. Israeli Status Law, Articles 1, 4 and 5, *Israel Government Year Book, 1953–54*, pp. 243–4.
63. *Jewish Chronicle*, 7 November 1975.
64. *Ibid.*, 27 February 1976.
65. Edinger, *op. cit.*
66. Michael Elkins, 'From our own Correspondent', BBC radio report, 7 February 1975.
67. *The Jewish Outlook*, London, May 1946.
68. *Ibid.*
69. Roumani, *op. cit.*, citing 'Ismat', Abd al-Rahman Sami, *al-Sahyuniyya wa al-Masuniyya* (Zionism and Freemasonry), pp. 49–50.
70. F. Lafitte, *The Internment of Aliens*, Penguin Books, Harmondsworth, 1940, pp. 165–8.
71. Robert Lacey, *Majesty: Elizabeth II and the House of Windsor*, Sphere Books, 1978, p. 155.
72. David Ben Gurion, 'Jewish Survival', *Israel Government Year Book, 1953–54*, p. 35.
73. Zionist Ideological Conference, Jerusalem, Spring, 1957.
74. *Jewish Daily Forward*, New York, 9 January 1959.
75. *Zionist Newsletter*, Jerusalem, 2 May 1950.
76. Bat Yeor, 'Zionism in Islamic Lands: The Case of Egypt', *The Wiener Library Bulletin*, Vol. XXX, New Series, 43–44, 1977, pp. 16–17.
77. Chouraqui, *op. cit.*, pp. 258–9.
78. Bat Yeor, *op. cit.* pp. 24–5.
79. *The Jewish Encyclopedia, op. cit.*, Vol. V, p. 67.
80. Jon Kimche and David Kimche, *The Secret Roads: The 'Illegal' Migration of a People 1938–1948*, Secker and Warburg, London, 1954, pp. 26–7.
81. 6 June 1975.
82. *Daily Telegraph*, 4 June 1976.
83. *Jewish Chronicle*, 13 September 1974.
84. Alfred M. Lilienthal, *The Other Side of the Coin*, The Devin-Adair Co., New York, 1965, p. 47.

85. Goitein, *Jews and Arabs*, *op. cit.*, p. 73.
86. Raphael Shapiro, in *Khamsin No. Five*, *op. cit.*, pp. 10–13. See also Baruch Nadel, citing David Siton in 'The Sephardi Communities in Recent Times', *Yediot Aharonot*, 23 July 1976.
87. Kimche, *op. cit.*, pp. 59–60.
88. Bracha Habas, *The Gate Breakers: A Dramatic Chronicle of Jewish Immigration into Palestine*, Herzl Press, New York, 1963, pp. 237–8.
89. *Ibid.*, pp. 238–9.
90. Munya M. Mardor, *Strictly Illegal*, trans. H. A. G. Shmucklev, Foreword by David Ben Gurion, Robert Hale, London, 1964, pp. 89–90.
91. Kimche, *op. cit.*, pp. 64–5.
92. See Habas, *op. cit.*, pp. 240–1, and Ruth Bondy, *The Emissary: A Life of Enzo Sereni*, Afterword by Golda Meir, Robson Books, London, 1978, p. 61.
93. Habas, *op. cit.*, p. 178.
94. *Ibid.*, pp. 186–7.
95. *Ibid.*, p. 187.
96. *Ibid.*, pp. 178–81.
97. Bondy, *op. cit.*, p. 175.
98. *Ibid.*, pp. 230–41.
99. *Ibid.*, p. 195.
100. *Ibid.*, pp. 196–9.
101. *Ibid.*, p. 203.
102. *Ibid.*, p. 202.
103. Moshe Dayan, *Story of my Life*, Weidenfeld and Nicolson, London, 1976, p. 55.
104. Mardor, *op. cit.*, pp. 96–9.
105. Yigal Allon, *The Making of Israel's Army*, Vallentine-Mitchell, in association with Weidenfeld and Nicolson, London, 1970, pp. 134–5.
106. Habas, *op. cit.*, p. 260.
107. *Ibid.*, p. 261.
108. *Ibid.*, p. 271.
109. *Ibid.*, p. 272.
110. *Ibid.*, pp. 274–8.
111. See Bondy, *op. cit.*, pp. 200–1, and Mardor, *op. cit.*, p. 92.
112. Habas, *op. cit.*, pp. 279–80.
113. Mardor (*op. cit.*, p. 92) refers to Jewish girls in Iraq as 'excellent material'. See also Herzl, *Diaries*, *op. cit.*, p. 62.
114. Habas, *op. cit.*, p. 294.
115. *Ibid.*, p. 295.
116. *Ibid.*, p. 226.

Seven

The Violent Years

No matter what they did, the unfortunate Jews of the Arab countries were hopelessly compromised. If they claimed to have totally rejected Zionism, they were not believed because of the Zionist insistence on speaking in their name. If, on the other hand, their increasing feelings of insecurity led them to turn to Zionism as a possible solution to their problems, this merely 'proved' to their non-Jewish fellow-citizens that they were 'traitors'. Then, too, many had relatives and friends who, faced with growing suspicions against them, had already fled to Palestine, and any links with them merely confirmed the opinion that the Jews were maintaining 'contact with the enemy'. Also, for the reactionary leaders of some Arab countries, it was better to deflect the anger of the masses, who had suffered greatly under feudalistic and repressive régimes, to victims who were in no position to defend themselves, than to risk popular uprisings against their own tyranny.

Events in Palestine inevitably had their repercussions in other Arab countries, and the situation of the Jews grew more precarious when in 1946 and 1947, the Irgun Zvai Leumi and Stern Gang terrorists were indulging in an orgy of murder, the taking of hostages, bank robberies and other crimes in Palestine,[1] in addition to the blowing up of the King David Hotel on 22 July 1946, and, a month before the establishment of the State of Israel, the massacre of Deir Yassin, two atrocities which are too well-known to require description here.[2] The leader of Irgun was Mr Menachem Begin, who was to become Israel's Prime Minister in 1977.[3]

When the former Ottoman Empire was carved up into a series of artificially created states, the situation of minorities deteriorated. The Jews were even more affected than the Christians and other minorities because, from the time that the question of Palestine arose, the Jews tended to be singled out and their position became even more difficult after the establishment of the state of Israel. Members of other minority groups, for example, sought to show their loyalty to their countries at the expense of the Jews. The situation of Jews in Islamic countries should, therefore, be examined in the light of these facts because, as Dr Landshut wrote, 'it is evident that the general anti-Jewish attitude in these countries is not to be mistaken for what is called anti-Semitism elsewhere.'[4]

Although anti-Jewish propaganda spread by Nazis in Arab countries had some effect (mainly as a result of the reaction towards Allied support for Zionist aims and not, as has often been said, because of agreement with Nazi anti-Semitism), this only had a fleeting effect because, as Landshut added: 'Anti-Semitism, that form of cold and theoretical hatred which endows its imaginary object with abstract qualities, is entirely a European creation and does not yet exist in Muslim countries to any marked degree.'[5]

Although the riots mainly erupted following the United Nations partition recommendation, there had been earlier outbreaks and one of the first, the most severe and the most surprising, took place in Baghdad. The *farhud* (a term which, in Iraq, denotes a breakdown of law and order) which took place against the Jews in Baghdad on 1 and 2 June 1941, was at any rate the first to have occurred for a hundred years. Many observers wondered what were the reasons behind it and why it was restricted to Baghdad, while there was almost no damage nor serious harm done in the many other cities in Iraq where Jews lived.

Although the *farhud* lasted for thirty-six hours, during which thousands of Muslims, some of whom were armed and among whom were soldiers and police, attacked the Jews, and although Baghdad's eighty thousand Jews were unprepared for such violence, the casualties were considered to be relatively small with only between one hundred and sixty and one hundred and eighty Jews killed and a few hundred injured.[6]

Writing as he was in 1966, Professor Cohen, who described the *farhud*, expressed the hope that, when the British archives were opened to the public, documents would be available which would throw further light on what had happened in Baghdad in 1941.[7] Unfortunately, however, these documents only make the situation more mystifying.

King Feisal, the puppet ruler of Iraq, was the eldest son of the Hashemite family of Mecca who had been placed on the throne by the British. He and his successors, who became the nominal rulers of Iraq, were just as much disliked by the majority of Iraqis as were the British who were viewed with suspicion and hatred not only because they were an imperial power but also because of their role in Palestine and, of course, during the war the Axis exploited this situation.

It is interesting to note how Professor Luks, who has written from a pro-Zionist standpoint, has linked the Jews with the British by writing: 'Pro-German, anti-British officers in the Iraqi army, influential student leaders educated in Germany, Axis radio propaganda and the presence of German agents helped to poison the atmosphere for the British and the Jews.'[8] In direct contradiction to all the other historians who, even although they were writing in support of Zionism, stressed that there was no anti-Jewish feeling as such, this writer tended to see the increasing antipathy towards the Jews as evidence of 'anti-Semitism'.[9] His attitude, however, is the classical one of the European (or, in this case, American) Zionist who ignores the glaringly obvious factors which contributed to anti-Jewish attitudes and attributes these to what they see as a basic defect in the character of the non-Jewish population of the world which 'hates Jews simply because they are Jews'. Luks has, however, provided evidence of Jewish support for British rule in Iraq[10] which makes it seem highly likely that the Jews had become linked, in the average Iraqi mind, with the British.

On 2 April 1941, Rasheed Ali al-Gailani, who was a former Prime Minister, staged a *coup d'état* with the aid of four colonels and refused to allow British troops to cross the country—which conveniently provided the British with a pretext to invade and occupy Iraq.[11] A number of Arab writers have claimed that Rasheed Ali was opposed to the Nazi hatred of Jews and, certainly, it is true that the Iraqi Jews were not harmed physically while he was at the head of the government, 'but,' wrote Dr Landshut, 'during the three-day interval between his flight and the arrival of the British in Baghdad a terrible massacre broke out.'[12]

This account is not, however, completely accurate because the British forces were already in Baghdad when the massacre took place. The sequence of events was that, at the end of April, British troops entered Mosul[13] and, at the beginning of May, the airport, dock areas and power station at Basra were occupied,[14] then the Iraqi airforce was destroyed[15] and the commercial quarters of Basra were occupied on 4 May.[16] On 12 May it was reported from Jerusalem that the Regent had announced that he was 'a true friend of Britain', and on the same date it was also reported that the 'revolt was collapsing'.[17]

On 14 May soldiers of a Ghurka regiment, which had participated in occupying Basra, began, along with Arab youths, to loot shops in the town which were mainly Jewish, and this continued for two days until a distinguished Muslim notable, Salih Bashayan, assumed the leadership and sent his own men to guard the Jewish shops. On 19 May 'Assyrian troops, under British command, captured the town and robbed houses and shops, though making no distinction between Jewish and non-Jewish property.'[18]

Rasheed Ali escaped from Baghdad on 30 May and fled to Iran, by which time the British forces were within three miles of the capital.[19] British troops entered Baghdad on 1 June and 'found the city quiet and the British Embassy untouched.'[20] On 5 June *The Times* published a report, dated 1 June and marked 'delayed', saying that the Regent had returned in triumph and that several sheep were sacrificed in honour of the occasion, while the Regent's dog gave him an ecstatic welcome.[21] Although *The Times* had a correspondent in Baghdad who was sending lengthy daily despatches from the capital, there was no mention in the paper, either then or in the days following, of what had happened to the Jews of Baghdad.

What, in fact, occurred on 1 June was totally unexpected. On Friday, 30 May the Jews were preparing for the Feast of Shevuoth (Pentecost) which was to be celebrated on 1 and 2 June. They were very happy because the Committee for Internal Security had announced that Younis as-Sabawi, a former Minister in the Rasheed Ali Cabinet, had been deported, that all youth organizations had been dissolved and their members ordered to surrender their weapons at police stations, and also that any disorder would be severely punished.

The following day the Jews were delighted by the news that the Regent would return on the Sunday morning, the first day of the festival. The next morning some of them, including leading members of the community, went to the airport to greet the Regent and his entourage on their return from Amman. All was quiet and the Jews were cheerful. Then some of those who had gone to the airport were attacked as they returned to the city, and one Jew was killed and sixteen injured, according to an official Iraqi report written by an investigating committee whose members, all Muslims, added that police and soldiers were on the spot 'but did not intervene on behalf of the Jews'.[22]

Unfortunately the British archives throw little light on what occurred, and this may be because there are some documents missing. One of these has been 'transferred to the Public Record Office Safe Room' and is closed until 1992,[23] while another has been 'retained in the Department of origin' and is closed until the year 2017.[24] Mr David Watkins, Labour Member of Parliament for Consett, raised the matter in the House of Commons on 6 and 8 April 1976, when he asked, first, the Foreign Secretary and, then, the Attorney-General if these documents 'relating to events in Iraq in 1941' would be made available; on each occasion, however, he was told that 'it would not be in the public interest to release these papers.'[25]

A long despatch dated 11 July 1941, from Sir Kinahan Cornwallis, the British Ambassador in Baghdad, to the Foreign Office, described how:

> The Regent's return on June 1st was not welcomed by all classes. Rasheed Ali's forceful propaganda had made too deep an impression for so sudden a change of public feeling to be possible. The army and police were largely sullen and resentful and the people in the streets looked angrily at those who passed on their return from greeting His Highness at the Palace. Sensitive observers of public feeling forecast trouble and events soon justified them. Shooting, looting and rioting began in the streets of Baghdad about three o'clock in the afternoon and continued spasmodically throughout the night. The next morning (June 2nd) the situation became steadily worse and by about ten o'clock, the mob was out of hand, looting shops at will. Malicious persons deliberately encouraged attacks on Jews. A large number of Jewish shops and homes were looted and several hundred Jews

were brutally murdered. The police force was for a time useless. Its discipline had been undermined by the political manipulations and fanatical propaganda of Rasheed Ali's régime, and officers and men joined recklessly with the mob in breaking into and looting shops and houses all over the town.

The Lord Mayor who, pending the formation of a new government, was still nominally in control, begged the Director-General of police to use his reserves and to order them to clear the streets and shoot to kill, but the Director-General pleaded that he could not accept responsibility for such a drastic action unless specific orders were given by the Regent. After some delay, the Regent sent the order in writing and also arranged for the despatch of troops to take control. The soldiers did their work well. There was no more aimless firing into the air; their machine-guns swept the streets clear of people and quickly put a stop to looting and rioting. In those few hours however, hundreds of families were ruined and brutal outrages were committed which all right-minded persons will for long remember with shame and horror. . . .

There is evidence to show that the riots were instigated by certain officers in the army and police who took advantage of the temporary absence of responsible authority. . . .[26]

On 24 July the British Embassy in Baghdad received a cable from the Foreign Office referring to a letter from the Jewish Agency in London, which quoted a message from the Jewish Agency in Jerusalem that: 'Massacre began upon return of Jewish delegation from Regent who had returned that day to Baghdad. Jews removed from cars and brutally murdered, then mob began attack on Jewish holiday crowds walking in street. . . . Official report states Moslem, Christian, Jewish victims. Apparently, some non-Jews involved, but mob excesses which resulted in previous fighting clearly directed against Jews, incriminated police not removed. No investigation, no punishment. . . . Implore help and immigrant permits to Palestine.'[27]

A cable from Sir Kinahan Cornwallis said: 'The Jewish report of the anti-Jewish excesses in Baghdad, though highly coloured, is substantially true. The statements that the rioting and pillaging was approved by British troops is wholly inaccurate. . . .' The telegram added that a large number of rioters were shot down and that Iraqi troops probably killed as many rioters as rioters killed Jews, while a military court, which had been set up in Baghdad to try those responsible for the massacre, had already sentenced many of the guilty to long terms of imprisonment, while three (including one policeman) had been publicly executed.[28]

Commenting on the British explanation (which is given in the correspondence between the British Embassy in Baghdad and the Foreign Office) that the riot was instigated by agents of Rasheed Ali, Professor Luks wrote: 'This explanation avoided the actual causes of the outrage against the Jews. By blaming the riot on the machinations of a few individuals, the British absolved the general population of responsibility for the murdering and pillaging. With this aim in mind, Britain did not want to appear as the protector of the Jews by ferreting out the perpetrators of the bloodshed.'[29]

Professor Cohen wrote, however, that '... in general, it was soldiers, officers, policemen and youngsters imbued with hatred against Jews who were the main perpetrators of the slaughter, while civilians, the common people and uneducated masses, were responsible for most of the looting. It was thought,' he added, 'that the number killed did not exceed one hundred and eighty while about eight hundred were injured....'[30]

Cohen also explained that: 'The fact that the masses did not hate the Jews or thirst for their blood, but only the small group influenced by imported Nazi propaganda, can further be supported by the point that no outbreak took place in any other town of Iraq. The few educated among the younger generation of Basra, Mosul, Amara, Hilla and Irbil, usually lived in Baghdad while completing their studies and then stayed on in the capital, so that there were few with any education living outside Baghdad.... Muslims felt that they were responsible for the Jews, whom they knew mostly by their first names and with whom they had daily contact. So that, outside Baghdad, if any youngsters tried to molest Jews, they would be stopped by any Muslim passer-by.'[31]

Two years after the *farhud*, the United States Minister in Baghdad wrote that 'one of the immediate causes of this attack on the Jews by the mob was the jubilant attitude ... of the Baghdadi Jews, many of whom openly celebrated the British victory and did not conceal their scorn and contempt for Arab-Muslims in general.' Luks commented: 'In other words, the Jews were blamed for their own destruction.'[32]

F

While it is obvious who was responsible for the massacre, the question remains as to why no action was taken at the very beginning to stop the attacks, and why orders to fire on the looters were not given in the first hours of the disturbances but only on the evening of the second day. The Regent, Abd al-Ilah, was already in Baghdad before the first Jew was killed, and although it was claimed that he gave no orders which would have stopped the carnage because 'there was no government', this seemed a very weak explanation. It appeared that he was reluctant to antagonize the army because its members were anti-British, pro-Nazi and not loyal to him, so that he had to wait for the arrival of Kurdish soldiers from the north, who were loyal to both him and to Great Britain.

Another question which must be asked is why the British, who were at the gates of Baghdad, did not take some action on the first day. According to a British source, the British troops were unwilling to enter the city unless invited, while the Iraqi authorities were equally anxious not to seek assistance. Professor Cohen has written: 'In other words, the British Forces waited patiently in their camps and were not moved to rescue people from the hands of the murderers, not only because they were not invited to do so by the Regent, but also because the British did not want to antagonize the Iraqis by intervening in an internal affair of Iraq.' He explained that, while they may have been right from a strictly legal point of view, 'it is doubtful whether their indifference to the *farhud* in Baghdad was due to the restrictions imposed by laws and agreements. It is well known that they did not hurry to stop the outbreaks in Libya in November 1945, nor that which took place against the Jews in Aden in December 1947, and only did so after three days. In Aden and in Libya, they were in power and the only ones responsible for the lives of the citizens.'

This account also claims that Jews from Baghdad maintained that they were sure the British distributed arms among the Arab youths and incited the crowds against the Jews. Such charges have not been proved, but what is certain is that neither the Regent nor the British made any effort to stop the *farhud* when it began.

In Professor Cohen's opinion 'The only outbreak known to the Jews of Iraq in the last century was not caused by any hatred for

Jews on the part of Muslims, but was the result of imported
foreign anti-Jewish propaganda, which penetrated into the hearts
of the younger generation of Baghdad Muslims, from among
whom the murderers came. . . .'[33]

In 1943, when the anti-Zionist press campaign in Iraq was at
its height US military intelligence confirmed a suspicion held by
many Jews. Based upon accumulated evidence, it was reported to
Washington that the anti-Zionist campaign in the Baghdadi press
and radio was a well-organized propaganda scheme originating
with the Prime Minister and approved by the British Embassy.[34]
In the index of the file in the Public Record Office, which is concerned with events in Iraq in 1943, there is an item relating to
'the anti-Zionist campaign in the Iraqi press in 1943 and actions
taken by the Iraqi Government' but there is no such material in
the file. There is, however, a note in the file that a certain
document has been 'retained in the Department of origin', but
no release date has been given.[35]

There is also a telegram marked 'of particular secrecy' which
was sent to the Foreign Office from the British Ambassador in
Baghdad on 17 February 1943, and said:

> Having heard rumours that the Prime Minister had approached
> local Jewish community in the hope that they would agree to the
> issue of a declaration dissociating themselves from Zionism, I
> asked Nuri Pasha recently what the position was. His Excellency
> replied he had in fact been in touch with local Jewish leaders as
> he felt that if they did not believe in extreme Zionist ambitions
> they should make their attitude quite plain. But if, on the other
> hand, they were sympathetic to Zionist aspirations, etc., he felt
> their best course would be to keep quiet and so avoid being
> provoked. 2. I report foregoing primarily for purposes of record
> and not because I consider Prime Minister intends any further
> initiative at the moment.
>
> Action he has so far taken has however given rise to the belief
> in some local Jewish circles that Prime Minister in contacting
> their leaders had my support. In actual fact, he acted without
> consulting me at all.[36]

TROUBLES IN NORTH AFRICA

The Jewish Outlook has described how:

> Libya is the worst example of the mischief done by the military
> authorities and Zionist missionaries, who seem to have combined
> in an effort to turn the country, where the Jews and Muslims
> have lived together in friendship for generations, into another
> Palestine.
>
> With the liberation, Palestinian Jewish soldiers stationed there
> seemed to have spent all their leisure in doing Zionist propa-
> ganda, para-military organization of Zionist boy-scouts, who
> used to march in a provocative manner through the streets
> singing Zionist songs. The Jewish population, who had suffered
> a great deal from Axis brutality, were attracted more by the
> plentiful stores of food and clothing offered them by these troops
> than by the propaganda, but the combination proved a powerful
> bait—especially to the younger generation.[37]

Obviously, as this account was written in 1946, there were
frictions even before the establishment of the State of Israel, and
the population of Libya was not surprised when rioting broke
out. This resulted in thirteen Jews and five Arabs being killed
and twenty-two Jews and thirteen Arabs seriously wounded.
Reporting these events, one newspaper commented that: 'Most
of these Jews, like those of French North Africa, have lived on
the spot for many, many centuries and have generally lived in
perfect peace with their Muslim neighbours, being more acceptable to the latter than are Christians.'[38]

Italian Government officials complained that the Arab-Jewish
riots were giving the former Italian colony of Libya a bad name.
They added that they blamed the British for the disturbances
and pointed out that this was the second anti-Jewish outburst
under British administration in two and a half years although,
during the preceding thirty years of Italian rule, there had been
no such troubles. Official spokesmen for the Jewish communities
of Italy had, apparently, asked for special protection for the Jews
of Tripoli after the 'pogrom' which occurred there in the autumn
of 1945, but seemingly their request had been ignored. At that
time the rioting had gone on for three days and about one
hundred and fifty Jews were killed. Investigations made at that

time disclosed that British troops did not intervene until the damage was done, with the official explanation that the Tripoli garrison could take orders only from British headquarters in Egypt and that orders did not come through. In view of what had happened previously and, also, in 1948, the Italian press publicized the second riot and *Avanti*, a socialist newspaper, bore a headline which said: 'The English Stand By as "Spectators".'

Commenting on the events in Tripoli, the Italians claimed that the British had absolutely no right to allow Tunisian volunteers for the Palestinian front to enter Libya, and that they could not compensate for this lack of foresight by sending them back when it was too late and the damage had been done. They also emphasized that 'Britain's attitude in Palestine' had had a great deal to do with the troubles, and that, as Libya was then full of British troops who had been evacuated from Palestine, immediate action by the British authorities at the first signs of trouble could have prevented it from spreading.[39]

The following year it was announced that, as a result of Britain's *de facto* recognition of Israel, which had been celebrated with great rejoicing by Jews in Tripoli, the British military administration had lifted its ban on the issue of exit permits to Jews of military age, and it was estimated that, out of thirty thousand Jews in Tripolitania, ten thousand had applied for permission to emigrate to Israel. The administration, apparently on instructions from the War Office in London (Tripolitania had then come under the jurisdiction of the British Foreign Office), had made drastic alterations in its 'Jewish policy' and was doing its utmost to facilitate the emigration of the Jews.[40] Shortly afterwards, five young Jews, who were accused of illegal possession of arms and explosives, appeared in court in Tripoli. They were also charged with throwing hand-grenades at Arabs during the riots of June 1948, and of injuring two Arabs in a later incident.[41]

A few months later it was reported that, when the last contingent of six hundred Jews arrived in Tripoli from Cyrenaica *en route* to Israel, the Jewish community of Benghazi would almost cease to exist and that only a few hundred would remain out of the five thousand Jews whose ancestors had settled in Libya after the destruction of the second Temple. Most Jews from the

interior of the country had been brought to Tripoli, but many
were not being allowed to emigrate until they had been treated
for trachoma and other diseases. The report added that the Arabs
had asked the Jews to stay, but such pleas were unlikely to have
any effect 'since the Jews of North Africa are anxious to leave
this area, which has so many unhappy memories for them.'[42]

In June 1951 Tripoli's remaining eight thousand Jews rejected a suggestion that a special institution should be established
for what were described as the 'hard-core' cases—in other words
eight hundred sick and aged Jews whom Israel refused to admit.
The proposal, which was made by the Zionists, would have
enabled the 'able-bodied' Jews to leave for Israel immediately,
but they refused to emigrate without their sick and elderly
relatives.[43]

It was reported the following month that of the seven thousand
Jews who remained in Tripoli, three thousand were expected to
emigrate before the Jewish Agency offices in Tripoli were closed
towards the end of the year, but many wealthy Libyan Jews
were waiting for the Constitution of the new Libyan State to be
published before deciding whether to emigrate, as they had decided that, if they were to be allowed to transfer their assets and
to emigrate in the future, should they wish to do so, they would
probably decide to remain, at least for the time being. Relations
between Jews and Arabs at that time were good, and there was
nothing to suggest that the position of the Jews would change
when the Libyan Government assumed full powers later that
year.[44]

By the time Libya gained its independence on 1 January 1952,
however, only a few hundred Jews still remained in Tripoli,
while elsewhere 'the Jewish quarters were entirely deserted, the
synagogues locked and abandoned: a history of more than two
thousand years of Jewish settlement had come to an end.'[45]

As tensions which had originally only manifested themselves in
those countries which bordered, or were in reasonably close
proximity to, Palestine, continued to spread throughout the Arab
world, some Arab rulers went out of their way to protect the
Jews. The Sultan of Morocco, for example, who had already refused to implement the anti-Jewish laws of the Vichy government
during the war[46] now reminded his subjects (on 23 May 1948) of
the protection which Morocco had always accorded the Jews,

and he appealed to them to maintain this tradition, while he also appealed to the Jews to refrain from all manifestations of Zionism. In spite of the efforts of the government to prevent outbreaks of violence, however, riots broke out against the Jews in the north of the country because anti-Jewish propaganda, probably from foreign sources, had been disseminated among the Muslims of Oujda since the end of May. On 7 June a small incident set off a reaction among the crowd, which poured into the Jewish quarter and, in the three hours before the mob could be brought under control by the army, five persons had been killed and thirty severely injured, while shops and houses were destroyed. The same night, there was an even more serious outbreak of violence at Djerada where the Jews were sávagely attacked and thirty-nine of them were killed.[47] Large numbers of those responsible for the attacks were arrested and brought to trial; two of them were sentenced to death and others were imprisoned.[48]

On 2 September 1949 it was reported that: 'Over three hundred youths from North Africa who immigrated to Israel earlier this year, returned to North Africa last week. Their return was arranged after they had repeatedly demonstrated in front of the French Legation in Tel Aviv demanding to be sent back.'[49]

After the French were defeated in 1940, the Cremieux Decree was abrogated in Algeria and the Jewish inhabitants, who numbered more than one hundred thousand, suffered discrimination because the Algerian administration applied the racial laws of Vichy with excessive severity. The Algerian resistance movement had many Jewish members and their activity led to the insurrection of Algiers, under the leadership of Jose Abulker, on 8 November 1942, which facilitated the landing of the Americans in the country, but, paradoxically, after this victory of the Allies in Algeria, 'General Giraud, Admiral Darlan, and Governor Yves Chatel, with the complicity of the local diplomatic representative of the USA, Robert Murphy, took new measures against the Jews, including the establishment of detention camps.'

Protests were made by international Jewish and Algerian organizations as well as by distinguished Jews, Muslims and Christians throughout the world, but the campaign was ineffective until, following the personal intervention of President

Roosevelt, the Cremieux Decree was again put into force on 20 October 1943, but it was not until 1947 that all inhabitants of Algeria were granted equality.[50]

It was the Algerian struggle for independence which decided the fate of the Jews, because the Jews were reluctant to adopt Algerian nationality although, in August 1956, members of the FLN (Front de Libération Nationale) appealed to Algerian Jews who 'have not yet overcome their troubled consciences, or have not decided which side they will choose' to assume Algerian nationality.

On 18 February 1958, records the *Encyclopedia Judaica*, 'two emissaries of the Jewish Agency were kidnapped and assassinated by the FLN.' This account adds that, until 1961, the majority of Algerian Jews had hoped for partition or a system of dual nationality, but, as the struggle intensified, 'they increasingly feared that popular reaction would be directed against them not only as Europeans but as Jews and Zionists.' Therefore, although the Jews did not officially adopt an anti-independence position, a delegation in March 1961 urged that the negotiations which were then about to be undertaken should 'obtain official recognition of the French nature of the Algerian Jewish community'.

The Algerian Jews were mainly pro-French,[51] and this was bound to lead to problems for them because of the hatred for the French felt by practically all Algerians. Jews began to leave Algeria until, in 1962, Jewish emigration increased as a result of OAS (Organisation Armée Secrete, which was opposed to an independent Algeria) violence, and fears that there would be even more violence on the proclamation of independence. By the end of July that year, seventy thousand Jews had left for France and another five thousand for Israel.[52]

THE YEMEN RIOTS

Victor Halba, an Israeli writer, referred to the distorted picture presented of Jews in Yemen in Albert Memmi's book, *Jews and Arabs*,[53] and he wrote that Memmi appeared to have an inferiority complex because of the sufferings of the Jews in Christian countries which reached a peak in Hitler's holocaust. Victor Halba added that Memmi had tried to rid himself of this complex by inventing a doubtful and distorted parallel between traditional Christian European anti-Semitism and the condition of the Jews in Islamic countries in recent years. Memmi had written that there was no significant difference between Jewish suffering in Christian and in Muslim countries, and it was as if one were asked to choose between cholera and the plague. He based his views on the 'shocking poverty' which he had observed in the 'ghettos' of North Africa.

While, wrote Halba, it was difficult to ignore the existence of Jewish poverty in Muslim countries, this did not exist because of the machinations of the state: it was a feature of a general condition of privation which existed in those countries. In fact, the Jews, being a relatively educated and urban element, enjoyed a higher standard of living than the non-Jews. In general, they comprised, both economically and socially, an élite. Memmi had included in his book a long list of anti-Jewish riots in Arab countries during the twentieth century. Although, Halba continued, critics would question his account, he had presented no documentary or bibliographic support for his contentions.

Halba also drew attention to the omission of Tunisia, Memmi's birthplace, from the list, and he asked whether Memmi's conscience had prevented him from falsifying the facts 'and publishing lies and slanders'. An example was given of what was described as the superficial and dubious nature of his arguments. He had written that: 'In South Yemen in 1946, following the local authorities' declaration that Jews need not live like other human beings, eighty-two Jews were killed and seventy-six badly injured.' Yet, Halba pointed out, it was known that the only people who held power in Aden in 1946 were the British, and he asked whether the British had declared that Jews did not need to live like other human beings. He added that, while it could not truthfully be denied that harm was done to Jews in Muslim countries, especially as a result of the political conflict over Palestine, persecution was marginal and was far from representing the general feeling.[54]

Victor Halba also wrote that, when he looked up 'anti-Semitism' in the *Hebrew Encyclopedia*, he found no reference to the Muslim countries, although Memmi had insisted that what he called the 'Arab pogroms' had claimed more victims than the Russian, Polish and German ones. Halba emphasized that, as a native of an Arab country, Lebanon, in which he had spent his

childhood, he could testify, with the support of his parents and
friends there, that they had never observed any 'pogroms' nor
had they ever sensed any atmosphere of hatred on the part of the
Arab population. He quoted Mr Charles Hadad, the former
president of the Jewish community in Tunisia, who had said:
'For hundreds of years, we lived together in joy rather than
privation.' According to Halba, the final proof which destroyed
the entire structure Memmi had tried so hard to build was the
known fact that the extent of emigration of Jews from Muslim
countries before the foundation of the State of Israel was comparatively small, in spite of Palestine's geographical proximity.[55]

As we have already seen, however, one Arab country from
which there had been some early emigration to Palestine—for
reasons which have been explained—was Yemen; but, even so,
the Jews who remained behind were treated tolerantly under the
rule of the Imam Yahya who was murdered in 1948 at the age of
eighty. The *Jewish Chronicle* reported that he appeared to have
been generally liked and respected by the Jews of Yemen and, in
1942, when he was seriously ill, Yemenite Jews in Palestine
offered prayers for his recovery of their own free will. This was
due to the general feeling among them that he had done his best
to protect their lives and property.[56] Yet in 1949 the *Palestine
Post* described how the Imam Yahya had re-enacted the Covenant of Umar when he had come to power after the First World
War. This account, which was headed 'The World's Oldest
Jewish Community', reported that the Jewish community of
Yemen was approaching the end of its 'exile' from a country
where the early Jewish settlers had built themselves palaces and
planted gardens and orchards. They were intelligent and graceful
and were respected by the local inhabitants for these qualities.
Later, religious observance was compulsory because Yemen was
a theocratic state. Those who failed to practise their religion
might be reported by the police to the Muslim mullah or the
Jewish rabbi. Under the law of Yemen, orphan children were
wards of the state; and Jewish orphans were therefore liable to be
taken away forcibly and converted to Islam.[57]

At the beginning of 1949, Yahya's son, the Imam Ahmad,
became the first Arab ruler to allow the Jews to leave for Israel,
and he prohibited the collection of taxes or other payments from
them.[58] Dr Schechtman, a Russian-born Zionist envoy to various

European countries, wrote, however, that after the establishment
of the State of Israel, efforts were made to obtain the consent of
the Imam for the departure of his Jewish subjects, but it was
said that he would never receive a Jew in audience. Yoseph
Zadok, a Yemenite Jew who had settled in Palestine as a boy and
who had been sent to Yemen, dressed as an Arab, six times in
1948 and 1949 'to prepare and organize the exodus' said that
there had never at any time been negotiations between outside
Jewish bodies and the Imam.[59]

Yet the *Jewish Chronicle* reported that, in any dispute between
a Jew and a Muslim, the Jew was allowed direct access to the
Imam. Jews were also allowed to make wine but not to sell it to
Muslims, and they had almost complete autonomy in their
quarter. In Sanaa, where the majority of Jews lived, their position was reasonably good, and the same was true of other cities,
but in the villages they were at the mercy of local despots. In
general, there was no suggestion of emancipation for either Jews
or Muslims.

The new régime (after the death of Yahya) had decided to
make Yemen into a modern state, with a constitution, parliament,
representative institutions and self-government. In the opinion
of the *Jewish Chronicle*, however, it was feared that a deterioration would take place in the position of the Jews of Yemen 'in
view of the general deterioration of the Jewish position in the
transition from despotism to the pseudo-democratic state'.[60]

This account was written four months after the United
Nations partition recommendation for Palestine, but it made no
mention of the reason for the changing situation of the Jews in
Arab countries, although it did emphasize one point which many
other writers have consistently ignored, and that is that discrimination towards Jews, under the feudalistic conditions of the
past, was not caused by 'anti-Semitism' but by the fact that the
Jews were non-Islamic: and the reason why the Jews in Yemen
were the only people to suffer in this way is because there were
no other non-Muslims in the country. The article in the *Jewish
Chronicle* ended: 'It is interesting to recall, also, that although
there were Christian settlements existent in the Yemen up to the
tenth century, there are no traces of Christianity in the country
at the present day.'[61]

The Imam, in fact, allowed his Jewish subjects to leave the

country freely and, when the leaders of the Jewish community of Sanaa arrived in Israel, they said that he had mainly acted out of *hassidut* (a Hebrew word implying various things from simple human kindness to piety and saintliness).[62]

On 2 December 1947, following the United Nations partition recommendation, Aden's Arab population began a three-day protest strike and, when fighting broke out between Arabs and Jews, one person was killed and twenty injured.[63] The disturbances which followed this initial outbreak of violence resulted in one hundred and twenty-two deaths because of the increasing friction between Jews and Arabs caused by events in Palestine.[64]

Many innocent people were killed and wounded by 'trigger-happy', locally-recruited troops who fired indiscriminately with rifles and Bren guns. Some of these troops took part in the looting which they were supposed to suppress, and the majority showed sympathy towards the looters. These facts were publicized in a report by Sir Harry Trusted, KC, who had been commissioned to enquire into the riots in Aden in December 1947, when eighty-two Jews and thirty-eight Arabs were killed. Criticizing the way in which the riots had been handled by the authorities, Sir Harry said there had been no justification for the promiscuous use of rifle and Bren gun fire. Four days of rioting, looting and fire-raising by local mobs had begun when regional Arab politicians organized a demonstration against the United Nations decision to partition Palestine. The Aden Protectorate Levies, who had been invited by the local authorities to restore order, had been recruited from local Arabs, under the command of British and Arab officers. (Aden was at that time a major coal bunkering port for Britain's trade routes to the Far East and India; the town itself was a British colony, and the adjoining territory a protectorate,[65] but the remainder of Arabia was independent.)

Witnesses said that, in one Jewish quarter alone, thirty-one Jews had been shot and killed, some of them by the local troops. After the riots, nine members of the forces were imprisoned for looting, and there was one incident involving British troops.[66]

An article in the journal of a pro-Zionist Jewish organization said that most people had the impression that the entire Jewish community of Yemen had flown to Israel 'on the wings of eagles' (a term commonly used, along with 'on magic carpets', in

Zionist accounts of the emigration of Arab Jews to Israel) just
after the establishment of the State of Israel, but this was not
correct because *'informed sources have estimated* [emphasis in
text] that the Jewish community in Yemen numbers about five
thousand people. For over twenty years, this part of the world
has been considered as a place of the past existence of a Jewish
community.'[67]

A Time of Turmoil in Syria

Although those Zionist historians who specialize in the subject of
the Jews of the Middle East present a balanced picture of events
before the Zionist colonization of Palestine, they seem, on the
whole, unable to comprehend or to place in their true perspective,
Arab feelings of outrage and betrayal over the Palestine question.
All their writings fail to take into account the contradiction between ultimate developments and early assurances, such as a
Statement of Policy issued by the British Government in May
1939, which reaffirmed the principle, originally laid down in the
Churchill White Paper of 1922, that the government had at no
time contemplated 'the subordination of the Arabic population,
language or culture in Palestine'. The British authorities also
stated categorically that this meant that it was 'not part of their
policy that Palestine should become a Jewish state', and their
ultimate objective was, they claimed, the establishment of an independent state 'in which the two peoples in Palestine, Arabs and
Jews, share authority in such a way that the eventual interests of
each are secured.'

Another statement made in 1939, by an Anglo-Arab committee presided over by Britain's Lord Chancellor, was to the
effect that the committee reported unanimously that in 1918 the
British Government had not been free to dispose of Palestine
'without regard for the wishes and interests of the inhabitants of
Palestine'.[68] Arab anger was also intensified by the recollection
that the Arabs had been promised independence by the British
Government shortly before the Balfour Declaration was issued.[69]

The Zionist chroniclers, however, seem to consider the Arab
attitudes towards Zionism and Israel as being totally unjustified
and the particularly strong feelings of fury in Syria outrageous,
although Syria, as has been shown, had suffered greatly because

of its dismemberment. Thus a report to the Foreign Office had explained that Dr Chaim Weizmann '. . . states that Jewry as a whole considers Arab national ambitions fully realized in the new Arabo-Syrian State. . . .'[70]

The position of the Syrian Jews was especially precarious because they had, for years, been subjected to the attentions of Zionist emissaries who were extremely active in Syria (as has already been described) owing to the proximity of the country to Palestine, and it was precisely as a result of this proximity that the Arab population of Syria was particularly affected by events in Palestine even before the UN partition recommendation. Increasing nationalism, coupled with political instability and hatred of foreigners, all combined to create a tense climate in which the slightest provocation was bound to unleash a wave of fury against some scapegoat or other. The Jews were the obvious target because, on the one hand, the Syrians were attempting to force them to renounce Zionism while, on the other, the Zionists were urging them to embrace it.

In October 1945 the leader of the 'Young Muslims' Association', Sheikh Mustafa al-Sibaj, in a speech after the Friday midday prayers in the Umayyad Mosque in Damascus, prophesied disaster for the Jews in Arab countries if a solution for the Palestine problem was not forthcoming. Since the first Parliament had been convened in December 1936, there had been one Jewish representative in the Chamber of Deputies. He was allowed to retain his seat even when anti-Zionist feelings reached their height, but there was little he could do to improve the situation.[71]

On the Muslim holiday of Qurban Bairam on 18 November, an enraged mob, led by a group of students, broke into the Great Synagogue in Aleppo, smashed the candle burning in front of the Ark, attacked some old Jews who were praying and burnt the prayer-books. This was the signal for the outbreak of a general anti-Jewish campaign which was exacerbated by the agitation of nationalist orators among the Arab mobs. The murder of Jacques Franco, assistant headmaster of the Alliance Française school in Damascus raised suspicions that his death was the result of the situation at the time, but these were never proved.

Rabbi Moshe Nahum of the Jewish community of Jezirah

issued a statement which was made, claimed the Zionists, under duress, protesting against Jewish immigration into Palestine. There was also what Dr Landshut referred to as 'the humiliating spectacle' of the leaders of the three Jewish communities 'being compelled' in November 1945, to participate in a demonstration against the Balfour Declaration, and Jewish shopkeepers 'being ordered' to close their shops as a sign of solidarity with the Muslims.[72]

The assumption on the part of the Zionists that the Jews supported Zionism rather than the aspirations of their Syrian fellow-citizens is interesting because it gives an insight into the difficulties which existed at that time. If, as Dr Landshut believed, the Jews were acting 'under duress' when, in fact, they supported Zionism, the hostility of other Syrians towards them is understandable. If, on the other hand, their espousal of the Syrian cause was genuine, the European Zionists did them a great disservice by loudly proclaiming their so-called pro-Zionist attitudes.

Public hysteria against the Jews in Syria was whipped up to such an extent that, within four days of the announcement of the United Nations recommendation on Palestine, the crowds were sufficiently worked up for rioting to break out in Aleppo. On 2 December 1947 a crowd, instigated by agitators, burnt down the four large synagogues in the city as well as fourteen smaller ones, and one hundred and fifty houses were destroyed. An unknown number of Jews were killed.

By the time the State of Israel was declared, on 15 May 1948, the Jewish communities in Syria were cut off from their contacts abroad. The commercial life of the Jews practically ceased as they were not allowed to open their shops or to continue in their employment.[73]

On 30 March 1949 the Syrian régime was overthrown by a bloodless coup led by Brigadier Husni Zayim who installed a military dictatorship and then announced that all citizens, irrespective of creed, were to have 'complete equality in rights and liabilities', and that the restrictions which had been imposed, preventing Jews from travelling freely, from running their businesses, and from transferring properties, were to be removed.

A bomb thrown into the entrance of a synagogue in Damascus on 5 August killed twelve Jews and injured twenty-six. President

Zayim sent a representative to visit the wounded and ordered the
arrest of those responsible 'without fail' so that numerous suspects were rounded up and, on 9 August, a seventeen-year-old
Syrian who had fought in the Palestinian war admitted that he
and two friends had thrown hand-grenades into the synagogue.
The President announced that the three criminals had been imprisoned and would be judged and condemned to death if found
guilty. He also ordered the authorities to prevent further anti-
Jewish terrorism at all costs. Shortly afterwards—on 14 August—
there was another military coup, led by Colonel Sami Hinnavi,
and the Zayim régime was overthrown. Zayim was executed by a
firing-squad and the new régime adopted the attitude that the
fate of the Jews in Syria was connected with that of the Palestinian refugees. As soon as the refugee problem was settled
satisfactorily, it was said, full rights would be restored to the
Syrian Jews.[74]

One of the main causes of the troubles was, of course, the fact
that the Zionist underground movement had, for years, been
organizing the clandestine passage of young Jews into Palestine
and these Jews, along with their co-religionists from other Arab
countries, formed the bulk of Israel's army. The Arabs looked
upon the actions of their former citizens as unforgivable treachery
and, although it could be contested that the Jews who left Syria in
the late 1940s had every justification for leaving because of the treatment they had received, it was also a fact that when the Zionist
activities began, there was no discrimination against Jews in Syria.

In September 1949 thirty Syrian Jews were sentenced to terms
of imprisonment ranging from one to three months for attempting
to cross into Israel illegally; two months later twenty-two Jews
from Aleppo were arrested for trying to cross the Lebanese
border into Israel, and, in December, the police in Beirut
arrested two hundred Syrian Jews and seized nine motor-boats
after coming upon a large Arab-Jewish gang smuggling Syrian
and Lebanese Jews into Israel.[75]

The tragedy was that the initial violence, sparked off by the
actions of the Zionists, was often directed against those who had
been in no way involved in such actions, and the resulting feelings
of insecurity led to increased determination on the part of a
growing number of Jews to leave their country illegally: this, of
course, caused further repressive measures against them.

While it could be argued that there is no excuse or justification for the way the Jews of Syria and other Arab countries were treated during this unhappy period, it is necessary to understand why such a situation arose instead of merely dismissing it as 'typical anti-Semitism' as many writers have done. As has already been pointed out, even in Western countries much hysteria has been directed against people thought to have links with an enemy in times of war, yet the Arabs who were, especially some thirty years ago, at a totally different stage of development from Western nations have been reviled for not displaying almost superhuman restraint and understanding. One has only to reflect on the amount of hatred generated by the British role in Northern Ireland and the numbers of people killed and injured there—and in Britain too—as a result of the troubles, to understand that Arab behaviour, although often reprehensible, was not surprising.

EGYPTIAN UNREST

In 1939 an Egyptian nationalist organization accused the Jews of raising money for the Zionists in Palestine, and bombs were discovered near three synagogues in Cairo; these were wrapped in notices warning the Jews not to support Zionism. They were obviously not intended to explode for, if they had been, the warning notices would have been somewhat superfluous. Anyhow, the Jews did not take them seriously and paid no particular attention to them.[76]

At the end of 1945, anti-Jewish riots—the first in Egypt since the middle of the nineteenth century—took place in Cairo, and these disturbances were instigated by members of the Misr-al-Fatat (Young Egypt) movement which had threatened, some weeks earlier, to attack the Jews if they did not dissociate themselves from Zionism. A synagogue and various Jewish institutions were set on fire, and many Jews left Egypt. The Egyptian press began to feature the Palestine issue prominently, and the authorities voiced their opposition to Zionism. Five days before the UN partition recommendation, the Egyptian representative in the United Nations General Assembly, announced that: 'The Arab governments will do all in their power to defend the Jewish citizens in their countries, but we all know that an excited crowd is sometimes stronger than the police. Unintentionally, you are about to spark an anti-Jewish fire in the Middle East which will be more difficult to extinguish than it was in Germany.'[77]

On the day that the State of Israel came into existence, King Faruq proclaimed a state of emergency in Egypt, and shortly afterwards an order was issued which gave the government the power to confiscate the property of persons whose activities were considered to be detrimental to the state and provided for the confiscated property to be transferred to a special appointee. Professor Cohen has written that: 'In theory, this was not specifically directed against the Jews. Nevertheless, out of more than a hundred individuals and companies whose property was confiscated within a short period thereafter, the great majority were Jews. . . . During this period, hundreds of Jews were arrested, accused of Zionism or communism and placed in detention camps, despite the fact that Zionism was not prohibited in Egypt then.'[78]

Between June and November 1948 there were numerous acts of violence against Jews and a number were killed and wounded; but the following year scores of those who had been imprisoned in May 1948 were released, their property was returned to them and they were allowed to leave Egypt—it was no longer necessary to have a special exit permit—and when the Wafd Government assumed power at the beginning of 1950, the detention camps were emptied of Jews, with the exception of those who were communists. The revolution of 1952 and the deposition of King Faruq did not alter the situation of the Jews: General Naguib, who ruled Egypt after the monarch was overthrown, was friendly towards them and, although he permitted them to leave the country if they wished, only a few did so in 1953.[79]

REFERENCES

1. *New York Times*, 24 July 1946; 5 August 1946; 27 January 1947; 28 January 1947; 2 March 1947; 25 March 1947; 3 July 1947. See also *Hansard*, 31 January 1947, cols. 1302–1360.
2. See David Hirst, *The Gun and the Olive Branch: The Roots of Violence in the Middle East*, Faber and Faber, 1977. Chapter 4, headed 'Gun Zionism' (pp. 108–43) deals specifically with the blowing up of the King David Hotel and the massacre at Deir Yassin, but the book contains much detailed evidence of other Zionist atrocities.

3. See Israel Shahak (ed.) *Begin and Company: As They Really Are: An Anthology*, Professor Israel Shahak, Jerusalem, September 1977.
4. Landshut, *op. cit.*, p. 97.
5. *Ibid.*, p. 97.
6. Hayyim J. Cohen, 'The Anti-Jewish *Farhud* in Baghdad 1941', *Middle Eastern Studies*, 1966, p. 2.
7. *Ibid.*, p. 17.
8. Luks, *op. cit.*, p. 33.
9. *Ibid.*, p. 32.
10. *Ibid.*, p. 32.
11. *Ibid.*, p. 33.
12. Landshut, *op. cit.*, p. 46.
13. *The Times*, 26 April 1941.
14. *Ibid.*, 5 May 1941.
15. *Ibid.*, 6 May 1941.
16. *Ibid.*, 10 May 1941.
17. *Ibid.*, 12 May 1941.
18. Cohen, *Farhud*, p. 8.
19. *The Times*, 31 May 1941.
20. *Ibid.*, 2 June 1941.
21. *Ibid.*, 5 June 1941.
22. Cohen, *Farhud*, pp. 10–11.
23. PRO/FO E4209/1/93.
24. PRO/FO E4154/1/93.
25. *Hansard*, 6 April 1976, col. 110; 8 April 1976, col. 249. (Mr Watkins raised the matter at the request of the author.)
26. PRO/CAB 185 5/9101/41.
27. Message, dated 19 July 1941, accompanying letter, dated 21 July 1941, from Zionist leader, Professor Lewis Namier to Lord Moyne (who was later murdered by Zionist terrorists).
28. PRO/FO E4242/1/93.
29. Luks, *op. cit.*, p. 33.
30. Cohen, *Farhud*, *op. cit.*, p. 12.
31. *Ibid.*, p. 13.
32. Luks, *op. cit.*, p. 33.
33. Cohen, *Farhud*, *op. cit.*, p. 16.
34. Luks, *op. cit.*, p. 35, citing Seton Lloyd, *Iraq*, London, 1944, p. 20, MID, Military Attaché Report No. 147, 24 September 1943, Sidelights of the Arab Unity Movement, Iraq G2 Regional File, Folder 3800, GAD-RG 165.
35. PRO/FO E5810/87/31.
36. PRO/FO, War Cabinet Distribution from Iraq, 173.
37. *Jewish Outlook*, London, May 1946.
38. *Christian Science Monitor*, 15 June 1948.
39. *Ibid.*
40. *Jewish Chronicle*, 11 March 1949.
41. *Ibid.*, 22 April 1949.
42. *Ibid.*, 16 September 1949.

43. *Ibid.*, 29 June 1951.
44. *Ibid.*, 24 August 1951.
45. Chouraqui, *op. cit.*, p. 183.
46. Baruch Nadel, *op. cit.*
47. Chouraqui, *op. cit.*, pp. 181–2.
48. *Encyclopedia Judaica, op. cit.*, Vol. XII, col. 344.
49. *Jewish Chronicle*, 2 September 1949.
50. *Encyclopedia Judaica, op. cit.*, Vol. II, cols, 616–17.
51. *Ibid.*, col. 618.
52. *Ibid.*, col. 619.
53. Translated from the French by Eleanor Levieux, J. Philip O'Hara, Chicago, 1975.
54. *Haolam Hazeh*, 28 September 1976. Albert Memmi's book contains virtually no documentation. The few notes which exist are mainly comments by the author, such as the following, which is typical and is the only note for the particular chapter to which it is appended: 'Although Zionism is a national movement, it must also be more socialist than other such movements, because of the specific conditions of the Jewish people, whose very body needs to be made strong and firm' (p. 141).
55. *Haolam Hazeh*, 28 September 1976.
56. 12 March 1948.
57. 8 November 1949. Professor Cohen (*Jews of the Middle East, op. cit.*, p. 64) wrote that, in 1921, Yahya 'even revived a decree of previous centuries—the orphans' decree.'
58. 8 November 1949. Cohen, *Jews of the Middle East, op. cit.*, p. 64.
59. Joseph B. Schechtman, *On Wings of Eagles: The Plight, Exodus and Homecoming of Oriental Jewry*, Thomas Yoseloff, New York, 1961, p. 59.
60. 12 March 1948.
61. *Ibid.*
62. Schechtman, *op. cit.*, p. 60.
63. *New York Herald Tribune*, 3 December 1947.
64. Report of Commission of Enquiry 22 September 1948, cited in *The Economist*, 9 October 1948.
65. *New York Times*, 6 December 1947.
66. *Daily Worker*, 5 September 1948.
67. *Bnai Brith Messenger*, Los Angeles, 14 June 1974.
68. Nevill Barbour, *Nisi Dominus: A Survey of the Palestine Controversy*, George G. Harrap, London, 1946. Reprinted by *Institute for Palestine Studies*, Beirut, 1969, pp. 200–1.
69. Ingrams, *op. cit.*, p. 3.
70. *Ibid.*, p. 43.
71. Landshut, *op. cit.*, pp. 57–8.
72. *Ibid.*, pp. 58–9.
73. *Ibid.*, pp. 59–60.
74. Schechtman, *op. cit.*, p. 163.
75. *Ibid.*, p. 174.

76. Cohen, *Jews of the Middle East, op. cit.,* pp. 48–9.
77. *Ibid.,* p. 49.
78. *Ibid.,* p. 50.
79. *Ibid.,* pp. 50–1.

Eight

Subversive Activities

THE BAGHDAD BOMBS

EVEN after the riots of 1941, few Jews emigrated from Iraq and the majority carried on their lives as before because it was felt that there was no further danger since the exceptional circumstances which had existed when the country was without a government were not likely to arise again; and the Jews were also confident that, as long as the régime of Abd al-Ilah and Nuri es-Said was in power, they would not be harmed. In addition, they were enjoying great economic prosperity at that time.[1]

After his visit to Iraq in 1941, Munya Mardor wrote that: 'It had become obvious to me that Iraqi Jewry was not yet ready for mass emigration even if that could be organized. . . .'[2] Nevertheless, the underground activities of the Zionists compromised many innocent Jews all over Iraq and, after 15 May 1948, when Iraq was in a state of war with Israel, the tension heightened enormously, and even those Jews who had not welcomed the attentions of the emissaries were looked upon as traitors to their country. Munya Mardor described how, on one occasion, when members of the Zionist underground had returned to Baghdad from a visit to the Jews in Kurdistan, they learned that British Intelligence had received a detailed report from the town of Irbil that two men, one in British uniform, the other in civilian clothes, had called on the head of the Jewish community there.[3]

A method of bringing about the mass emigration of the Jews of Iraq had not yet been devised by the Zionists although they had given the matter much thought. Munya Mardor wrote about the enormous efforts which were required to persuade the Jews to embrace Zionism because they were shocked by the thought of doing work which might soil their hands.[4] Although, as we saw in the previous chapter, the Jews had had sufficient confidence in the situation after 1941 to invest a great deal of money in Iraq, it is not difficult to understand why feelings of suspicion gradually built up against them in the years which followed. Munya Mardor wrote, for example, that it was his firm opinion that someone should be sent from Palestine exclusively to organize the Haganah units in Iraq and that this person should act quite independently of other Zionist emissaries and organizations. He considered this essential, not only on grounds of efficiency but also for reasons of security. If, he pointed out, Haganah activities became familiar to all the Zionist workers in Iraq, there was a risk that, should any of them be discovered by the authorities and questioned, they might reveal the extent of the Haganah network as well as details of any arsenal which might be set up and of the training centre that would consequently be necessary. Such revelations would be disastrous not only to those directly concerned but to the entire scheme 'for the rescue of Iraqi Jewry'.[5]

The fact that—as Mardor had already made clear—the Jews of Iraq did not want to be 'rescued' seemed quite immaterial to the Zionists.

Although Zionism had never existed in Iraq before the arrival of the European Zionists who, as we have seen, had an immensely difficult task attempting to convert the Iraqi Jews to their creed, Bracha Habas referred to 'the revival' of Zionism in the provincial towns of Iraq as one of the 'prominent achievements of the emissaries'. She described conditions among Jews in the Kurdish mountains in the 1930s when a Zionist traveller found small Jewish communities or families 'isolated among non-Jews'. A short while earlier, she wrote, there had been Jewish slaves in the Kurdish mountain villages where entire families of Jews were sold to Kurdish masters who did what they pleased with them, made them work, sold them, or gave them to friends as gifts. Often, she added, children and parents would be 'cruelly separated', and all this took place under Turkish law. She quoted the Zionist traveller, Ben-Zion Israeli, who, referring to the sufferings of the Jews in this 'Arab diaspora', said that it was likely that they would be among the first to pay with their lives for the actions of the Zionists in Palestine.[6] Miss Habas did not, however, provide any documentation to support her claim about Jewish slavery, and the accounts of writers of that period do not mention it.

In October 1949 the *Jewish Chronicle* quoted 'an Iraqi Jew who left Baghdad a week ago and who arrived in Israel yesterday'. His name was not revealed, but he 'gave the full story of the recent persecutions' and said that Jews were taken to police headquarters and tortured to force them to disclose any connection they might have had with the 'Zionist Underground' which, he added, 'the Iraqi authorities' imagination has created.' It was also reported in the same issue that: 'The Foreign Office reaction to the Israel declarations that a new wave of persecution of Jews was taking place in Iraq appears to be one of caution, both in accepting the accuracy of the stories and in taking any action.'[7]

Although readers of the *Jewish Chronicle* in 1949 may have seen nothing wrong with the supposed statement of an anonymous Iraqi Jew that the Zionist underground existed only in the imagination of the Iraqi authorities, it is absolutely inconceivable that any Iraqi Jew would have made such a claim. Even those who had no direct dealings with the underground and were therefore unaware of the scope and extent of its activities certainly knew about its existence.

A few days after the establishment of the State of Israel, Jews in Iraq were told that there was no danger of riots although there would be difficult times ahead for them. Then Jews began to be arrested and brought before military courts on charges of receiving messages from relatives and friends in Palestine. In July 1948 the word 'Zionism' was entered into Article Fifty-One of the criminal law and, as a result, hundreds of Jews were placed on trial between June and September 1948. Most of them were fined, others were sentenced to various terms of imprisonment and one was sentenced to death.[8]

The Jew who received the death sentence was Shafiq Adas, a rich inhabitant of Basra and, according to Rabbi Dr Elmer Berger, who stressed the similarity of the treatment of Jews in Iraq and of Japanese citizens of the United States at the time of Pearl Harbor, the trial was public and conducted with due process of law. Adas had been accused and convicted of 'trading with the enemy' for smuggling materials out of Iraq to Israel during the war in Palestine. (It was, in fact, reported that Adas, who had made a fortune by dealing in British Army surplus goods, had been tried for supplying weapons to Israel.) The

Chief Rabbi of Baghdad and Jewish leaders believed that the trial was as fair as it could possibly have been in view of the general atmosphere in the country and they agreed that a great deal of circumstantial evidence pointed to Adas's guilt.

There were no specific acts of hostility involving Jews, and no Jewish shops were attacked. The main anger and frustration were directed towards Britain and the United States which were considered to be primarily responsible for the Palestine tragedy and the main supporters of Zionism.[9]

Referring to David Hirst's account of the events leading up to the eventual departure of the majority of Iraqi Jews for Israel,[10] a reviewer in the *Jewish Chronicle* wrote: 'Occasionally, Hirst becomes quite absurd, as when he tries to show how the Zionists tricked the Iraqi Jews into exchanging a happy and secure existence in Iraq for a life of poverty, shame and discrimination in Israel.'[11] Since Mr Hirst's book was published, further material has come to light which amply confirms and reinforces what he wrote. All this material is from Israeli sources, and it will be described. In spite of all the efforts of the Zionists to make it appear that the Iraqi Jews were 'longing for Zion', an account entitled 'Zionism and its Oriental Subjects' in *Khamsin* describes how Zionism was not popular in Iraq even after 1948. While one section of the Baghdad Jewish community consisted of rich merchants and bankers, many of the young people were members of the communist party and a large number of its leaders were Jews. According to one Zionist historian[12] a Zionist meeting organized in 1946 was attended by three dozen people, while the Jewish Communist Anti-Zionist Alliance was publishing a daily paper in Baghdad, printing six thousand copies a day. Referring to the actions of Zionist provocateurs in Iraq (which will be described) a Zionist writer asked: 'But does the State of Israel have duties towards the Jews who are able, but do not wish, to come here? Moreover, do we have the right to tell them: We know better than you what is best *for you*—and we shall, therefore, act to make you come here, and we shall perhaps even try to make your position more severe, so that you will have no choice but to immigrate to Israel. Note that this last question is not imaginary. We have confronted it in some very concrete situations and we may still have to confront it again.'[13]

This seems similar to the attitude of Dr Eliyahu Ben Elissar,

director-general of the Israeli premier's office, who was chosen
by Mr Menachem Begin to act as his chief representative at
the negotiations with President Sadat of Egypt. He said: 'If
the United States turns against Israel, and American Jews are
made to feel unwelcome because of their support for Israel, if
they are driven out of the United States, then we will have
achieved the real goal of revolutionary Zionism: the American
Jews and their money will come to Israel, and an Israel that is
eight million strong will make us self-sufficient.'[14]

From 5 to 7 March 1950, the Iraqi Parliament suddenly announced that any Jew who chose to leave Iraq of his own free
will could renounce his citizenship and be free to leave the
country.[15] According to one of the most distinguished of Arab
historians, this law was passed as a result of a British initiative,
and the move had two objectives, the first being to strengthen
the State of Israel and the second to encourage instability in those
sectors of the Iraqi economy that were controlled by Jews.[16] It
was reported that the law had been passed because of the
smuggling of Jews to Persia during the previous few months. The
government had decided that it was best to allow those Jews who
wished to leave to do so in order to enable the others, who were
in a majority, to settle down. The government intended to
restore to the Jews, at the earliest opportunity, full rights and
citizenship.

The Jews had been flying from Persia to Israel in Israeli
planes, and the cost from Basra, one of the centres of smuggling,
had been £70 which included the air fare to Tel Aviv. It was
mostly the young Jews who had gone but the movement had been
nothing like a Jewish exodus and, the report added, it was unlikely that the 'establishment' Jews, many of whose families had
been in Iraq for one thousand years, would wish to leave although
it was possible that there might be an exodus of poorer Jews.[17]
Indeed, the middle-class, educated Jews still had no wish to leave
although they were, in Zionist eyes, the most sought-after members of the community. Shortly before Passover, it was announced that Jews wishing to leave the country should register
at the Central Synagogue in Baghdad, but the Jews felt that this
might be a trap to round up suspected Zionists and only four
thousand registered.[18]

On 19 March 1950 a bomb exploded at the American Cultural

Centre in Baghdad which was a favourite meeting-place for young Jews. There were some casualties then, but no one was injured in the later bomb explosions which occurred at two Jewish concerns, the Betlawi Automobile Company on 10 May and the Stanley Shasha Trading Company on 5 June.[19]

On 8 April 1950, the last day of Passover, the Jews of Baghdad were strolling, as was their custom, along Abu Nawas Street beside the River Tigris, which is flanked by public gardens on the river's edge and buildings on the other side. Many of these buildings were—and still are—cafés. One of them, the Dar al-Beida coffee-house, was very popular with young Jewish intellectuals who, on warm evenings such as this one at the end of Passover when Baghdad's weather was approaching its fierce summer heat, would sit at tables in the garden in front of the café, under strings of coloured lights, sipping Turkish coffee and soft drinks.

At half-past nine, a bomb exploded near the Dar al-Beida and four people were seriously injured. Abd al-Jabbar Fahmi, Baghdad's chief of police, and his men spent several hours interviewing those who had been in the café,[20] and, the following day, it was reported that the police had announced that the bomb had been thrown from the neighbouring Al Hanna restaurant and bar, and the names of the injured were Akram Ezra, Mourad Khadouri, Shaool Yusef and Elias Yusef. The report added that some arrests had been made.[21]

Later, the *Jewish Chronicle* reported that: 'Four Jews were seriously injured in Baghdad recently when a bomb was thrown into a crowded café frequented by Jews. The police later announced that three Jews had been arrested in connection with the incident.[22] The day after the explosion, many Jews flocked into the offices which had been set aside for those who wished to renounce their citizenship and to apply for permission to leave for Israel. Most of them were poor Jews who had nothing to lose. Many of them recalled the riots of 1941 and wondered if there was to be a repetition of those days. Faced with this rush of applications, the police asked the Jewish community to put Jewish schools and synagogues at their disposal to use as registration offices for the emigrants. The large Ezra Daoud synagogue was given over to this purpose, and police officers and volunteer clerks, who were members of the Zionist underground movement, worked in shifts, both day and night, registering those who wished to emigrate. A special kitchen was set up to provide food for the police and their helpers so that the work of registration could continue without interruption. When the initial panic had subsided, however, it became evident that by no means all Iraqi Jews wished to leave. In addition, the pace of transportation to Israel was very slow because only one plane arrived daily and this flew no more than one hundred and fifty Jews to Cyprus and from there to Israel.[23]

The Jews stopped registering and then, on 14 January 1951, a bomb exploded at the Masauda Shemtov synagogue; Ekhak Salman, a seven-year-old Jewish boy, was killed, and twenty-seven Jews were injured (two of them eventually died). An Iraqi newspaper asked: 'Are there some Jews behind the incident?' and it went on to report that, two minutes after the explosion which blew a large crater in the ground between the two doors of the synagogue, a taxi had driven away from the building, carrying some Jewish passengers on their way to the airport. The bomb was reported to be of British manufacture.[24]

Dr Schechtman wrote that in January 1951 'a series of bomb outrages causing several deaths and scores of wounded precipitated a virtual stampede. Between 14 January and 10 March, forty thousand registered, over twenty thousand per month.' Each applicant was required to sign the following statement:

> I declare willingly and voluntarily that I have decided to leave Iraq permanently and that I am aware this statement of mine will have the effect of depriving me of Iraqi nationality and of causing my deportation from Iraq and of preventing me forever afterward from returning.[25]

(Dr Schechtman did not, however, mention that members of the Zionist underground had been found guilty of the bomb outrages.) When the registers were completed, it was found that all the Jews of Iraq, with the exception of some five thousand, had registered to emigrate to Israel.[26]

A few days later, the government, led by Nuri es-Said, went into secret session, following which the Majlis (legislative assembly) also went into secret session; as it was a Saturday, most Jewish businesses, and also most of the banks, were closed. For additional security, the telephones between the Majlis and the rest of the city were disconnected so that none of the members would leak details of the discussions to their Jewish friends. It was proposed that the property of every Jew who had renounced his citizenship prior to departing for Israel should be confiscated and the law, which was passed immediately, required the banks to stop trading and all Jewish businesses to close down, while anyone found removing goods from a Jewish shop was liable to seven years' imprisonment. All those who had not given up their citizenship had to present themselves at special registration offices to be provided with new identification certificates. They would continue to be regarded as citizens with equal rights and they could have passports and travel abroad, but they had to return to Iraq within three months or they would lose their citizenship. The five thousand Jews who remained were permitted to carry on their businesses without any restrictions.

Suddenly, one of the richest and most splendid Jewish communities in the world had lost everything. Planes were arriving at the rate of three or four a day, and the Jews were flown to Nicosia, accompanied by an Iraqi police officer; but, after a while, the pretence ceased and the planes went directly from Baghdad to Israel, the Iraqi officer continuing to accompany the passengers and to return in the empty plane. The rapid and total destruction of an ancient and cultured Jewish community had taken place.[27] In Israel, its members became paupers, and from a highly educated group with a very large proportion of university graduates, it was reduced to one that was poorly educated, oppressed and discriminated against in every way, trapped in the Ashkenazi culture that was totally foreign and entirely hateful to it.[28]

THE ONE-EYED MAN

The subject of the Baghdad bombs and the question of who was responsible for them would probably not have arisen years after the event if it had not been for the Israeli government's habit of constantly reminding the country's Jewish inhabitants of the past sufferings of the Jews. When it comes to European Jews there is ample material concerning past persecutions, but, with those from Arab countries, it is a little more difficult, as Victor Halba pointed out. He described how he had gone to Kiryat-Gat in connection with his work and had found that a stage had been erected in the town's central square for the forthcoming Israeli Independence Day celebrations. Across the whole length of the stage was a placard with a list of all the terrible names which were so familiar to people in Israel: Auschwitz, Dachau, Bergen-Belsen, Buchenwald, etc. At the end of the macabre list, he wrote, there was a name which he had never heard before and which did not seem to fit into the list. He asked a friend who lived in the area what the name signified and he was told that a large number of the town's population were of North African origin. The commemoration of the Holocaust, therefore, conveyed little to them, and so the organizers of the ceremony had tried to find some area of Jewish suffering with which they could identify and had got hold of the name of a site in Tunisia where the Nazis had started to build a concentration camp during the short time that they were in control there.

Needless to say, this gesture was unsuccessful as hardly any of the town's residents had ever heard the name of the site and even the few who recalled its significance were unmoved by it.[29]

It was because of a stone memorial, built in 1966 in Or Yehuda, the place where thousands of Iraqi Jewish immigrants live in Israel, that the events of 1950 and 1951 were re-examined. The memorial was erected in memory of two Baghdad Jews 'who were hanged for their part in the unfortunate Iraqi affair after their trial according to the principles of international law.' This account, in *Haolam Hazeh*, described how: 'Twenty-five years ago, there were whispers about "Cruel Zionism" but only now is the most secret affair in the history of the State of Israel revealed.'[30]

Under the heading of 'Self-defence against persecution', the *Encyclopedia Judaica* explains that: 'The Iraqi authorities contended that the bombs were planted by Jews, to humiliate Iraq in the eyes of the world. In June 1951 several dozen Jews were arrested, a few of whom were accused of planting bombs. In December 1951 two of them, a lawyer, Joseph Basri, and a shoemaker, Abraham Salih, were condemned to death. They were hanged publicly in January 1952. These two young men had been active in the clandestine Zionist organization Hehalutz, established in 1942. They organized small cells, which gathered secretly to study Hebrew and follow developments in Palestine. About six hundred members of the Haganah were instructed in the use of weapons in Baghdad, Basra, and Kirkuk. In 1949–50 the Haganah helped to organize the illegal exodus to Israel, and in 1951 it was decided to hide the arms. In this last activity Basri and Salih were caught, together with dozens of other members of the Haganah.'[31]

A Zionist publication, citing the *Jerusalem Post*, wrote: 'To accuse Jews of the crime is a refinement of cruelty which even the Iraqi Government should have outgrown. ... Regarding the "intention to murder for political purposes" the Court was hard put to prove any intention to murder whatsoever—no one had in fact been killed by the three explosions. ...'[32]

It was a combination of circumstances at the time of the unveiling of the memorial which led to many disclosures about the past being made by those who felt, perhaps, that they had remained silent for long enough. The Israeli magazine *Haolam Hazeh*, published by Uri Avnery who was then a member of the Knesset, wrote that it had decided to tell the story because all those who had been involved in the events in Iraq, with the exception of the two who had been hanged, were in Israel.

The account in *Haolam Hazeh*, when checked against other descriptions of the events in question, is accurate in most important respects except for details of the casualties, because the magazine claimed that there were no casualties at the Dar al-Beida and, also, that the bomb had been thrown from a passing car, although newspaper reports at the time said it had been thrown from the roof of a neighbouring building. *Haolam Hazeh* said, too, that there had been only two casualties at the synagogue when 'a young boy was killed and a man was injured.'[33]

Part of the article was later reprinted in *Black Panther*,[34] a journal devoted to the grievances of the non-European Jews in Israel, and also in *Middle East International*.[35]

We are told by *Haolam Hazeh* that: 'On one point, all the immigrants who followed the "Iraqi Affair" closely, or were involved in it, including the families of those who were hanged ... were agreed that they praised *Haolam Hazeh* for its decision to expose the secret. "The time has come," they said, "for the people of Israel to know what efforts were made to bring the Jews of Iraq to Israel and what they left behind them." ' *Haolam Hazeh* made it clear that its informants were those who had been involved in the events in Baghdad, and it seems fairly obvious

that if they were responsible for the bombs, they were not prepared to admit that they had deliberately caused more than the
minimal number of casualties.

The account referred to the supposedly sole wounded person
(whose claims for compensation as a result of his injuries helped
to publicize the matter) in the following words: 'Kadouri Saleem
is a man of forty-nine who looks at least sixty, thin, bent, with
a wrinkled face and a glass eye. He lost his eye at the doorway of
the Masauda Shemtov synagogue.'

Kadouri Saleem said that he had given up his citizenship and
was standing beside the door of the synagogue when, suddenly,
the bomb exploded and he felt blood running down his cheek. He
remained in Iraq for three months after leaving hospital and, on
his arrival in Israel, he was thrown into an immigrants' camp and
all his efforts since to get compensation have been fruitless. He
claimed: 'I was wounded by the bomb. The court ruled that the
bomb had been thrown by the Movement [Zionist under-
ground]. The government of Israel should give me compensation. . . . I am willing to make a sacrifice for the good of the
state, but when the situation at home is bad, when my wife
wants money and there is none, what use is there in making
sacrifices out of goodwill?'[36]

Another of those involved who had decided to unburden himself was Yehuda Tajar, an official of the Israeli Foreign Ministry
who eventually became an attaché at the Israeli Embassy in
London. He was a Zionist agent who was sent to Baghdad from
Israel in 1950 on what he described as 'a national mission', and
he added that he was caught out through a Palestinian Arab who
served the coffee in the office of the military police in Acre,
where Tajar had been an officer. One day the Palestinian was ill,
so his cousin arrived in his place and served the Turkish coffee
for a week. This cousin ended up in Iraq and recognized Tajar
when he saw him in Baghdad. Tajar, who admitted to the police
that he was an Israeli and explained that he had gone to Baghdad
to marry a young Iraqi Jewish girl, was arrested along with
Salih, a young native of Baghdad who was in charge of the
Haganah arms caches. He broke down under questioning and
took the police from one synagogue to another, showing them
how he had hidden his weapons which had been stockpiled from
the Second World War.[37]

Also arrested was Mourad Kazzaz who was later to become a member of the Knesset under the name of Mordechai Ben Porat. He was known to other members of the Zionist underground as 'Zaki' and he served as the local commander of the underground. Kadouri Eluyah, a former member of the local council of Or Yehuda was quoted as saying that Tajar had been arrested because he had gone into Orozdibak, a department store where the Palestinian refugee worked, but the many Jewish salesmen who worked in the store succeeded in confusing the Palestinian in order to give Tajar a chance to escape. 'From then on,' said Eluyah, 'he should have stayed in his house, and left Iraq as quickly as possible, but, instead, he visited Orozdibak a second time the following week with the leader of the immigrant organization, Mordechai Ben Porat. It was then that the refugee ran outside and called a policeman and Yehuda was arrested. Ben Porat was arrested too, but he succeeded in convincing the police that he did not know Tajar and he was released on bail of two thousand dinars. He jumped bail and left for Israel.'

An Iraqi lawyer, who lived in Tel Aviv, was also quoted. He pointed out that at four o'clock in the morning, after the explosion of the bomb at the Dar al-Beida café, handwritten leaflets were already being distributed among the worshippers at the first morning service in the synagogue. The leaflets warned of the dangers that were revealed by the explosion of the bombs and advised the worshippers to emigrate to Israel. Salman al-Biyat, an examining magistrate for south Baghdad, considered this a strange phenomenon because the distribution of the leaflets so early in the morning meant that those who had prepared them must have had prior knowledge of the intended bombing. He advised the police to make investigations among the Jews and, as a result, two youths of the Muallim family were arrested.

Suddenly, because of the intervention of the Ministry of Justice, the prisoners were released and the case was transferred to the examining magistrate of north Baghdad, Kamal Shahin.

The Iraqi lawyer added that, at that stage, it was considered justifiable to turn a blind eye because of an active agreement between the government and the Zionist representatives. After two further explosions, however, and the arrest of the envoy from Israel, this was too much and the police went into action. After that, it was impossible to stem the tide. He added that the trial

G

that took place was conducted according to international law, but the facts were such that there was no alternative to passing sentences of that sort.[38]

Haolam Hazeh referred to Yehuda Tajar as 'the big fish'[39] in the affair and, indeed, as Ben Porat pointed out later: 'For the police, I was no more than a poor idiot of a local Jew. They were interested in the big catch, in the Israeli Tajar.'[40]

A few weeks after its previous story of the Iraqi Jews, *Haolam Hazeh* published more revelations. This later account mentioned that the President of the State of Israel was to take part in the unveiling of the memorial at Or Yehuda and added: 'Zionists in Iraq have suddenly become famous. Those who led the underground now hold different posts in Israel, and they have begun to recall the past. . . . Basically, their movement was no different from its counterparts in other Arab countries. It was given a push by the Second World War: Europe went up in flames and the Jewish population in Palestine was cut off from its roots there. For this reason, the Zionist movement turned towards other sources, nearer ones. The fact that a large number of Jewish soldiers served in these countries, as members of the British army, greatly facilitated these activities.'

The article added that envoys of the Jewish Agency and Haganah arrived in Iraq with forged documents wearing the uniforms of British soldiers which they discarded once they had reached their destination, and assimilated themselves among the local Jews. The envoys were helped by *bona fide* Jewish soldiers who assisted them to set up the first arms caches of Haganah in Iraq. These soldiers also transferred young Iraqi Jews to Palestine in the guise of soldiers; and drivers of Eged (a Palestine transport company) which was then transporting British soldiers from Palestine to Iraq took back illegal immigrants, who pretended to be relief drivers, with them.

The account also revealed that Ben Porat had blamed Tajar for the arrests which took place as the Iraqi detectives found in the pocket of the Israeli agent a notebook in which were written the telephone numbers of all the members of the network.

Referring to what it described as 'cruel Zionism' (deliberately stimulating anti-Jewish manifestations), the article explained that a number of Iraqi lawyers who followed the military trial which sentenced Salih and Basri to be hanged and Yehuda Tajar to life imprisonment (he was released after ten years under the terms of an amnesty granted by General Qasim) were prepared to agree that the conclusion of the trial had been correct and the bombs were thrown by the underground. Mordechai Ben Porat, however, disagreed and claimed that anti-Jewish elements in Baghdad had thrown the bombs. One man who challenged Ben Porat's version and who wrote to Israel's Prime Minister and to the Minister of Justice, demanding that an enquiry should be held into the whole matter, expressed the hope that Ben Porat would prosecute him so as to bring certain facts to light, but Ben Porat commented: 'I would not prosecute such small fry.'[41]

Other facts have been revealed. For example, an Iraqi Jew who went to Israel in 1951 described how a poor Baghdad shoemaker, E.M. (name supplied) who, he said, now lives in Israel and is a rich man, left his job and was seen 'living the life of a pasha, dressed in new clothes', in 1950. It became known among the Jews in Baghdad that the shoemaker had been approached by the Zionist underground and had been given one hundred and fifty dinars 'to perform a simple task'. He was asked to travel to Zakhou in the north of Iraq, dressed as a Muslim Arab and, on the Sabbath, when Rabbi Nahum and the congregation emerged from the synagogue after the service, he was instructed to approach the rabbi, spit in his face and strike him. He did these things and, when the Jews saw them, they became afraid that they were going to be attacked and persecuted. Eventually, because of such incidents (we are told that there were probably many similar ones) and because of the bomb explosions, all the Jews left Zakhou.[42]

Then, too, Mr Reuben Naji Elias, a cinema and property-owner and president of the Baghdad Jewish community, and Mr Naji Chachak, a lawyer, who is secretary of the community, both said that there was no doubt in their minds that the bombs were the work of the Zionist underground.[43]

An Iraqi Jew, who was a member of the communist party and who, as a result, was imprisoned from 1949 until 1958 and then from 1959 until 1961, explained how he had been sentenced to life imprisonment while his wife was also jailed for five years. When she was released in 1953, she went to Israel. This is his story:

I was born in Baghdad in 1919 of a poor family. I joined the communist party, as many young people, both Jewish and Muslim, did because of the exploitation we had suffered. I was not a Zionist and had no wish to go to Israel. The prison in which I served my sentence was built by the Americans, especially for communists and other political prisoners, and the Americans used to visit the prison and complain if we were not being treated harshly enough. I really think that, after the State of Israel was established, the Western powers wanted the Iraqi Jews to go to Israel to avoid any dangers of the spread of communism in Iraq.

While I was in prison, members of the Zionist underground were brought in to serve their sentences and they used to talk quite openly about their exploits. They spoke about a British man in Baghdad who was known as 'Mr Rodney'; he was a notorious fascist who had been in an internment camp in India during the Second World War. He ran a brothel in Baghdad which was called the Red Palace and this house was used for meetings between the Zionists and Iraqi leaders. The Zionists paid the Iraqis ten dinars for every Jew who emigrated.

The Zionist prisoners told me that their instructions had been that, if it was necessary, they could kill up to twenty per cent of the Jews of Iraq in order to send the remainder to Israel. When I was released from prison, I was taken straight to the plane and I was flown to Iran. From there, I went to Israel because my wife was there and, anyway, I had no money. Some of my relatives are still in Israel, but I never want to go back. [He left for good in the 1960s.][44]

After the revolution of 1958 in Iraq, the former head of the government, Tawfiq as-Suaidi, was put on trial for treason, and one of the clauses in the indictment was that he had aided Israel 'by allowing one hundred thousand Iraqis to become Israeli citizens'.[45]

The exodus of the Iraqi Jews to Israel was described in the introduction to an article headed 'Give us the bodies of the Jews and take their possessions', by Shalom Cohen, an Iraqi-born Jew and a former member of the Knesset, and it was explained that the bomb outrages were clearly brought to mind twenty-five years later through legal proceedings concerning the conflict between two men, both of them Israelis, Baruch Nadel and Mordechai Ben Porat. Baruch Nadel was described as a journalist, well-known for his investigative work in the spheres of corruption

in political and financial circles in Israel, and the account added:
'He is also known for having denounced the discrimination and
exploitation of the oriental Jews in Israel. . . . Baruch Nadel is
the author of a document which specifically accuses the Israeli
establishment of having deliberately perpetrated the outrages in
Baghdad.'

Born in Baghdad fifty-four years ago, Mordechai Ben Porat
was an illegal immigrant from Iraq who had joined the Israeli
army in 1945 and had taken part, as an officer, in the conflict
which followed the creation of the State of Israel in 1948. He was,
until May 1977, a labour member and vice-president of the
Knesset. He was accused by Baruch Nadel of participating in the
activities of a group of politicians who had 'succeeded in imposing themselves on the Jewish people by a thirst for power'.
From October 1977 until January 1978, he had been on a
mission to the United States, sent by the Israeli Foreign Ministry
in an endeavour to convince responsible American politicians
and the foreign representatives of the United Nations that the
same international status should be accorded to the organization
over which he presides (the World Organization of Jews from
Arab Countries) as that which is received by Palestinian organizations, and on his return to Israel at the end of January, he wrote
to the Prime Minister, Menachem Begin, to demand the right to
participate in the peace negotiations with Egypt.

But first, he made his way to the law courts in Tel Aviv where
proceedings for defamation which he had raised against Baruch
Nadel were taking place.

The article stated that it was going to reveal the preliminary
results of the enquiry of Baruch Nadel and the first disclosures
made at the court hearing, and that Shalom Cohen, correspondent in Israel of the Parisian daily newspaper, *Le Matin*, had
devoted himself to the rights of non-European Jews in Israel and
was also militating for the recognition of the rights of the
Palestinians. But this did not prevent him from declaring himself
to be a Zionist and, according to the magazine's editors, it was
that which made his article so valuable.

He wrote that a scandal which had shaken the Israeli public
for nearly a year had been caused by an article written by Baruch
Nadel and first published in the journal of the Sephardic community in Jerusalem. (The word 'Sephardic' originally meant a

Spanish or Portuguese Jew but, now, along with the word
'oriental', it is used in Israel to describe Jews from all Islamic
countries.) This article dealt with the 'forced' exodus of the Iraqi
Jews who were, in fact, driven to emigrate to Israel in the 1950s
by terrorist measures for which those responsible were Israelis.
A passage of the text which triggered off the outcry indicates the
tone of the piece:

'Zionism,' wrote Baruch Nadel, 'not having saved the Jews of
Europe found itself after the Second World War without a useful
objective. To give a moral justification to the existence of their
country, the Zionists looked for a way to "save" other Jews in
spite of themselves. The only Jews with whom this would be
possible were those of the Arab world.'

The author asserted that David Ben Gurion and his men
arrived at an agreement with the Imam Yahya of Yemen, Nuri
es-Said of Iraq, and other Arab rulers. The agreement, said
Nadel, was simple. The Zionists told the Arabs to take the
possessions of the Jews in return for allowing them to emigrate
to Israel, but, in Iraq, this agreement met with difficulties because the Jews who lived in prosperity had no wish to emigrate.
The official Israeli emissaries then threw bombs in Jewish areas,
causing panic and forcing practically all the Jews of Iraq to leave
for Israel in less than a year.[46]

Mordechai Ben Porat was quoted as saying: 'All those who
know me and who know that I was sent by Israel to Iraq during
this period hold me responsible for bombs thrown at this time.
This is an untrue accusation, totally without foundation.' Shalom
Cohen commented that this was the argument put forward by
the plaintiff but, he asked, what was the reality? He described the
events which had taken place in Baghdad before and after the
bomb explosions and then he reported a clandestine radio message sent to Israel which said: 'The situation of the Jews is very
bad. They have lost their nationality. They have left their homes
and their jobs. Why did you force us to lie to them and to
promise them unlimited immigration?'

The Zionist underground was worried because letters were
arriving describing the appalling treatment being meted out to
the Iraqi immigrants in Israel where directors of banks, important officials, doctors, businessmen, lawyers and artisans, who had
left Iraq were received like unclean animals by officials in Tel

Aviv. They were disinfected with DDT. . . . In the maabaroth
(transit camps), their spirits were broken. Iraqi doctors and
lawyers were crowded into tents on the bare earth, far from
centres of population. To earn a living, they were hired twelve
days per month to weed the roadsides. Heads of families were
treated as inferior beings. The officials constantly told them that
their children came from a primitive community without culture
and that they ought to initiate themselves into the supremely important culture of the Polish Jews.[47]

In the maabaroth, rumours on the subject of the bombs in
Baghdad kept circulating. After all, it was pointed out, the Iraqi
court itself had found the Zionist organization guilty of these
acts, and also, when some years later there burst on Israel the
scandal of the revelations concerning the activities of a net which
had planted bombs in Alexandria and Cairo, the Israeli Defence
Minister himself remarked: 'This method of operation was not
invented for Egypt. It was first tried in Iraq', and other Israeli
leaders saw in these outrages acts of 'cruel Zionism'. The term is
attributed to David Ben Gurion concerning anti-Jewish acts
carried out by the Zionist movement to force certain Jewish
communities to emigrate to Israel 'in their own interest'.[48]

Israeli law allows someone accused of libel to submit to his
accuser a list of questions to which he must reply, so Nadel took
three months off work from his newspaper to research the
documents which supported his accusations. As a result, three
hundred and sixty-five questions were presented to the court.
Among them was one which asked Ben Porat whether it was true
that, when he was nominated for the presidency of the local
council of Or Yehuda, people called after him in the streets and
treated him with hostility because they considered the Zionist
underground to be responsible for the bombs in Baghdad.

He was also asked whether he knew that Mr Avraham Dar, the
agent of Mossad (the Israeli Secret Service) who had formed the
network which was responsible for acts of sabotage in Egypt
(which will be described in another section of this chapter),
happened to be on a mission to Baghdad shortly before the bombs
were thrown. Another question was whether he was aware that,
shortly after the bomb explosions in Baghdad, other bombs were
thrown in Morocco by Israeli emissaries and by militant local
Jews in the areas of densest Jewish population and that, during

the same year of 1951, Israeli agents were delivering to the homes of Jews in Morocco pamphlets which advised them to send their children to Israel so that they could take refuge from future outrages. A further question concerned the fact that the select group of agents who were concerned with the falsification, in Baghdad, of documents for illegal emigration, had specifically named the member of the Zionist underground who had, they claimed, thrown the grenade.

Mr Amnon Sayegh, who had been under Ben Porat's orders in Baghdad, made the following deposition: 'The explosions accelerated the emigration. Those who were hesitant decided to leave their country and those who had had no thought whatever of emigration began to think about it. It could have been that the bombs were thrown in order that the government in Israel would realize the gravity of the situation and take some action.' The question was asked whether the facts and conclusions set out in this deposition were true, while a final query was: 'Is it true that, before the explosions, the Zionist underground paid the journal of the Istiqlal Party, *al-Yaqza*, to publish articles against the Jews and to drive the Jews to leave their country?'

Shalom Cohen claimed that WOJAC (the World Organization of Jews from Arab Countries), 'manipulated by Moshe Dayan, to counter the claims of the Palestinians, could only be successful if international public opinion admitted his basic premise, that Jews were kicked out of the Arab countries and had, in consequence, the right to claim the status of refugees.' He added that Baruch Nadel had declared that now the truth had to come out and this truth, he said, concerned not only the five bombs in Baghdad, but also the attitude of Israel in general towards the Arab world. 'Ben Gurion,' wrote Baruch Nadel, 'founded his entire political career on an everlasting war against the Arabs, and all Israeli governments have succeeded him in not wishing peace. After the exodus of the Iraqi Jews, the prevailing memory was of the place where the two Israeli agents were executed. All the better. Because of that, no Iraqi Jew would dream of returning there, and no Israeli would ever think that peace would one day be possible with people who hanged Jews in a public place.'[49]

An interesting insight into Zionist beliefs is provided by the following passage in Shalom Cohen's article: 'We must admit that we do not see in the act itself [the throwing of the bombs] an absolute evil. In our opinion, it is allowed, in special circumstances, to lead people towards national liberation and to personal safety against their wishes as did Lehi [the Stern Gang] during the fight against the British in Palestine.'[50]

THE 'SECURITY MISHAP'

Commenting on what later came to be known in Israel as 'the security mishap',[51] Dr Schechtman wrote: 'In February 1954, Naguib was overthrown by his second-in-command, Gamal Abdul Nasser. Under the new régime, the Jewish position considerably deteriorated. In July, three young Jews were arrested on trumped-up charges of having set fire to the United States Library, the Alexandria Post Office, and a number of cinemas.'[52] Israel's Prime Minister, Moshe Sharett, referred in the Knesset to the Egyptian government's 'wicked plot' against this group of Jews who had 'fallen victims to false accusations and from whom it seems attempts are being made to extract confessions of imaginary crimes by threats and torture. . . .'[53]

Over the years, since those events took place, the truth has been gradually leaking out. Four of those who were responsible for the acts of sabotage in Egypt, Robert Dassa, Marcelle Ninio, Philip Natanson and Victor Levy, have now given a full account[54] of their actions which began when an agent of Israeli Intelligence, Avraham Dar, arrived in Cairo in April 1951, armed with a British passport and using the name of John Darling, in order to set up an espionage network. As he had been instructed, he contacted an emissary of the Mossad and asked for assistance in recruiting 'a group of loyal and dependable youngsters' for the underground cell he intended to establish. Ovadia Danun found what were, in his opinion, three of the finest young men in Alexandria, and Victor Saadiya recommended Dr Moshe Marzouk, Meir Zafran and Eli Naim from Cairo as well as his 'star pupil', Robert Dassa from Alexandria.

Dar trained his subordinates in simple sabotage techniques, teaching them how to manufacture incendiary materials and explosives from chemicals which were freely available, and, at the end of August, he left Egypt, having established two underground cells.

At the end of June 1954, another emissary arrived from Israel;

his name was Avraham Seidenberg and, having been born in Austria, he was blond and 'Aryan-looking' so that he was able to masquerade as a German under the name of Paul Frank. He told the young Jews that the first target for their 'operations' was to be Alexandria's central post office where they were to leave an incendiary device which would ignite after the post office closed.[55] After the 'success' of this first 'experiment', it was decided to bomb United States libraries in Alexandria and Cairo as well as Egyptian cinemas showing British and American films, in order to disrupt Egypt's relations with Britain and the United States and, it was hoped, wreck the negotiations for the British evacuation of the Suez Canal zone. The Israelis had feared that evacuation would leave valuable military installations in the hands of their enemies.[56]

The bombs were placed in spectacle cases which were then laid on the library shelves, behind the books. Seidenberg mentioned that he had been with Zacharia Mohieddin (the Egyptian Minister of the Interior) when the latter was told of the fire at the American library in Cairo, and the two men went to the scene of the fire, with 'Robert', as Seidenberg was called by his 'team', 'making angry sounds to demonstrate his displeasure at the dastardly deeds of the arsonists'.[57]

The next 'action' was planned for 23 July, Revolution Day, and this was to be the biggest of all, with five targets being attacked simultaneously in Cairo and Alexandria; these were to be two cinemas in Cairo, two in Alexandria and the Cairo railway station. Shmuel Azar and Robert Dassa went to Cairo and booked into a small hotel where, locked in their room, they assembled the bombs. Then they separated, and Dassa went to the Radio Cinema where he deposited his bomb. The following day, he bought all the papers and read them carefully but found no mention of any fires in either the Radio Cinema or the Rivoli where Shmuel Azar had gone to deposit his incendiary device.

Dassa returned to his home in Alexandria where he was arrested by men from the military intelligence.[58] It was only later that he learned that Philip Natanson had gone to the Metro Cinema in Alexandria to plant his bomb, but as the cinema was full, he went to another one nearby, the Amir. Later, at the military tribunal which tried the members of the espionage group, the prosecutor presented a policeman who testified that on the evening of 23 July he had been ordered to 'take up a post outside the Metro Cinema to protect it from terrorists'. Apart from the four members of the cell, the only person who knew that the Metro had been chosen as the target was Seidenberg.

Philip Natanson was about to plant his bomb when it ignited in his pocket in the foyer of the cinema and there was an explosion. He was badly injured and thought he had lost a leg. He was arrested, and later the other members of the network were rounded up. It seemed, at first, as if the Alexandria cell had been unmasked because of the premature explosion of the bomb, but it then became apparent that the accident was a cover which the Egyptian police used to conceal their prior knowledge about the cell and its members, as well as the operations planned for 23 July.[59]

Commenting on the trial, Robert Dassa said: 'It was an embarrassing situation. The Egyptians accused us of betraying our homeland. To this, there could be only one answer: Egypt was not our homeland! Israel was our homeland! But we could not say that. The State of Israel dissociated itself from us, denying that we had anything to do with it, and consequently, we could not claim that we *did* belong.' He added that nobody in Israel took any responsibility for the actions of the cell and 'Everyone wriggled out. Everyone hastened to blame someone else for "giving the order".'

Two of the accused, Dr Moshe Marzouk and Shmuel Azar, were sentenced to death, and Victor Levy and Philip Natanson were condemned to life imprisonment, while Marcelle Ninio and Robert Dassa received sentences of fifteen years and two others, Meir Mayuhas and Meir Zaafran, seven years; Eli Naim and Cesar Cohen were acquitted. Max Bennet committed suicide in his cell.

After the sentences were passed, the Egyptian Government was inundated with appeals for clemency from public figures and governments all over the world. President Eisenhower, the Pope and Nehru all intervened. In his diary, Moshe Sharett wrote that the Israeli Government considered publishing an official statement denouncing the death sentences, but decided against this.[60]

Polish-born Pinhas Lavon, who was Israel's Defence Minister in 1954, said he had not known of the sabotage plan, but Colonel

Benjamin Gibli, the chief of military intelligence, insisted that Lavon had personally instructed him to carry it out.[61] In January 1955 Moshe Sharett appointed Lieutenant-General Yaakov Dori and Yitzhak Olshan, the president of the Supreme Court, as a commission of enquiry to attempt to ascertain whether Lavon had in fact given the order for the 'security mishap', but the commission was unable to reach any conclusion on the matter and, on 2 February, Lavon resigned and Sharett asked David Ben Gurion to serve as Minister of Defence, which he agreed to do. After the general elections, he formed a coalition Cabinet and became Prime Minister while retaining the Defence portfolio.[62]

Issar Harel, the head of Mossad, began to have suspicions that Seidenberg might be a double agent and so he was tried *in camera* in 1960. He denied the charges of possessing classified material and trying to set up contact with an enemy agent, and claimed that his trial was an attempt by Israeli intelligence to silence him by sending him to prison for the rest of his life. He alleged that his trial and the evidence presented at it were a plot to frame him, but he was nevertheless sentenced to twelve years' imprisonment which was reduced, on appeal, to ten years.[63]

What was revealed at the trial, however, was that false evidence had been given on behalf of Gibli, and although he could not be prosecuted because of the statute of limitations, he was dismissed from the armed forces; later, a typist who had worked for him provided information which convinced most of the Cabinet that the evidence against Lavon had been fabricated.[64]

There were further investigations and these revealed that witnesses had been induced to commit perjury in 1954 and that important documents had vanished, while there was a great deal of testimony concerning lies and forgeries by heads of the intelligence services.[65] If it had not been for all the lies, it was said, Lavon would have been acquitted of all blame for the events of 1954, and thus began what came to be known as the 'Lavon Affair' which arose because of Lavon's request that Ben Gurion should clear him of all responsibility for the sabotage in Egypt, but Ben Gurion refused to do this.[66]

The Cabinet, with Ben Gurion in a minority, passed a resolution stating that the 1954 operation had been ordered without the knowledge of Pinhas Lavon, but Ben Gurion attacked this decision and claimed that in exonerating Lavon, the Cabinet had implicitly condemned Gibli without a trial. The Prime Minister, therefore, resigned the Premiership and brought down the government, and he announced that he would not return to office as long as Lavon represented the Mapai (Labour) party as secretary-general of the Histadrut (Labour Federation). Lavon was ousted and he held no further public office until his death in 1976. Ben Gurion had turned against Lavon because, in his efforts to exonerate himself, Lavon claimed that many people in the Ministry of Defence, who had been appointed by Ben Gurion, had plotted against him.[67]

Meanwhile, Seidenberg was in Ramleh prison. After serving his full sentence he went to Tel Aviv where he sold television sets, but, in 1972, he emigrated to the United States and settled in California.[68] After the publication in Israel of a book by Seidenberg in August 1976, Issar Harel appeared on Israeli television and flatly accused him of having betrayed the spy ring to the Egyptian security services, and demanded that he should be tried on this charge. Harel also urged that details of the sentence passed on Seidenberg in 1960 should be revealed. The following week, Victor Levy appeared on Israeli television and pointed out that Seidenberg's book had been 'full of falsifications' because in it he had claimed that he had not told Dr Marzouk that he was in danger after learning that the Alexandria cell of the spy-ring had been exposed 'because he had never heard of Marzouk'; but Levy maintained that he had personally attended a meeting which had taken place between the two men at the Cairo Jewish Hospital where Dr Marzouk had worked.

Seidenberg had also claimed that Shmuel Azar had decided against leaving Egypt when the other members of the network were unmasked, but, in fact, Levy said he had met Azar in prison just before he was executed, and Azar had told him that Seidenberg had reassured him and said he had nothing to fear although the others had been captured. Levy added that only those who had been in contact with Seidenberg had been arrested and that others who had not known him had all escaped.[69]

The blame for the arrests could not, however, be entirely directed to Seidenberg. Marcelle Ninio, who worked for the Grunberg Travel Agency, had also played her part. The travel agency was a front for the head office of the organization set up in Egypt by the Jewish Agency, which was the Zionist move-

ment's executive and formed a shadow Government for the
Jewish State. The Grunberg office, which occupied one floor of
the imposing Immobilia building in Cairo, also had a branch
office in Alexandria. Max Bennet was a German Jew who was not
connected with the sabotage campaign, and he had been sent to
Egypt by Israeli Intelligence and had 'rendered them invaluable
service'. He had arrived in Egypt as the representative of a
German firm which specialized in artificial limbs for wounded
soldiers, and he had succeeded in establishing contact with
General Naguib himself. The 'Darling-Frank group' had lost
contact with him for some time and, in spite of strict orders from
Tel Aviv that his activities were to be conducted independently of
other groups under Israeli command, they had asked Marcelle
Ninio to track him down, and she had been indiscreet enough to
have more than one meeting with the solitary spy.[70]

Meir Mayuhas was released on 5 August 1961 and Meir
Zaafran six days later, and a firm decision was said to have been
taken in Israel in 1967 to arrange for the release of the remaining
prisoners. General Meir Amit, head of Mossad, had not been
concerned with the events of 1954, which took place long before
his appointment, but, nevertheless, he stated: 'They acted on
instructions from Israel and under the command of an emissary
sent from Israel. Even though the instructions are a subject of
disagreement and the emissary was a dubious person, Israel is
responsible for their fate.' Therefore it was said, in the first un-
official talks on an exchange of prisoners which took place after
the 1967 war, 'Israel insisted on an exchange of prisoners', but
it was claimed that the Egyptians refused to exchange soldiers for
civilians, and General Amit then pointed out that the former
agents were officers in the Israeli army and had been since 1953,
and 'he even gave their military numbers.'[71]

However, three of the agents appeared on Israeli television in
1975, and they then levelled serious accusations against the
Israeli leaders. Marcelle Ninio, Victor Levy and Robert Dassa
all said that the Egyptians had been prepared to repatriate them
to Israel in 1957, after the Sinai campaign, in exchange for
Egyptian prisoners-of-war sent home by the Israelis. They
would thus have been released two years after being sent to
prison, but they were not returned to Israel until 1968. Robert
Dassa said: 'Maybe they did not want us to come back . . .

there was so much intrigue in Israel. . . . It would have been so easy to get us back in 1957.' Avraham Dar also appeared on the programme and he said that Moshe Dayan had been one of those responsible for the 'security mishap' and that if Israel had requested the repatriation of the group in 1957, the Egyptians would have agreed, but because of the political climate in Israel at that time, 'those in authority would not hear of it.' The four added that, after they had arrived in Israel in 1968, they had met Moshe Dayan who had told them that, even after the 1967 war, he had not been prepared to press for their release by the Egyptians.[72]

The revelation that a group of Egyptian Jews living in Egypt had been, from 1953 onwards, officers in the army of a foreign power with which Egypt was in a state of war makes it easy to understand why Jews in Arab countries have been viewed with suspicion by their fellow-countrymen.

Totally ignoring the fact that the agents had been imprisoned because they had planted bombs in cinemas and other places, Mrs Golda Meir, Israel's former Prime Minister, who acted *in loco parentis* for Marcelle Ninio at her wedding, wrote, in the foreword of a book about the exploits of the saboteurs: 'Not only I, but everyone in Israel felt that these were our children when they came home. These are our sons, our children who were in exile, who were in prison, who suffered because they are Jews, because they are Zionists, and because they wanted to be pioneers in Israel together with our young generation. . . . I hope those who read this book will find it as fascinating and as exhilarating as I did. . . . Here is a group that can serve as an example not only to Jews, but to everyone. If only there were more like them, the world would be a better, happier, more decent place to live in.'[73]

The Exploits of Elie Cohen

One of the most famous of Israeli spies was Elie Cohen, who was born in Egypt although his family came from Syria where they had lived for generations in Aleppo, a city in which there had been a flourishing Jewish community for hundreds of years.[74]

One of the earliest and most serious influences on Elie Cohen which concerned 'the Jewish struggle in Palestine' was the

assassination of Lord Moyne in Cairo in 1944 by two members of
the Stern Gang, Eliahu ben Zuri and Eliahu Hakim. Cohen, it
is said, 'came to identify himself' with the two Eliahus who
shared his first name.[75] (There were considerable feelings of
outrage in Western countries when the remains of the two
murderers, who had been hanged in Cairo in 1945, were sent to
Israel in 1975, where the authorities held various ceremonies in
honour of their memory while the coffins were placed in the
Israeli Hall of Heroism.[76] There were similar feelings when it
was announced that Israel was to issue a postage stamp in
honour of Avraham Stern, the founder of the Stern Gang
in 1977.[77])

When he was twenty years old, Elie Cohen became a member of
the Zionist youth organization in Alexandria; this was in 1944,
and from then on he worked tirelessly for Zionism. He had
been introduced to the movement by Shmuel Azar (who, as we have
seen, was later to die for his acts of sabotage), and Cohen distinguished himself by his 'missionary work' among young Jews
of Alexandria who were won over to Zionism by his persuasive
methods. Because of his Zionist activities, he had to leave the
Faruq I University in 1947 before he had graduated, and he
subsequently spent most of his time in underground Zionist
work.[78]

He was arrested in 1952 for 'Zionist extremist activity', but
was released after intensive questioning. He was a member of the
sabotage team which carried out the bombings of 1954, and in
fact, in 1953, at the request of Shmuel Azar he had taken an
apartment in Cairo in his own name for the group's under-
cover work. When the members of the ring were arrested in
1954, he was again questioned but he succeeded in persuading
the police that he was innocent.[79]

After arriving in Israel in 1957, Cohen obtained a job as an
accountant in the Supply Department of Central Distributors,
and one morning in the spring of 1960 he received a visitor who
announced himself as 'Zalman' but refused to give a surname.
Zalman asked Elie Cohen to work for Israeli Intelligence, saying
that the work would be interesting and would involve travel,
probably to Arab countries; however, Cohen said he was not
interested in the offer as he had recently married and wanted to
stay with his wife, and besides, he added, he had become tired of

travelling and wanted to settle down. He was offered double the salary he was then receiving, but he was adamant.

The following month, Elie Cohen was dismissed from his job, and two days later Zalman reappeared and renewed his offer, saying he had heard 'by accident' that Cohen had been fired.[80] In this way Elie Cohen became a spy for Israel. He received training in espionage methods and in the course of his instruction he was given a French passport, made out in the name of Marcel Cowen, which belonged to an Egyptian-born Jew who was staying in Israel on his way to Africa; Cohen's photograph was substituted for that of the owner of the passport.[81] (It is common knowledge among the Arab Jews in Israel that the Western passports of Jews born in Arab countries who do not have Jewish names are 'borrowed' from time to time by Israeli Intelligence.)

Cohen was told that he was to be sent to Syria, using the name of Kamal Amin Taabes,[82] and he received instruction in Islamic practice.[83] At the end of 1960, it was decided to send him to Buenos Aires where he was to play the part of a rich Syrian who had settled there. A 'biography' was concocted for him, and he was even given a 'family album' with faked photographs of his supposed relatives superimposed on a Buenos Aires background. As his Spanish was not good enough for someone who was supposed to have lived in Argentina for years, he had to spend some time there perfecting his knowledge of the language.[84]

Armed with a radio transmitter concealed in an electric mixer in his baggage, Cohen set off for Damascus, posing as a Syrian patriot returning to his homeland.[85] He then took a five-room flat opposite Syrian army headquarters and began sending his radio messages to Tel Aviv.[86]

Cohen started to make contacts in Damascus, and his generosity and hospitality constantly widened his circle of friends, so that within a comparatively short time he was on terms of close friendship with political and military leaders who were encouraged to discuss Syria's problems with him by his pretence of deep patriotism and apparent determination to assist his country in every way possible. He broadcast frequently to Israel and his information was considered of great value. He described operation orders, government decisions and armament plans, and gave details of sensitive areas, and of all movements of the Syrian army, the dates of receipt of weapons and the effectiveness of the equipment and its operational possibilities. The information was transmitted to Israel by every possible means and was utilized to the full. When he had parties at his home, he chose suitable girls and, without arousing their suspicions, managed to persuade them to collect any information of value. When his parties were at their height he took many photographs which he reckoned would serve as excellent extortion material.[87]

One evening, he received an urgent message from Israel to make every attempt to 'locate the Nazi criminal Franz Raedemacher, who was hiding in Syria under the assumed name of John Rosalie'. Cohen asked what he was to do when he found the man and he was told to 'find a way to eliminate him', and so Cohen offered a man called Springer one thousand dollars 'to put him out of the way', promising that in return, a blind eye would be turned to the shady deals Springer conducted in Syria.[88]

Apart from occasional visits to Israel which were made via other countries, Cohen had been in Syria for three years—he had arrived in Damascus on 10 January 1962—when he was unmasked. At eight o'clock in the morning of Thursday 21 January 1965, he had just sent a radio message to Tel Aviv. At dinner with Colonel Saleem Hatoum the previous evening, he had learned that President al-Assad had called a meeting of senior officers of Syrian Intelligence to discuss a plan for merging the various Palestinian organizations, and so, after passing on this information, he sat on his bed, with his radio receiver switched on, waiting for his instructions from Tel Aviv. Just then, eight plain-clothes men burst into the room, and Cohen was arrested. Colonel Ahmed Sweidani, head of Syrian Intelligence and counter-espionage services, was in command of this group, and he said later: 'I am still amazed at the naivety of certain of my fellow-countrymen in letting themselves be fooled by Elie Cohen's stories. They really believed that he was going to send their goods to Europe, and were convinced that he had opened a Damascus branch of an import-export firm that was going to become one of the most prosperous businesses in Syria.' The colonel added that when he was given—unfortunately at a very late stage—a list of the people who regularly visited Cohen's flat, his suspicions were aroused because they were men in high positions in the economic, political and military life of Syria. He added that there were difficulties at first because Cohen had worked very discreetly; he had kept no maid, had cleaned his flat himself and had done his own laundry and even polished his own windows. In addition, he never met the same people during the day that he met in the evenings, and for certain visitors he had an agreed signal and would not open his front door unless the bell had been rung a given number of times.

The Israeli author of this account writes, however, that Colonel Sweidani's narrative was 'concocted' and that Cohen had not aroused the suspicions of the Syrian security service nor had he and his friends been shadowed; the truth was that the Syrian authorities had become aware that an illicit transmitter was operating in that area and they had traced it to the block of flats where Cohen lived and had decided that it could only belong to Cohen.[89] Another version has it that 'a humble ministry clerk recognized him as the little Jewish boy, Elie, with whom he had shared a school bench thirty years earlier.'[90]

The publisher's foreword to one account about Elie Cohen's exploits states: 'Elie Cohen, one of the most expert and resourceful secret agents in recent years, is a name known only to the most informed students of Middle East affairs. Yet it was due, in great measure, to this man that Israel, during the Six-Day War, defeated the forces of Syria within a matter of hours.'[91]

A number of Syrians who had been on terms of friendship with Cohen were arrested, and some of them received prison sentences. The Israelis claimed that Cohen had been tortured, and when his trial ended and the death sentence was passed, many prominent people in various parts of the world, including the Pope, issued appeals to the Syrian Government on behalf of Cohen, but he was hanged on 18 May 1965. The Israeli Government had briefed two French barristers to defend him, but they were not allowed to attend the trial. Two months earlier, Levi Eshkol, Israel's Prime Minister, had said: 'Civilized states no longer execute spies. The normal procedure is to arrange an exchange of agents or, at the worst, to inflict a term of imprisonment. We shall do everything in our power to save Cohen.'[92]

Exploits like those of Elie Cohen tended to increase feelings of suspicion towards other Arab Jews, and, inevitably, comparisons were made between what were seen as the double standards concerning Cohen's case and that, for example, of Mahmoud

Bakr Hijazi, a twenty-eight-year-old Palestinian refugee whose mother lived in a camp near Nablus. He had entered part of the territory of his homeland on 18 January 1965, as a member of Al-Fatah guerrilla organization; when his unit was intercepted by an Israeli army patrol, Hijazi was wounded and taken prisoner. The Israelis kept the matter secret for four months and then, in June, Hijazi appeared before a military court under the Emergency Regulations (which are still in existence in Israel at the time of writing and which were inaugurated during the British mandate and were bitterly denounced, at that time, by Jewish lawyers as 'fascist' and 'Nazi-like').

Hijazi was found guilty on four charges of 'using firearms against defence forces, infiltration, carrying explosives and attempted sabotage', and he was sentenced to death. Although Israel has always refused to recognize the Geneva Convention with regard to captured Palestinian guerrillas (even when taken in uniform) this was the first time one of them had been sentenced to death. A month before the trial, Hijazi had asked for an Arab lawyer, but the court appointed an Israeli to defend him. The lawyer appealed, and three weeks later a higher military court quashed the sentence because Hijazi had not been given the opportunity which Israeli law provided for a man charged with a capital offence to engage a foreign lawyer under special circumstances; this was the law which enabled Eichmann to engage a defence lawyer from abroad.

When Elie Cohen was tried and executed without being allowed to see his French lawyers, the Israeli press pointed to the higher court's ruling in the Hijazi case as an example of Israeli magnanimity. The lawyer Hijazi was allowed to choose to represent him as the result of the ruling was Jacques Mansour Verges, a Frenchman of Arab origin, and, when he arrived in Israel, an Israeli journalist asked him if, under the same conditions, a Jewish lawyer would have been allowed to plead for Cohen in Syria. Verges replied that there was no similarity in the two cases because Cohen was an Israeli agent who had entered an Arab country with a false passport for purposes of espionage, and spies are not protected by any international convention. Verges added that Hijazi, on the other hand, was a soldier who had been captured 'in his own homeland—Palestine—and as a militant protected by the Geneva Convention.' Verges also observed that, aside from documents issued by the British colonial office, the only claim to legality that Israel has ever been able to muster is the 1947 UN General Assembly resolution on partition, which designated the region where Hijazi was captured as part of an Arab state. Verges went on to say that Hijazi would be defended, on a political level, as a freedom-fighter, and that when he returned with his two legal colleagues from Mali and Senegal, he would 'review the entire Palestine question in the course of the trial as the basis for defence'.[93]

Such a scrutiny was the very last thing desired by Israel, and, in December, Hijazi's request was refused on the grounds that there were 'no special circumstances' to justify the presence of a foreign lawyer and that Hijazi could be adequately defended by an Israeli. In spite of a subsequent higher court ruling which required the Minister of Justice to show cause for his ruling, the Minister of Justice again rejected the request, and when the case was due for retrial at the military tribunal, Verges arrived to defend his client but was detained at the airport and put on the next plane back to Europe. Hijazi decided to conduct his own defence and, after having been described for months by the Israeli press as an illiterate, uncouth mercenary, Hijazi stunned the courtroom with an articulate self-defence, delivered in flawless classical Arabic.[94]

Sentence was delayed until April 1966, when the Israeli press reported that Hijazi had to undergo an emergency operation for ulcers. This time, the prosecutor asked only for life imprisonment, and the defence lawyer, who had been appointed by the court, pleaded mitigating circumstances on the grounds that his client was 'a wretch, rejected and disowned by his own country' (meaning Jordan). Hijazi was sentenced to thirty years in prison and, wrote Abdallah Schleifer:

> What remained after Hijazi was led away was the memory of the Eichmann trial, itself a legal process that was subject to challenge but, nevertheless, an Israeli procedure that allowed a Nazi mass-murderer the right to a foreign counsel, who in turn developed, in dialogue with the state attorney, such broad political questions as Nazi ideology and the moral responsibility of bureaucrats. Yet Hijazi, an Arab patriot—by Israeli or partisan Western standards, at worst a 'terrorist'—was denied this right, and men of conscience who read about the trial abroad began to under-

stand that this was because Hijazi, unlike Eichmann, had a case.[95]

ESPIONAGE IN EGYPT

Wolfgang Lotz, who called himself 'the champagne spy' because of his love for champagne and other luxuries, was born in Germany of a Jewish mother and non-Jewish father and, although he was not circumcized (a factor, which he explained, substantiated his cover story and later saved his life when he was unmasked), he was considered by Jewish law to be a Jew because according to this criterion, a child takes the religion of the mother. In 1933 Lotz emigrated to Palestine with his mother and, on the outbreak of the Second World War, he joined the British Army and was sent to Egypt, and later participated in smuggling arms for Haganah.[96]

Because Lotz was blond and 'Teutonic-looking', he was chosen by Israeli Intelligence to go to Egypt as a spy. He was instructed to use his own name and he retained his birth certificate and identification documents from which his mother's Jewish origin was removed. After instruction in the performance of espionage activities, he arrived in Egypt, armed with letters of introduction which had been obtained because 'Western Intelligence chiefs, while outwardly maintaining a strict neutrality towards Israel, nonetheless look upon her as a secret ally who should be unofficially helped whenever possible. In the late 1950s this help came abundantly from both the CIA and the West German Intelligence Service, with the tacit approval of General Gehlen (the chief of West German Intelligence) himself.'[97]

Lotz posed as a rich man who was interested in horses, and he used the large sum of money with which the Israelis had provided him to start a riding-school and stud farm in the exclusive residential suburb of Zamalek in Cairo. He was told to 'lie low' or, in other words, to act as 'a sleeper' for a year before commencing his espionage activities.

He posed as an ex-Nazi and became very friendly with some of the German scientists at the rocket and aircraft research establishments and also with several of the senior officers in the Egyptian army and on the President's personal staff.[98] After establishing his identity and contacts in Egypt, Lotz travelled to

Europe for a meeting with his Israeli superior. According to his own account he was lonely, having been divorced twice,[99] and on 3 June 1961, he claimed, he met an attractive blonde on a train, fell in love with her, married her shortly afterwards and persuaded the Israelis, despite their misgivings, to allow her to accompany him when he returned to Egypt.[100] Another account maintains, however, that the experts of Israeli Intelligence, in deciding how best to develop cover stories, strongly believed that it would help Lotz and lend credence to his assumed identity if he could have the ideal Aryan wife. There was, however, an obstacle in the form of an existing wife who was not, unfortunately, a Nordic type but a typical Israeli girl by whom he had had two children. Discreet arrangements were made nonetheless, and when it was pointed out that certain acts had to be undertaken for the sake of Israel's honour and security, a loyal and patriotic wife finally agreed to the proposal. Her husband therefore consented to be 'married' to the German blonde whose name was Waltraud Neumann.[101]

Lotz met a man called Heinrich Bolter and his wife, Caroline, in Cairo. Dr Bolter was a German archaeologist and head of a Yale expedition who spent most of his time working in Upper Egypt, while his wife and small child remained in Cairo in a villa near where Lotz lived. The wife, Caroline, claimed to be half Dutch and half Hungarian and she denied having any links with Germany although she spoke fluent German. Lotz became suspicious of her because she was always attempting to obtain information about rockets and, whenever she was slightly drunk, she began to speak Yiddish. She also tried to strike up a friendship with Marlis Knupfer, the wife of one of the leading German rocket experts. Mrs Bolter joined the Heleopolis Sporting Club, which was about an hour's drive from her home, because Mrs Knupfer was a member there, but she never went to any of the clubs near her home.

Karl Knupfer's office was next to his house and, from his bedroom, one could see the room in his office where detailed diagrams of rockets were kept and plans were drawn. Knupfer always kept the shutters of his bedroom window closed and the door locked although the key would be left in the lock.

One night Knupfer confided in Lotz that he thought Caroline Bolter was an Israeli spy because, that day, she had met his wife

at the club and had asked her for a lift, attaching herself to Mrs
Knupfer in such a way that it would have seemed rude not to in-
vite her in for a drink. While Mrs Knupfer was in the kitchen
giving some instructions to her cook, Caroline Bolter disappeared
from the sitting-room. Puzzled, Mrs Knupfer went to look for
her and found her in the bedroom, with the door unlocked and
the shutters open. Moreover, she was taking photographs from
the bedroom window. She stammered some excuse about looking
for her child's ball. . . . Now, Knupfer said, he was going to
report the matter to the Egyptian authorities.

Lotz decided that the woman was probably working for Israeli
Intelligence and that he must prevent her arrest, so he told
Knupfer that, as he had not taken the film from her camera, he
had no evidence and, therefore, Lotz would ask his contacts in
Egyptian security to keep her under surveillance until there was
'enough rope to hang her'. Knupfer agreed, and the next morning
Lotz sent a message to his superiors in Israel on the radio
transmitter which he kept hidden inside a pair of bathroom
scales, saying that the woman was obviously working for some
organization and suggesting that if it was for Israeli Intelligence,
she should be withdrawn immediately.

The following afternoon Mrs Bolter received a cable from her
'aunt' in Germany, saying that she was critically ill and that her
'niece' should return home. She left with her child that night, and
the next morning Lotz received a message of thanks from Israel.[102]

Eventually, Lotz was caught transmitting his information and
he and his wife and some of their close associates were arrested.
The trial lasted from 27 July until 21 August 1965;[103] Lotz
succeeded in escaping a death penalty by insisting he was a
German and not an Israeli, and he was sentenced to life imprisonment and his wife to three years.[104] (When they were both released, in 1968, they went to Israel.) During the trial, it was
revealed that Lotz had been in possession of dangerous explosives, and he was also charged with 'causing severe bodily
harm to foreign nationals employed by the Government of the
United Arab Republic as well as to citizens of the United Arab
Republic' and 'attempting to kill foreign nationals employed by
the Government of the United Arab Republic as well as citizens
of the United Arab Republic by means of dangerous
explosives.'[105]

Lotz described how, during the trial, an officer 'produced the explosives found in my possession . . .' and a postmaster testified 'to having lost an eye when a letter addressed to one of the German scientists exploded in his hand. . . .' Although it had taken the Egyptians some time to trace the transmitter to Lotz, his messages had all been recorded and some of these were read out in court; one of them was the despatch advising the Israelis to recall Caroline Bolter and another said: 'The letter which was sent to Kirmeir did not explode. Another letter did explode in the Meadi post office. This made a strong impression on the German scientists.' A further message said: 'I am sure we can induce additional German scientists to leave by despatching more threatening letters. . . .' At the beginning, Lotz had maintained that the letters which contained explosives had merely been threatening letters, but, eventually, when he remembered that his messages asking for additional explosives had been intercepted, he admitted that some of the letters could have contained explosives. At the trial, the prosecution also said that Lotz had replaced John Leon Thomas, an Israeli spy, who had been executed; he had been caught on 5 January 1961, and Lotz had arrived in Egypt two days later.[106]

While he was in prison, Lotz met, and became a close friend of, three other convicted Israeli spies, Robert Dassa, Victor Levy and Philip Natanson,[107] and his wife met Marcelle Ninio in the women's prison.[108]

Although Lotz had dual German and Israeli nationality and although he had not admitted to being a Jew at his trial, he boasted about this after his return to Israel, and this knowledge, coupled with the fact that those involved in the 'security mishap' had been Egyptians, seemed to confirm to some Arabs that all Jews, irrespective of their origins or nationality, appeared to give a prior allegiance to Israel.

CLANDESTINE ACTS IN KURDISTAN

In recent years much evidence has come to light of CIA destabilization attempts in various parts of the world. In certain Arab countries these activities were often carried out with Israeli assistance, and internal conflicts were deliberately exploited by outside agencies for their own political purposes.

Iraq was a typical case in point. During the period of British domination over the country, the Kurdish revolt was subdued 'by the intervention of the British airforce which ruthlessly strafed and destroyed Kurd villages and forced the insurgents into submission'. In August 1945 Mulla Mustafa Barzani, leader of the Kurdish insurgents, defeated Iraqi troops, but 'the RAF intervened, destroying fifty-five villages.'[109]

After General Abd al-Karim Qasim and his fellow-officers seized power on 14 July 1958,[110] Mulla Mustafa, who had been living in exile in the Soviet Union following the collapse of his revolt in 1946, returned from Moscow at Qasim's invitation,[111] but the honeymoon between them was short-lived and there was soon bitter fighting between the Barzanis and other Kurdish tribes, supported by government forces. By the beginning of 1961 Qasim was hated throughout Iraq, and the people, who had had high hopes of an improvement in conditions with the overthrow of the monarchy, felt that Qasim's main preoccupation was to keep himself in power.[112]

Though ineffectual in many other spheres, Qasim dealt savagely with the Kurdish rebels so that, in the first year of the fighting, some five hundred villages were destroyed by air attack and, in that first winter, eighty thousand persons had been rendered homeless.[113]

On 8 February 1963 the Qasim régime was overthrown by the Baath Party, and the following day Qasim was shot.[114] Although Abd as-Salaam Arif was said to have led the coup d'état and he also claimed to have organized it, it later transpired that he had been chosen by the Baath leaders to serve as a figurehead.[115] The hopes of the Iraqi people for a better leadership were soon shattered as Arif began to institute more and more reactionary measures. There were rumours, a few years later, that the régime was planning to appoint two ministers approved by Mulla Mustafa which was felt, in some circles, to imply the granting of autonomy to the Kurds without actually admitting it. On 17 July 1968 the régime was overthrown by a bloodless coup, and Brigadier Ahmad Hasan al-Bakr replaced Arif as President.[116]

Barzani and his followers were accused of being 'feudalists, reactionaries and allies of imperialism and Zionism . . .' and there was renewed fighting in Kurdistan. Later, the Baath government spoke of plans to develop the Kurdistan region when the insurgents had ceased to be a problem. The President said that ten million pounds had been allocated to rehabilitate the area 'destroyed by Barzani'. In Israel, a group of Jews from Kurdistan asked the government to protest 'against the war on the Kurds', but the Israeli Foreign Ministry said that the matter had not been discussed. The account, which reveals these facts, adds: 'Despite the apparent mutual advantages in some kind of Israeli-Kurdish alliance none appears to have been sought by the Kurds . . . the Kurds regard the Palestine question as an Arab affair which does not directly concern them. They have been careful not to antagonize the Arab world by further seeking help from the Israelis. Such a connection has nevertheless been alleged by the Baghdad government.'[117]

These allegations were treated with ridicule and contempt, but, as had happened in other instances of Israeli interference in the affairs of the Arab countries, evidence began to emerge, in the 1970s, that the Iraqis had been right. The first hint of Israeli involvement came in 1969 when it was reported that the Kurds in Iraq had purchased, by way of Iran, Soviet-manufactured small arms captured by the Israelis during the 1967 war and, although American officials had been unable to confirm these reports, they found it 'plausible that Israel and Iran would thus make trouble for Iraq'.[118]

Then Jack Anderson, the American columnist, wrote:

Israeli agents—immigrants whose families had lived in Arab lands for generations—have a perfect knowledge of Arab dialects and customs. They have been able to infiltrate Arab governments with ease, gaining access to the innermost circles. . . .

The Israelis are also skilful at exploiting Arab rivalries and turning Arab against Arab. Every month, for example, a secret Israeli envoy slips into the mountains in northern Iraq to deliver fifty thousand dollars to Mulla Mustafa al Barzani, leader of the Kurdish tribes. The subsidy ensures Kurdish hostility against Iraq, whose government is militantly anti-Israel. The Central Intelligence Agency . . . gives this secret account: 'An Israeli Intelligence officer regularly delivers to al Barzani Israel's fifty thousand dollar monthly subsidy. . . .

'On at least one occasion, General Zvi Zamir, the Israeli Intelligence chief, called on al Barzani in his mountain stronghold.

'One purpose of General Zamir's visit,' reported the CIA, 'was to discuss the possibility of having al Barzani assist Iraqi

Jews to emigrate from Iraq.' General Zamir also was seeking assurance from al Barzani of continued Kurdish hostility toward the Iraqi régime.[119]

Questions were raised about whether Mulla Mustafa's so-called 'national liberation movement' was quite what it had been made out to be the following year when it was reported that Iraq had 'agreed to a peace treaty which promised the Kurdish insurgents the autonomy they have fought for through a century', and Barzani had made 'a direct appeal for American support'. Voicing his opposition to the Iraqi nationalization of the Western-owned Kirkuk oil-fields the previous year, he said he had been ignored when the government reached a settlement with the Western oil companies three months before, and he added: 'We are ready to do what goes with American policy in this area. . . . If support were strong enough, we could control the Kirkuk field and give it to an American company to operate. . . .' The report disclosed that there were indications that he had received some military and financial help from Israel, but he was 'uncharacteristically evasive when asked about this, finally saying: "There are things that may be true that are better not spoken about," although he admitted that he would be willing to accept American aid channelled through Iran or Israel.'[120]

Later, it was revealed by a senior US Intelligence official that the CIA had supplied millions of dollars' worth of weapons and ammunition to Kurdish rebels in Iraq in 1972, at the request of the Iranian Government.[121] It was also reported that Barzani had been brought secretly to the United States by the CIA, and that disclosure of the visit had been made in connection with a leak from the House (of Representatives) Intelligence Committee that President Nixon, by agreement with the Shah of Iran, had ordered the CIA in 1972 to acquire Soviet or Chinese arms and send them to the Kurds.[122] Two months later, it was revealed that the United States Secretary of State, Henry Kissinger, had received a gift of three valuable oriental rugs from Barzani, while Kissinger's wife, Nancy, had been presented with a gold and pearl necklace by the Kurdish leader.[123] During his visit to the United States, Barzani had 'begged to see' Dr Kissinger, but he was kept in total isolation and then, in spite of his protests, sent back to Iran. He had tolerated his incarceration up to the last moment in the belief that this was the condition of his meeting Dr Kissinger and other American leaders. He was kept at a house in the woods of McLean, Virginia, near CIA headquarters, where he was guarded by a joint escort of agents of the CIA and Savak, the Iranian secret police. He did, however, succeed in meeting Joseph J. Sisco, Under-Secretary of State for Political Affairs.[124]

The reason for Barzani's alarm was also the cause of Israeli anger and loss of confidence in the US because the Americans knew in advance—and failed to tell Israel—about the sudden decision of the Shah of Iran to stop helping the Kurdish rebels in Iraq. For five years Israel had supplied arms and military advisers to the Kurds in a three-way deal with the US and Iran.[125]

In 1978 an article headed 'A Secret Mission to Mustafa Barzani—in an eyrie in Kurdistan', written by Arieh Luveh Eliav, appeared in an Israeli newspaper. This article claimed that it was 'the first published account of the amazing affair of Israeli help to the Kurds', and it described how, at the end of 1966, Israel's Prime Minister, Levi Eshkol, had asked Luveh Eliav, at the time a member of the Knesset and a deputy minister, to travel to Kurdistan to meet Mulla Mustafa Barzani. He had set off with a delegation from Israel which included doctors and nurses; and a field hospital, complete with equipment, was transported to the area in jeeps and lorries. The members of the delegation arrived at the place where they had arranged to meet Barzani's men and found the armed Pash Marga fighters awaiting them. The party made its way to Barzani on horseback by night; the meeting with the Kurdish leader was an emotional one and the discussion, in Russian, was lengthy. Eliav presented the greetings of the government of Israel and its head and the greetings of the Knesset to Barzani, and he also bestowed a gift on him—a special gold medallion struck to celebrate the opening of the new Knesset.

Various kinds of assistance were discussed, and the field hospital, which the article described as 'a big present' to Barzani, was set up. A dentist had also accompanied the party and he fixed Barzani's teeth which had been causing him 'hellish pain'.

Before the departure of the Israelis from Kurdistan, Barzani asked Eliav to 'tell the Prime Minister and the Ministers that we are brothers and we will never forget that you, the Jews, were the only ones of all the people and countries to help us in our hour of need.' With those words, he removed the knife from his belt and presented it to the Israeli, and he gave him another one for the chairman of the Knesset.

Eliav concluded: 'Barzani is now drawing to the end of his life, in exile in the United States. A few months ago, I received warm regards from him by way of Congressman Stephen Solarz, a Jew and one of the best friends Israel has in Congress.' He added: 'I hope and believe that it is not all over for the Kurds and that the final chapter has not been written about the deeds and the brave aspirations to break the stranglehold of strangers and to live their lives in liberty and freedom.'[126]

REFERENCES

1. Cohen, *Jews of the Middle East*, *op. cit.*, pp. 31–2.
2. Mardor, *op. cit.*, p. 90.
3. *Ibid.*, p. 93.
4. *Ibid.*, p. 92.
5. *Ibid.*, pp. 90–1.
6. Habas, *op. cit.*, pp. 216–17.
7. 28 October 1949.
8. Cohen, *Jews of the Middle East*, *op. cit.*, pp. 31–2.
9. Elmer Berger, *Who Knows Better Must Say So*, The American Council for Judaism, 1955. Reprinted by The Institute for Palestine Studies, Beirut, 1970, p. 31. See also Colin Legum in the *Observer*, 2 February 1969.
10. Hirst, *op. cit.*, pp. 155–64.
11. 7 October 1977.
12. A. Ben-Yaakov, *History of the Jews in Iraq* (Hebrew), Jerusalem, 1965, p. 257, cited in *Khamsin*, *op. cit.*, p. 16.
13. Uri Harari, 'Our Responsibility towards Jews in the Arab Countries', in *Yediot Aharonot*, 9 February 1969, cited in *Khamsin*.
14. Cited by Michael J. Berlin, writing from Tel Aviv, *New York Post*, 28 December 1973.
15. Schechtman, *op. cit.*, pp. 109–10.
16. Abdul Razzak al-Hassan, *History of Iraqi Ministries* (Arabic), Dar al-Kutub, Beirut, 1974, Vols. VII-VIII, pp. 173–4.
17. *The Times*, 4 March 1950.
18. Schechtman, *op. cit.*, p. 111.
19. Abdul Razzak al-Hassan, *History of Iraqi Ministries* (Arabic), Al Arafa Press, Sidon, 1968, Vol. VIII, p. 194.
20. *Al Zaman* (Iraqi newspaper), 15 January 1951.
21. *Ibid.*, 10 April 1950.

22. 19 May 1950.
23. *Haolam Hazeh*, 20 April 1966.
24. *Lwa al-Istiqlal* (Iraqi newspaper), 15 January 1951.
25. Schechtman, *op. cit.*, p. 112.
26. *Ibid.*, p. 106.
27. *Haolam Hazeh*, 20 April 1966. In a letter to the Israeli newspaper *Maariv* (8 June 1966) Kadouri Eluyah of Or Yehuda wrote that the law was not passed in secret and only the draft was secret.
28. *Black Panther*, 9 November 1972.
29. *Haolam Hazeh*, 28 September 1976.
30. *Ibid.*, 20 April 1966.
31. *Encyclopedia Judaica, op. cit.*, Vol. VIII, cols. 1453–4.
32. 10 December 1951, cited in Jewish Agency's Digest, 21 December 1951.
33. 20 April 1966.
34. 9 November 1972.
35. January 1973.
36. *Haolam Hazeh*, 20 April 1966.
37. *Ibid.*
38. *Ibid.*
39. *Ibid.*
40. *Jeune Afrique*, 22 February 1978.
41. 1 June 1966. Kadouri Eluyah wrote (*Maariv*, 8 June 1966) that the trial was not a military one and the court was presided over by three judges and, in accordance with Iraqi criminal law, the judgement of this court had to be approved by a higher court, presided over by five judges in every case where the indictment included offences incurring sentences of death or life imprisonment.
42. Memorandum from Eliahu Yusef to the author, 12 December 1977.
43. Testimony to the author, Baghdad, 25 April 1978.
44. Memorandum from Ezra Cohen to the author, 5 June 1978.
45. *Haolam Hazeh*, 20 April 1966.
46. *Jeune Afrique, op. cit.*
47. *Ibid.*
48. *Ibid.*
49. *Ibid.*
50. *Ibid.*
51. *Jewish Observer and Middle East Review*, London, 20 August 1976.
52. Schechtman, *op. cit.*, p. 194.
53. *Jerusalem Post*, 12 December 1954.
54. *Jewish Chronicle*, 8 September 1978.
55. *Ibid.*
56. *The Times*, 26 January 1976.
57. Marcelle Ninio, Victor Levy, Robert Dassa and Philip Natanson as told to Aviezer Golan, *Operation Susannah*, Harper and Row, London, 1978, cited in *Jewish Chronicle*, 8 September 1978.
58. *Ibid.*
59. *Ibid.*, 16 September 1978.

60. *Ibid.*, 22 September 1978.
61. *The Times*, 26 January 1976.
62. Shabtai Teveth, *Moshe Dayan: The Soldier, The Man, The Legend*, Weidenfeld and Nicolson, 1972, pp. 230–1.
63. *Jewish Chronicle*, 22 September 1978.
64. *The Times*, 26 January 1976.
65. *Jewish Chronicle*, 22 September 1978.
66. Teveth, *op. cit.*, p. 297.
67. *The Times*, 26 January 1976.
68. *Jewish Chronicle*, 22 September 1978.
69. *Jewish Observer*, 20 August 1976.
70. Ben Dan, *The Spy from Israel*, Vallentine, Mitchell, London, 1969, pp. 14–19.
71. *Jewish Chronicle*, 22 September 1978.
72. *Ibid.*, 21 March 1975.
73. *Ibid.*, 22 September 1978.
74. Dan, *op. cit.*, p. 7.
75. *Ibid.*, p. 12.
76. *The Times*, 26 June 1975.
77. *Ibid.*, 13 August 1977.
78. Dan, pp. 13–14.
79. *Ibid.*, p. 20.
80. Eli Ben-Hanan, *Elie Cohen: Our Man in Damascus*, A.D.M. Publishing House, Tel Aviv, 1967, pp. 11–13.
81. Dan, *op. cit.*, p. 43.
82. *Ibid.*, p. 49. (In 'Amid this Susurration of Spies', in the *Daily Telegraph Magazine*, 23 July 1976, Cohen was described as 'a Syrian-born Jew' who 'appeared in the Syrian capital as Harnhan Attasi, an American-naturalized member of a wealthy Syrian family'.)
83. Dan, *op. cit.*, p. 48.
84. *Ibid.*, pp. 59–62.
85. *Ibid.*, pp. 85–9.
86. *Ibid.*, pp. 103–4.
87. Ben-Hanan, *op. cit.*, pp. 100–1.
88. *Ibid.*, pp. 76–81.
89. Dan, pp. 182–5.
90. *Daily Telegraph Magazine*, 23 July 1976.
91. Dan, *op. cit.*, p. xi.
92. *Ibid.*, pp. 196–9.
93. Abdullah Schleifer, *The Fall of Jerusalem*, The Bertrand Russell Peace Foundation, Nottingham, 1972, pp. 80–2.
94. *Ibid.*, p. 82.
95. *Ibid.*, p. 83.
96. Wolfgang Lotz, *The Champagne Spy*, Vallentine, Mitchell, London, 1972, pp. 12–13.
97. Richard Deacon, *The Israeli Secret Service*, Hamish Hamilton, London, 1977, pp. 140–1.

98. *Ibid.*, pp. 141–2.
99. Lotz, *op. cit.*, p. 14.
100. *Ibid.*, pp. 27–9.
101. Deacon, *op. cit.*, pp. 143–4.
102. Lotz, *op. cit.*, pp. 115–17.
103. *Ibid.*, p. 158.
104. Deacon, *op. cit.*, p. 174.
105. Lotz, *op. cit.*, p. 159.
106. *Ibid.*, pp. 171–5.
107. *Ibid.*, p. 212.
108. *Ibid.*, p. 189.
109. Schechtman, *op. cit.*, p. 26.
110. Majid Khadduri, *Republican Iraq: A Study in Iraqi Politics Since the Revolution of 1958*, Oxford University Press, London, 1969, p. 40.
111. Derk Kinnane, *The Kurds and Kurdistan*, Oxford University Press, London, 1970, pp. 59–60.
112. *Ibid.*, pp. 64–5.
113. *Ibid.*, p. 67.
114. *Ibid.*, p. 72.
115. Khadduri, *op. cit.*, p. 192.
116. *Ibid.*, p. 296.
117. Kinnane, *op. cit.*, pp. 75–7.
118. *Washington Post*, 12 May 1969.
119. *Ibid.*, 17 September 1972.
120. *International Herald Tribune*, 22 June 1973.
121. *Ibid.*, 3 November 1975.
122. *Christian Science Monitor*, 10 November 1975.
123. *New York Times*, 26 January 1976.
124. *Christian Science Monitor*, 10 November 1975.
125. *Newsweek*, 7 April 1975.
126. *Yediot Aharonot*, 10 May 1978.

H

Nine

The Myths and the Facts

A COMPARATIVELY UNTROUBLED EXISTENCE

SINCE the exodus of the majority of Jews from Arab countries, a set of standard myths has been perpetrated about those who remained behind so that the general, and overwhelming, impression in Western countries is that 'the pitiful remnant' (a phrase used repeatedly) of Arab Jews still in their own countries are suffering from the cruellest forms of persecution and discrimination.

The facts, however, have been considerably distorted. In Sudan, for example, there was a small Jewish community of a few hundred families who settled, mainly in Khartoum, in comparatively recent times. Ronald Shaoul, a young man who is completing his studies in Britain, supported by a grant from the Sudanese Government, described how his family and some of their fellow-Jews from Iraq (many were engaged in the gold trade) went to live in Sudan, because of the excellent trading opportunities, about a century ago. These Jews prospered, and there was no discrimination of any kind although the Jews experienced economic problems after the 1967 war. Ronald Shaoul's family was not affected, however, because his father did not own his own business and worked for someone else. It seems that in 1967, owing to the tension in other Arab countries, some Sudanese began to avoid having business dealings with Jews, and so the majority of Jews left Sudan; but the Shaoul family remains although some relatives are now living in London.[1] The reason why there were reservations towards Jews in some quarters may be owing to the sympathy expressed by some of the Jews for Israel.

Lebanese Jews had comparatively few problems either. In 1947 there were estimated to be five thousand, nine hundred and fifty Jews in Lebanon,[2] and during the anti-Zionist demonstrations of

1947 and 1948 they came to no harm, while at the time of the June 1967 war the authorities posted guards in Jewish districts and, until 1972, Jews were free to leave the country with their money and possessions.³ A number stayed on and, when the civil war broke out in 1975, some of the most expensive shops in Beirut's fashionable Hamra district were still owned by Jews. Although the older and richer Jews supported the right-wing Phalangists, some of the young Jews were totally opposed to the Maronite Christian domination of their country (no census had been taken for years because of the fact that the Maronites held the balance of power although the Muslims seemed obviously to be in the majority): and they aligned themselves with the Palestinians and the leftists.⁴

The Palestinians, in fact, went out of their way to protect the Jews during the fighting, and on one occasion Yasser Arafat, head of the Palestine Liberation Organization, heard that some of Beirut's Jews were sheltering in two of the synagogues in Wadi Abu Jameel and that they were desperately short of food and water. He sent a special group of his men to their rescue although the area was very close to the front line and it was under regular mortar bombardment with snipers waiting to shoot anyone who moved about. Yet the group of Fatah members laid down their arms in order to take in lorry-loads of supplies.⁵

CONTEMPORARY SYRIA

There were increased feelings of bitterness in Syria after the 1967 war because the Israeli army had used napalm against villages as well as military installations, and they had levelled villages to the ground and destroyed buildings in the town of Quneitra. About thirty-five thousand people, who comprised a quarter of the population, fled from the Jolan plateau during the fighting, and during the next six months the Israeli occupation troops expelled a further ninety-five thousand people. Those who refused to leave their homes had their water and food supplies cut off; they were also threatened and some suffered torture while others were executed. Those who were expelled were forced to leave behind all their possessions so that shops fully stocked with goods, cattle, clothes and household articles, as well as lands, houses, orchards and vineyards all fell into the hands of the Israelis.

For a while, the dispossessed Syrians camped in open fields near Deraa, and the majority had no shelter of any kind; later, they were accommodated in tents near Damascus and Deraa. Only about eight thousand Syrians—five per cent of the population—remained under Israeli occupation; and most of them were Druzes. With the exception of four hundred persons, mainly Druzes, Israel prohibited everyone from returning. Once the region had been cleared of its indigenous population, the Israelis called on Jewish people from all over the world to come and settle in the Jolan area, and a dozen or more military settlements had soon been established. All these measures were in violation of the Fourth Geneva Convention, which had been drawn up after the Second World War to prevent a recurrence of the crimes committed by the Nazis against the Jews and other innocent victims.[6]

Under the disengagement agreement of 29 May 1974 between the Syrians and the Israelis, which had been negotiated by the US Secretary of State, Dr Henry Kissinger, Quneitra was returned to Syrian civilian administration by the Israelis on 26 June that year. When, however, the former inhabitants of Quneitra eagerly returned to their town, they found that nothing remained of it because the Israelis had deliberately and systematically razed it to the ground. Eye-witnesses, who included United Nations forces, described how the Israelis brought in a large number of bulldozers which demolished smaller buildings with a single attack. With larger buildings, however, earth ramps had to be built so that the upper floors could also be destroyed.

Not a single building was left standing and even the trees had been uprooted. Generators had been removed by the Israelis who also carted off all the pumps for both drinking and irrigation water. In addition, they poured diesel oil, petrol and garbage into the reservoirs. Every moveable object had been looted, and churches and mosques had not only been destroyed but stripped of their marble and all other ornamentation.

Although the inhabitants of Quneitra had peacefully surrendered to the Israelis before fleeing in 1967, the Israelis had at that time destroyed some of the buildings, but there had been nothing like the devastation and havoc which were created in 1974 before the Israelis finally left. The worst thing of all, however, was the discovery that the Greek Orthodox cemetery had not only been vandalized by the Israelis but coffins had been burst open and gold jewellery worn by the corpses (as is the custom), and even gold teeth, had been stolen. The macabre contents of the coffins were strewn all over the cemetery.[7]

At the beginning of 1971, a young man and woman who said that they had escaped from Syria some months previously reported that the five thousand Jews of Damascus were being forced to remain in a 'ghetto' and they were being threatened and harassed daily by the Syrian authorities. This report was delivered at a conference organized by the International Conference for the Deliverance of Jews in the Middle East, under the direction of Alain Poher, President of the French Senate. The names of the witnesses were not given and no one was permitted to photograph them for fear, it was said, that relatives in Syria might 'be endangered'. The man was heavily bearded and he wore a black hat pulled down over his face and a trench-coat, while the woman was draped in a black cloak and wore a floppy black hat which concealed her features and black boots (in case her feet might be recognized?). Both of them also wore dark glasses. These anonymous 'witnesses' said that Syrian Jews were being arrested and tortured and that crimes against the Jews were frequently perpetrated by the Palestinians who lived side by side with the Jews: these included the beating of children while the police looked on and laughed. The couple also declared that Jews were barred from public office and from the professions, and that they were reduced to manual or artisan work, such as carpentering or tailoring in their own neighbourhoods.

Arrests of Jews were said to take place daily, and Jews were supposedly forbidden to have any contact with the rest of the population which, it was said, was not allowed to buy in Jewish shops or to employ Jews. It was also alleged that the teaching of Hebrew was practically forbidden and that all teachers had to be Muslims except for a few Jews permitted to teach Arabic to Jewish students.[8]

The newspaper which had reported these restrictions later appeared to contradict itself by writing that there was no special state of alert or police guard in the Jewish quarter where many Christians and Muslims, including Palestinians, lived peacefully with the Jews. The Jewish community, it added, ran two schools in the quarter with a total of nine hundred pupils who studied Hebrew for prayers as well as the normal government curriculum. There were thirty-four Jewish students at Damascus University, of whom thirteen were studying medicine, nine pharmacy, four dentistry, two trade, two agriculture, three literature and one engineering. They had, said the report, no trouble in finding jobs; and a number of Jewish businessmen had left the old city and set up jewellery, perfumery and dry-goods stores and pharmacies in the new part of the city. This account also quoted Syria's Deputy Foreign Minister, Mr Abdul Ghani al-Rafei, who said: 'We cannot let our citizens go to swell the ranks of the Israeli army,' while a Syrian Foreign Ministry official had declared bitterly that: 'There are more than one hundred thousand Syrian refugees from the Jolan Heights and two hundred and fifty thousand Palestinian refugees here, but the Western press cares only for the fate of four thousand Jews.'[9]

The attitude of the Western press is, perhaps, indicated by reports which quite clearly emanate from Zionist sources even when these are not acknowledged, because the wording, in all of them, is identical and bears no relation to the facts. In a report headed 'Jews have no legal escape from Syria' and attributed to its 'Diplomatic Staff', for example, the *Daily Telegraph* quoted two anonymous young Syrian Jewish 'escapers' who had said that 'most Jews live in the Damascus ghetto, a poor, dirty quarter which they share with Palestinian refugees.' Jews were also said to have the word 'Jew' daubed on their houses, to be forbidden most white-collar jobs and to be paid only one-sixth of Muslim wages for other jobs.[10]

A letter to the editor of the newspaper from the author, who had just returned from Syria, commenting on the inaccuracy of the report[11] brought the strange reply that: 'I am informed that the story to which you refer was a straightforward report of what was actually said at a Press Conference. Therefore, any complaints should be addressed to the people who made those statements.'[12]

A further letter from the author to the *Daily Telegraph* pointed out that: 'Neither in your report nor in your letter is there any indication of (a) where the Press Conference was held, (b) under whose auspices it took place nor (c) the names of "the people who made those statements". Apart from the impossibility of making complaints to people whose identity you have not revealed, I think you must agree with me that, journalistically speaking, this is not the point at issue. The *Daily Telegraph* published certain statements (irrespective of their source) which I knew, from my own, personal observations, to be erroneous and I would, therefore, respectfully submit that I was entitled to take the matter up with the *Daily Telegraph* rather than with anyone else. In view of the fact that you published an unsigned report which gave neither the name of your informants nor the source of your information, I would have thought that you would have been equally prepared to publish a signed letter from a member of the journalistic profession which pointed out the inaccuracies.'[13] There was no reply to this letter.

Commenting on an article by Rabbi W. Gunther Plaut, president of the Canadian Jewish Congress, headed 'The Sad Plight of Jews in Syria',[14] a letter by Clifford G. Holland expressed the writer's surprise at the inaccuracies contained in the article. Mr Holland wrote that, when he was in Damascus in 1970 as part of a tour to survey the plight of Palestinian Arab refugees who, he pointed out, Rabbi Plaut had omitted to mention, he had made a special point of investigating conditions among Syrian Jews and had found that the Jews 'denied any interference in Jewish worship or education as claimed by Rabbi Plaut', although they did complain of verbal harassment from ordinary citizens at the time of the espionage trials when an Israeli spy ring was uncovered. He added:

> As for restrictions on profession, there are twelve Jewish professors on the faculty of medicine at the University of Damascus, nine of pharmacy, two of commerce, two of agriculture, one each of English literature and engineering and two of French literature.
> When I was there, five practising Jewish physicians and four lawyers practised in Damascus, while many Jews are merchants with shops, offices and residences in the city, though they tend to live close to their schools and synagogues.[15]

Commenting on the statement in the article to which he was replying, that the Canadian Government was not aware of the 'plight of this small group of people in a far-away land', he added that: 'it seems totally unaware and somewhat indifferent to the plight of two million Palestinian Arab refugees and the inhuman conditions now existing in the occupied Gaza Strip where mass detentions and deportations to camps in Sinai are taking place.'[16]

In June 1972 the Jewish community of Syria called a press conference and issued a statement which complained that: 'The scope of the campaign organized and led by Israel has widened lately.' They added that Israeli officials had recently issued false declarations about the 'bad conditions' under which they were living and, as Syrians, they considered such actions inadmissible meddling in their affairs and an attempt by Israel to speak on their behalf, an attitude which they flatly rejected and strongly denounced. They went on:

> ... we are fully aware that Israel, through its campaign, aims only at concealing its criminal acts and well-known racial practices against the Arab inhabitants as well as against the oriental and coloured Jews who have been deceived by Zionism which has brought them to its alleged paradise. Furthermore, Israel is trying to stir up sectarian strife between us and our fellow-citizens of all faiths. ... We, as good citizens, fully denounce the Israeli aggression against our country as well as the attempts being made by the Israeli organs to delude some naive Jews, using them as an easy prey for Zionist propaganda. Zionism, for the sake of achieving its malicious ends, does not hesitate to embroil these persons in certain trends to their detriment. ... We are also certain that the measures taken by our Syrian authorities aim only at protecting us from the wily methods of Zionism and its deceptive propaganda. ...[17]

Two months later, the Board of Deputies of British Jews issued a circular letter to Jewish organizations which declared: 'Please find enclosed herewith sample posters depicting the plight of Jews in Syria.' The posters stated: 'Jews incommunicado in Syrian prisons; night curfew in Jewish ghettos in Damascus, Aleppo and Kamishly; destructions of Jewish cemeteries; special identity cards for Jews; Jewish girls raped; confiscation of property; no freedom to travel; no employment; no permission to leave the country ... the Syrian version of universal human rights.'[18]

At this time, however, it was found that, although Jews were subjected to certain travel restrictions, there was no evidence to be found of the other allegations. The Harat al-Yahud in Damascus is constantly depicted as a 'ghetto' into which Jews are forcibly concentrated, but throughout history non-Jews have also lived in this quarter which contains Jewish, Christian and Muslim shops, and the Jewish businesses could only be identified by the fact that they were closed on a Saturday.

A publication distributed by the Zionist Federation of Great Britain states that: 'The Damascus Jews are segregated in a ghetto and Muslims are "advised" not to enter it; there is generally a curfew from ten p.m. . . .' (this, of course, is nonsense). The account adds: 'The Jewish communities in the Arab world have, as indicated, been reduced to a fraction of what they were thirty years ago. They have lost businesses, shops, homes and land worth thousands of millions of pounds. Responsibility for looking after three-quarters of a million destitute survivors has devolved on the State of Israel, and this responsibility has in turn saddled Israel with by far its biggest social problem. In the Arab treatment of the Jews, anti-Semitism has become interwoven with anti-Zionism, and has—particularly in Egypt, Libya and Iraq in the past, and in Syria today—produced savage racial discrimination. . . . It would seem that the Jewish communities in the Arab world are in the process of final and total liquidation. The State of Israel is today the sole effective guarantor of the lives and liberties of the survivors of discrimination and terror.'[19]

A pamphlet written by Martin Gilbert, a historian and a Zionist, gives the impression that, throughout history, the Jews were cruelly persecuted in the Arab countries. The booklet contains no documentation whatever, and some of the statements in it are unquestionably false. For example, the author (whose pamphlet was published in 1976) claims that the following restrictions have been in force in Syria since 1967: 'Government and military personnel are forbidden to purchase from Jewish shops', and 'Foreigners may not visit the Jewish quarter unescorted'; also 'Jews [are] forbidden to own radios or telephones or to maintain postal contact with [the] outside world', etc.[20] In the course of several visits to Syria between 1972 and 1976, however, the author of this book visited the Jewish quarter in Damascus many times alone and unescorted, and she accompanied a Syrian friend, Mrs Muawiya Shoura, personal assistant to the Minister of Health in Damascus, to various Jewish shops (in 1973, 1974 and 1975) where Mrs Shoura bought furniture and other goods; she also saw radios and telephones in Jewish houses.

A Christian who owns a large gift-shop in the Harat al Yahud said: 'If Jews really were suffering in the way that has been described abroad, we would be bound to know about it. You can't live in close proximity to people without being aware of what is happening to them, and yet we have heard nothing or seen nothing which supports the allegations.' He, incidentally, was a severe critic of the Syrian régime. Conversations with Mr Saleem Totah, the head of the Damascus Jewish community, and with other Jews made it clear that, although they did suffer from certain restrictive measures, their situation was nothing like the description given by the Zionist organizations.

For example, the claim that there was 'no employment' for Jews was patently untrue. The largest department store in Damascus, the Grand Magasin, which sells luxury imported goods such as French perfume, Italian silk clothing and leather goods is owned by two Jews, Yusuf Jajati and Jacques Katach. Although neither they nor Mr Totah made any complaints about their situation, the impression received was that they were under a certain amount of surveillance—as, indeed, were other Syrians at that time—but this seemed to be the worst of their disabilities; and subsequent visits to Syria conveyed a much happier impression when groups of Jews were encountered in restaurants, discotheques and mountain resorts such as Bludan. Although the educated and knowledgeable Jews realized why they had been compromised, some of the poorer and more ignorant ones simply failed to understand why they should be treated with suspicion just because their sons had left for Israel and were now members of the Israeli army. An Armenian in Damascus described how his best friend, who had been a Jew, had suddenly 'disappeared'. During the 1967 war, he was recognized on Syrian soil, fighting against his former compatriots.[21]

The activities of Elie Cohen, coupled with the intense anger which followed the 1967 war, were the main causes of the Syrian determination that Jews should not emigrate to Israel, and, while any restrictions on the citizens of any country are to be regretted and, indeed, condemned, it is surprising that no attempts have been made in the West to compare the Syrian attitude with that of, say, Britain during the Second World War when ordinary citizens were not allowed to travel abroad at all, let alone to travel to, and settle in, an enemy-occupied country. Illegal emigration from a country is invariably hazardous; in 1950 thirty Syrian Jews were smuggled out of Syria by a band of Arab seamen who promised to take them to Israel. Halfway between Beirut and Haifa, the Arabs turned on their passengers, stripped them of their valuables, murdered them and threw their bodies overboard.[22] In 1974 there was considerable Syrian embarrassment when a repetition of this incident occurred. It was announced on Damascus radio that four young Jewish women, who were carrying large sums of money and were attempting to reach Israel via Lebanon, had been murdered by members of a gang of smugglers, some of whom were Jews and some Muslims. In an effort to make it appear that the Syrian authorities had been responsible for the murders, Israeli radio announced that the young women 'had been tortured and then murdered and their bodies left in a Damascus street'. Rabbi Shlomo Goren, the Ashkenazi Chief Rabbi of Israel, sent cables to the Archbishop of Canterbury and the Pope denouncing the 'brutal murders' in Syria. In the same issue of the *Jewish Chronicle* which reported the Israeli radio account, there was a leading article which said: 'The reports of the brutal murder of four Jewish women in Syria during the past few days appear to be authentic. On the evidence at present available, the women were murdered in Damascus and their bodies dumped near the Lebanese border. . . . The outside world has been far too ready to listen to unfounded stories of Israeli brutality in occupied Arab territories and to ignore the real and continuous oppression of the Jews in Syria. Today there is only a reduced and pitiful remnant of what was once a flourishing community. . . . Syrian methods of discrimination are reminiscent of the Nazis; so is Syrian barbarism. . . .'[23] There was no mention of the Damascus radio report that the women had been murdered by a gang nor that the members had been arrested and, after interrogation, had confessed to the crime. Presumably the reason why it was alleged that the murders had taken place 'in Damascus' was to conceal the fact that the four women had been in the border region.

Four months after these events had been reported, a leading article in the *Guardian* pointed out that:

Pressure on the Soviet Union has been fairly successful in bringing about the release of Jews. The influx of Soviet Jews to Israel
has been an unexpected and welcome boost to a flagging immigration flow. Pressure on Syria, however, may be counter-
productive. Israel and Syria still live in a war atmosphere. It is an
important difference that Israel is not at war with the Soviet
Union. In these circumstances, Jews have become what Professor
Maxime Rodinson, a Jewish expert on Arab-Israeli relations,
calls the victims of 'war racialism'. This syndrome caused
Germans to be regarded as an accursed race during World War
Two, and the Japanese to be interned in the US.

Currently there is concern about the trial in Damascus of four
Syrians—two Jewish and two Muslims. They have confessed to
having robbed and murdered some months ago four Syrian
Jewish girls whom they had agreed to smuggle out of the country
into Lebanon. The issue is fundamentally criminal. Inevitably,
political overtones of persecutions have been introduced. This
interpretation probably does little more than make life uncom-
fortable for the Jewish community in Damascus. It also raises
additional awkward questions. If Syrian Jews are to be allowed
to leave their own country, Syria, for Israel, why should Palestinians not be allowed back to their own country? In the end,
only a peaceful political climate between Israel and Syria will
enable the freedom of movement for those who desire it.[24]

In an article attributed to the paper's 'foreign staff', the
Observer reported a story which had been told 'by a Syrian
Jewess', whose name, like those of 'two other recent emigrants . . .
cannot be disclosed for fear of jeopardizing the safety of their
families still living in Syria'. The article went on to describe how
Jews were being tortured, and how the 'small and frightened
community' was 'denied the means of sustaining itself'. Jews
could not hold jobs in government service, and 'they could not
work in the professions of their choice.' The article went on to
explain that the three anonymous informants 'had recent personal
experience' in Damascus, Aleppo and Kamishly where Jews
'have had to report to the police three times a day, giving details of everywhere they have been. . . . Security men burst into
Jewish houses at night and count the people there. . . . Jews
cannot work in banks, in the wholesale trades or in import-
export. . . .' The account added that no Jewish pupils were admitted to Syrian Government secondary schools and that Jewish

primary schools had 'Muslim headmasters and Muslim teachers, who are forbidden to teach Jewish subjects'. Harassment of Jews was said to be 'commonplace' and: 'Those who go out are molested by their neighbours—Palestinian refugees who moved into the houses left vacant in the Jewish ghettos. Young women never walk alone in the streets. Within the last six months four Jewish girls and two young men have been killed in the frontier zone. . . . The parents of escapers are invariably arrested and thrown in prison. . . . Three Jews have been in jail since the autumn of 1971 without charge or trial. They are Albert Elia, the 70-year-old secretary of the Damascus community, Joseph Swed and Nissim Katri. . . .'[25]

The press officer of the Syrian Embassy in London wrote a detailed refutation of the charges contained in the article, but the *Observer* only printed the first and last paragraphs of his letter the following week[26] and, as these consisted of no more than an introduction to, and a final comment on, his remarks, it is not surprising that the impression was given that there had been no adequate Syrian response to the allegations. The press counsellor of the Israeli Embassy in London wrote: 'The Syrian Embassy's response to your reports of the persecution of the Jewish minority in Syria is an insult to the intelligence of your readers.'[27] After protests by the Syrian Embassy, however, the newspaper consented to publish the major portion of the letter which said: 'The impression created by your article is that every move by every Syrian Jew is carefully watched and, if this were so, one must conclude that the identity of those who had left the country illegally—especially the women whose relatives were supposedly arrested—would be known to the Syrian authorities by now. . . . As for the implication contained in your article that the Syrian Government is in some way responsible for the murder of some Syrian Jews, the fact is that a gang of four men, headed by a Syrian Jew, Youssef Shaloh, and consisting of another Syrian Jew, Azoz Zalta, and two Syrian Muslims, had been carrying out bank raids and other crimes in the area bordering Lebanon. They were paid large sums of money to smuggle people carrying cash out of the country. The four girls mentioned in your article were tricked by this gang into parting with their life savings after which they were brutally murdered.' A footnote explained that: 'These passages were omitted from Mr Muallim's letter last week.'[28]

Precisely at the time when the *Observer* was reporting such distressing conditions as those allegedly existing in the 'ghetto' in Damascus, a number of visits to the district made it clear that there was no truth in the allegations. Jews were certainly not cowering in their homes, afraid to go out; and they denied that they were being 'molested' and that young women were unable to walk alone in the streets. Some new boutiques, which had been opened in central Damascus, were found to be owned by Jews.[29]

Practically without exception, journalists who have actually visited Syria and have studied conditions at first-hand among the Jews there have given accounts which have totally contradicted the claims made on the evidence produced by 'anonymous' sources. Invariably, the accounts of these journalists have been the subject of bitter attacks. Thus one finds the report of a Zionist organization which is headed 'American magazine misrepresents plight of Syrian Jewry', and which explains that the American Jewish Congress had made representations to the editor of the *National Geographic Magazine* concerning an article contained in the magazine in April 1974, and describes 'the editor's refusal to rectify the false impression about the position of Syrian Jews arising from that article'. We are told that: 'The *National Geographic Magazine* article conveys the notion that Syrian Jews live virtually normal lives although they may experience some minor inconvienience from time to time— usually brought about by Israel's military actions in the Middle East. The magazine concedes that Syrian Jews are not free to emigrate but, apart from that, are free virtually to live like other Syrian citizens. . . .' The report quoted an account in the *New York Times* of 14 April 1974 that:

> During and after the October war . . . Jews had remained in their houses . . . rarely venturing to the edge of the ghetto to buy food. After the fighting ended, Palestinian refugees who for years have been assaulting Jews on the streets were frequently joined by Syrians who claimed revenge against the Jews for Syrian casualties caused by Israel.

The report continued by citing Rabbi Ibrahim Hamra who had been described by the *National Geographic Magazine* as the 'spiritual leader of Syria's Jewish community', and who had said, 'we have many synagogues in Damascus . . . we have eight hundred students in two schools and many of our people go to the University of Damascus ... today we have rights like any other citizen.' The Zionist comment on this, however, was that: 'It is evident that a rabbi in Damascus under the menacing surveillance of the Syrian government can do nothing other than to laud his captors', and the report adds that: 'In recent years especially, arrests, torture, rape and murder have occurred. ... In March of this year the bodies of four young Jewish women were found. They had been murdered, robbed, raped and mutilated. It is unclear whether they were killed in an attempt to flee Syria or whether they were murdered in Damascus and their bodies removed to the border to try to make it appear that those helping them escape had murdered them. To shield the real murderers and to disguise governmental complicity, the Syrian authorities currently are framing four persons including two Jews. . . .'[30]

There was the customary reaction three months after the *National Geographic* article appeared when a correspondent of *The Times* visited Damascus and reported that, in the Harat al-Yahud:

> ... the ubiquitous secret police are obviously keeping a watchful eye—as they do among all communities throughout the country— but there is no evidence of the iron fist. Charges that the Jews suffer under laws similar to those enacted in Nazi Germany are without foundation. . . . Clearly the major point of confrontation between the régime and the Jewish community is illegal immigration. Jewish sources say this accounts for arrests of members of the community. Most of those who wish to take the 'escape route' from Syria travel with the aid of Syrian—Jewish and Muslim— middlemen through the Zebedani Pass into Lebanon. . . . It was here that four Jewish girls from the Damascus community were murdered last year. Coming at a time when Syria was anxious to project a favourable image internationally, the murders caused grave concern inside the régime. So much so that Colonel Ali Zaza, the Minister of Interior, announced after the four suspected murderers were arrested, that they were Syrians—'two of the Muslim faith and two of the Jewish faith.'

The article added that the Jews had staged a peaceful demonstration in Damascus, and they had called for a full government investigation. The police had moved in to disperse the demonstrators, but an enquiry was promised. A young Damascus Jew was reported as saying: 'When you think that Hafez Assad [Syria's President] used the army to put down riots by the Muslim majority in defence of his stand against making Islam the state religion, we were treated with kid gloves,' and 'a senior Jewish citizen' said: 'If the outside world starts to treat us as Soviet Jews then we see trouble ahead. We are too close to home to the Palestine question. If we are to be used in a propaganda war someone will win—but it will not be us. The one thing that I fear hearing each morning is the Arabic service of Israel radio. Not only Jews but all Syrians listen to that.'[31]

The following summer, the Columbia Broadcasting System repeated one of its 'Sixty Minute' programmes which had been shown on television the previous February. Entitled 'Israel's Toughest Enemy', the programme, which had as its reporters Mike Wallace and Morley Safer, revealed that the original broadcast had 'provoked a storm of criticism from Jewish groups, who charged that we misrepresented, distorted the status of the Syrian Jews. Among other things, our critics insist that conditions have not improved for the Jewish community in Syria, that emigration restrictions have been tightened again, that Jews are still harassed and kept under surveillance because they want to escape the country, and they say that Syria's explanation that Jews are suspect as a possible fifth column is untrue, a subterfuge to cover the Syrian Government's treatment of Jews. We are repeating that broadcast tonight. We'll have some comments after you've seen the report.'[32]

It was revealed during the programme that Jews could not leave the country except for emergencies, that they had to carry cards identifying them as Jews and, also, had to notify the authorities when travelling inside Syria although the government said this was for their own protection; but, 'having said all that, it must be added that today life for Syria's Jews is better than it was in years past.' Various aspects of Jewish life were shown and interviews took place with Syrian Jews. Mike Wallace reported that there were two Jewish schools in Damascus, one primary and one secondary, and that Palestinians also attended these schools which had a Jewish headmaster and a Muslim headmaster, while most of the teachers were Jewish who taught largely in Arabic although there were Hebrew lessons too. Mike Wallace asked one teacher: 'Where do all these stories come from about how badly the Jews are treated in Syria?' and the teacher replied: 'I think that it's Zionist propaganda.'[33]

A rich Damascus Jew, Mr Albert Nusseri, had been interviewed in the original programme, and the Zionists claimed that he would not be likely to say anything critical of the Syrian authorities on television because two of his sons had 'fled Syria' and, as a result, Albert Nusseri and other members of his family had been detained for questioning. It had been assumed that CBS was unaware of these facts, but it was revealed that the presenters of the programme had known of them all along.[34]

During the programme, Mike Wallace pointed out that Albert Nusseri had been chosen by the television company and not by the Syrians and that the CBS team had met him by chance in the synagogue where he had been 'carrying the Torah during the religious service'. CBS had originally arranged to interview his brother, whom they had also met in the synagogue, but his mother had explained that he had 'gone off to pick up his new car'.

Mike Wallace added: 'It has been suggested that, of course, the man we interviewed had no choice to say anything but what he did, because Syrian authorities were standing there in the room', but, in fact, Wallace had 'had a private talk with him prior to his consenting to be filmed. The Syrian authorities were not present for that. He could simply have turned me down.' He added that the Syrian Ambassador to the United States had pointed out that it was incorrect to say that Syrian Jews could not leave their country as some of them were permitted to go to Europe and the United States, and 'he gave us the names, passport numbers and visa numbers of two who are right now in this country on business.' He continued:

> We have gone to this length to explain because the criticism of the original broadcast has continued now for four months. Last week, the American Jewish Congress filed a complaint about our story with the National News Council, an organization which judges the validity of complaints of unfairness or inaccuracy in the news media. We'll keep you informed as to the News Council's decision. Meanwhile, our request for permission to go back to Syria to take another more detailed look at the status of the Syrian Jewish community has been granted. . . .[35]

One of the complaints made by the American Jewish Congress

was that, because Mike Wallace and many of his associates were Jewish, a large proportion of the audience would accept as 'doubly credible' any statements which were made that appeared to be 'sympathetic to Syria precisely because they would be regarded as against your own self-interest'.[36] In spite of the protests and the pressures, the Columbia Broadcasting System refused to be intimidated, and a further programme on Syrian Jews was broadcast. Following this, the American Jewish Congress dropped its complaint to the News Council.[37]

A month after the second CBS programme was screened, Irene Beeson reported that the case of the murders in Syria had been presented by Israel, Jewish organizations and some Western newspapers as one of persecution of Syrian Jews and that Syrian officials had complained that the facts had been 'viciously distorted in the foreign press, that a sordid crime of robbery and murder has been dressed up as a political cause célèbre. . . .' The Syrian Jews complained that they were 'utterly weary' of being 'used as political pawns', and a young Jewish teacher said that all their problems had come from outside Syria, from foreign newspapers and radio programmes and propaganda. An old man said that the Jews had lived in Syria 'for hundreds and hundreds of years and, until recently, were free to emigrate'. As for himself, Syria was his homeland and he had stayed because he belonged there.[38]

After complaints from the American Jewish Congress that: 'Life for Jews [in Syria] is so fraught with harassment, restrictions, terror, torture and even rape and murder, that the *National Geographic Magazine* article is actually shocking in the magnitude of its distortions', Margaret C. Bledsoe, chief of the Research Department of the *National Geographic*, conceded, in letters to three Zionist protestors, that it was possible that the magazine had failed to show the difficulties of Syrian Jews but, said the Zionist report, 'despite these repeated admissions of error, the *National Geographic Magazine* remains adamant in refusing to rectify its published report.'[39]

David Hirst wrote some months later, however, that the Syrians had no doubt that they were the target of venomous propaganda and that nothing irked them more than what they considered to be the obsessive preoccupation on the part of the Zionists and their supporters with the situation of Syria's five thousand Jews and the seeming readiness of the Western, especially the US, media to accept the Zionist version of the plight of the Jews. He pointed to the article in the *National Geographic* which 'produced such a storm that, for the first time in its eighty-four-year history, the magazine made an official retraction; it had to say, "We erred",' and, in this controversy, 'the most authoritative statement came in a pamphlet issued by the American Jewish Congress' which listed all the indignities under which the Syrian Jews supposedly suffer. He added that some of the claims made by the American Jewish Congress 'are false' because Jews 'are not forbidden to own cars, telephones and television sets. There is no ten o'clock curfew. "I'll take you to my favourite night-club",' said a young Jew, and 'Jewish property does not automatically revert to the State on death', as had been claimed.

Many Jews, he pointed out, ran profitable businesses in modern parts of Damascus. ' "I bought this place for one hundred and fifty thousand Syrian pounds, and I would not sell it for a million", said Yusuf Jajati, owner of Le Grand Magasin clothing store in the same central building as the mayor's office. "I close on Saturday and everyone knows that I am a Jew, but as you see I am doing very well." '

David Hirst added that all the teachers at the Alliance Israelite school are Jews although there were fifty Palestinian children among the five hundred and forty pupils while there were thirty-three Jews at Damascus University and more at Aleppo University, which was higher than the national average and twenty times more than the number of Palestinian students in Israeli universities. The Jews mainly agreed that, far from deteriorating, their situation had improved, along with that of most Syrians, since President Assad had taken full power in 1970. Jewish leaders, who were sometimes received by the president, argued that all the efforts to 'rescue' them and all the publicity on the subject was much more likely to slow down, rather than accelerate, the pace of improvement.[40]

In spite of all the pleas by Syria's Jews that the campaign should cease, it has continued unabated. For example, a report in the *Jewish Chronicle* described a visit to Damascus by Mr Benjamin Assa, a son of the Chief Rabbi of Damascus, Rabbi Itzhak Assa, who was also known as Rabbi Zaki Minfah. Mr

THE MYTHS AND THE FACTS

Assa, who had left Syria in 1948 and settled in Mexico where he is a businessman, described how he had celebrated the *seder* (Passover meal) with his parents and other members of his family like the rest of the Jewish community in Damascus, and he explained that matzot (unleavened bread) and other Passover food and requirements were freely available.

He added that the Jews of Aleppo had also celebrated the Passover and he said the Syrian authorities had lifted many of the previous restrictions on the Jewish community. No fewer than twenty-two synagogues were functioning in Damascus and daily morning and evening services were being held in all of them. Eight hundred children were attending the Moshe Ben-Maimon Talmud Torah (religious school), and the study of Hebrew was permitted. Jewish doctors were free to practise their profession and there were twenty-two of them in the capital, along with twelve licensed pharmacists, and some Syrian Jewish businessmen had been allowed to travel to Europe although their families had not been permitted to accompany them.[41]

The following week, a letter from the Midland Committee for Jews in Arab Countries said: 'We are shocked to read Arab propaganda in your May 7 issue under the heading "Syrians remove restrictions". For both the headline and content are misleading in the extreme.' The letter referred to 'the removal of some restrictions on the Jewish citizens' as 'no more than a slight reduction in the racial persecution from which they suffer. . . . This restriction on travel applies only to Jews. . . .'[42] (This is untrue as there have always been, and there are at the time of writing, restrictions on certain categories of Syrian citizens and on Palestinians, especially those with scientific, technical and other qualifications who have been educated at the expense of the State and who might, otherwise, take their badly needed expertise to highly paid posts in the Gulf states.) The letter from the Midland Committee for Jews in Arab Countries also referred to Syrian Jewish citizens as 'living in abject poverty'.[43]

The Zionist organizations frequently approach religious groups and ask them to intercede on behalf of Syrian Jews or to hold prayers for them. When Roman Catholics in the United States agreed to a suggestion that prayers should be offered for Syrian Jews in American Catholic churches, Mr Robert Swann, of the Eurabia Committee (European Co-ordinating Committee of

Friendship Societies with the Arab World), who is an English Catholic, suggested that special prayers for Syrian Jews 'may have been as ill-advised as they were clearly well-intentioned'. He referred to reports that 'the Syrian Jews do not want to be singled out from other Syrian citizens', and added: 'The decision of the Catholic Bishops to call for special prayers for the Syrian Jews will inevitably be contrasted with the lack of any such campaign on behalf of the Arab Christian community of Palestine.'[44]

In spite of all the evidence offered by the numerous trained observers who had actually visited Syria, the accusations continued. A report headed 'Arab terrorists living in Damascus ghetto' claimed that Jews were living 'in the same quarter as Palestinian Arabs, some of whom are being picked for terrorist activity against Israel'. (This claim was unfounded as, for some years, Syria had not permitted Palestinian guerrilla actions from its territory against Israel for fear of Israeli 'reprisals' such as took place in Lebanon, where the prime motive was the annihilation of the Palestinians, which led to large-scale evacuation of the south following massive Israeli bombardment of villages and refugee camps. The number of deaths and the influx of wounded, homeless and penniless refugees from the south caused much of the unrest which led, eventually, to the Lebanese civil war.) The report added that Israel's Public Committee for Jews from Arab Countries had designated a 'Syrian Jewry Day' at a press conference attended by a representative of the World Organization for Jews from Arab Countries.

The press conference had been organized by the Jews in Arab Lands Committee of the Zionist Federation and Lord Janner, who presided at the conference, spoke of the five hundred and twenty Jewish girls in Syria 'who have no chance whatsoever of getting married'. It was also announced that a motion had been tabled in the House of Commons calling upon the British Government 'to support every effort to secure the freedom and human rights of Syrian Jews'. At the same time, the British section of the Council for Jews in Arab Countries held vigils in London and Manchester.[45]

The 'plight of' the five hundred and twenty Syrian Jewish girls had been mentioned the previous year during Syrian Jewry Day rallies and meetings which took place in Israel, and 'an unnamed tourist' was quoted as referring to the restrictions suffered by Syrian Jews, while Mr Yaacov Tsur, the chairman of the Public Council for Syrian Jews, said in a broadcast that 'the Syrian authorities had made no real concessions in reply to world-wide representations on behalf of Syrian Jews and the young Syrian Jewish women in particular.'[46]

Two months later, fourteen Syrian Jewish women were permitted to leave Damascus for the United States and one of these girls was married to a Syrian-born Jew in New York five months after arriving in the United States. The bride said: 'I am thankful to President Assad for making this day possible.' It was reported that two of the other girls were planning to marry and that all of them, except two who had returned to Syria, were bridesmaids at the wedding.[47]

In a letter headed 'Syrian Jews' Plight', Mr Alex Gerlis, the secretary of the Jews in Arab Lands Committee of the Zionist Federation, wrote: 'The four thousand five hundred Jews now left in Syria are not allowed to emigrate, despite Article 13 (2) of the Universal Declaration of Human Rights (to which Syria is a party), which states that ". . . every person has the right to leave any country, including his own . . ." '[48] Mr Gerlis did not complete the quotation which continues '. . . and to return to his country', as this would, obviously, have raised awkward questions about the Palestinians.

The same portion of the quotation was contained in an article written by Percy Gourgey, chairman of the Jews in Arab Lands Committee who, once more, raised the matter of the four young women who had been murdered and added: 'Another atrocity concerned the former secretary of the Beirut Jewish community, Mr Albert Alia, who was imprisoned in Damascus in September 1971 and is now given up for dead, all efforts to trace his whereabouts having failed.' (No facts were ever offered to substantiate the allegations about Mr Alia.) Mr Gourgey also mentioned that: 'Two prominent Syrian Jewish citizens, Nissim Katri and Yousef Swed, were jailed for three years and released only after considerable international pressure.'[49]

In spite of reports such as that written by Anthony McDermott in the *Guardian*, that 'Syrian officials yesterday confirmed reports in the Kuwaiti newspaper *Al Qabas* that all restrictions on its Jewish nationals have been lifted and they will be treated on an equal footing with other citizens',[50] the allegations of ill-treatment continued. Anthony McDermott wrote that: 'Visiting correspondents have portrayed the community as being under-privileged and discriminated against but not oppressed', and he added that the Syrians Jews had 'undoubtedly been victims of the Arab-Israeli conflict'.

He pointed out that Syrians were, naturally, acutely conscious about security and that the activities of Elie Cohen contributed to and increased the suspicious attitude of the Syrian authorities.[51] The following day, *The Times* reported from Damascus that: 'The Syrian Government has lifted all travel restrictions on Syrian Jews, official sources said today. This means that members of the Jewish community, estimated between three thousand and four thousand, can move about Syria and travel abroad on the same footing as other Syrian citizens, they said.' The report added that the restrictions had previously forced Syrian Jews to put up bonds, sometimes amounting to more than £3,500, to gain permission for foreign travel in order to ensure that those leaving the country would return to it, because the Syrian Government said it was necessary to prevent Syrian Jews from emigrating to Israel and thereby strengthening Israel militarily. President Assad had told an American television interviewer earlier that year that all Syrian Jews who wished to emigrate could do so, provided they did not go to Israel. Syrian Jews interviewed by foreign journalists had said their living conditions were improving 'and the number seeking to emigrate has dropped'. The report went on that: 'An official of the Jewish Agency, which organizes immigration to Israel, said the struggle for Syrian Jews should be stepped up to test Syria's willingness to let the small community emigrate.'[52]

The following year, the *Jewish Chronicle* reported that Mr Saleem Totah, 'the president of the Damascus community', had said: 'Two years ago, all discriminatory measures against our community were lifted. They can move freely about the country. Their identity cards no longer have "Moussaoui" (Jew) stamped on them in large letters. Some Jews have their own cars, others a telephone at home. No Jew is in prison in Syria at present. Jews are allowed to buy property, but must obtain Government per-mission to sell it.' The paper's Jerusalem correspondent reported that Mr Yaacov Tsur, the chairman of the Public Council for

Syrian Jewry, had said 'that independent reports showed that
there had been a welcome easing of the previous stringent restrictions on Syrian Jews during the past two years, especially in
the field of religious observance as well as educational, travel and
business activities.' He pointed out, however, that the strict
prohibition on emigration remained.[53]

Referring to a report in the *Jewish Chronicle* headed 'Hope for
Syrian Jewry', Alex Gerlis wrote that he was very disturbed by
some of its implications because it was not the case that Syrian
Jews were free to leave the country, as the Syrian Ambassador in
London had assured four members of parliament when they
called on him. He added: 'Mr Shaw's belief in the assurances of
the Syrian Ambassador may well be as convincing and helpful as
Munich, 1938, or the acceptance at face value of what the Soviet
Union says about human rights and freedom in the USSR.

'The Jews in Arab Lands Committee of the Zionist Federation
is under no illusions as to the condition of Syrian Jewry and the
need to secure their right to emigrate, and to this end we have
undertaken a number of activities on their behalf.'[54]

This, then, seemed to be the motivating factor behind all the
activities which revealed themselves as being designed to arrange,
somehow, the emigration of the Jews of Syria, irrespective of
their wishes in the matter and of whether such renewed agitation
might, once more, compromise them and cause problems for
them.

Britain's former Prime Minister, Sir Harold Wilson, who has
frequently proclaimed his commitment to Zionism, acted as
chairman of a seminar on Jews in Arab Lands organized by the
Zionist Federation of Great Britain and Ireland and he said that
'the country now giving most cause for concern regarding its
Jewish population is Syria.'

He added: 'This emphasizes the urgency for them to be
allowed to emigrate', and he stressed 'that one of the aims of the
campaign on behalf of the four thousand five hundred Syrian
Jews was to help make articulate their desire to emigrate.'

In spite of the repeated and explicitly stated desire of the
Syrian Jews that the Zionists should stop interfering in their
affairs and that they should not be made a propaganda device
like the Soviet Jews, Sir Harold also said that 'the campaign had
to be seen in the same context as that on behalf of Jews and

others in the Soviet Union', and he signed a petition to be sent to the United Nations Secretary-General, Dr Kurt Waldheim, 'drawing attention to the plight of Syrian Jewry'.

Mr Eric Moonman, M.P., the chairman of the Zionist Federation, suggested that organizations such as the Women's Campaign for Soviet Jewry should 'be set up to fight for Jews in Arab lands',[55] while Sir Harold Wilson 'told the seminar that about thirty thousand Jews were left in Arab countries, mainly in Morocco'. He said: 'They have suffered persecution, particularly in Iraq where there are only two hundred Jews left, but the country causing most concern is Syria where the four thousand five hundred Jews can be threatened and treated as hostages at any moment.' He pointed out that: 'Their ill-treatment made it all the more urgent that they should be allowed to emigrate', and it was reported that 'the petition to Dr Waldheim says restrictions on Jews in Syria include loss of freedom of movement, arbitrary arrest and confiscation of property.'[56]

RETURN TO BABYLON?

In mid-1975, the Palestine Liberation Organization submitted a memorandum to the various Arab heads of state suggesting that they should issue invitations to their former citizens of the Jewish faith to return to their respective countries. The plan was based on an assumption that the Arab Jews were 'the subject of a Zionist conspiracy' which had taken the form of both persuasion and threats to urge them to leave their homes and settle in Palestine; their emigration from their own countries had been facilitated by the short-sightedness of the Arab régimes. On arriving in Israel, however, the Jews had encountered racial discrimination but they had lost all hope of finding any other refuge.[57]

A number of Arab countries (Morocco, Tunisia, Sudan, Iraq, South Yemen, Libya, Egypt) issued such an invitation, and one of the first to do so was Iraq which inserted an advertisement in various newspapers. Some newspapers published the advertisement in full but others (*The Times*, for example)[58] deleted parts of it; one of these was: 'The Jews, so long as they adhered to the true principles of Judaism, lived in peace and harmony among Christians and Muslims. However, along came the Zionists and

started propagating the myth of "A Chosen People". They converted Judaism into Zionism, a racist movement, and turned
religion into a nationality. The first outcome of this was the expulsion of the Arab Palestinians from their homeland. The
Zionists sinned against the very essence of Judaism. . . .'[59] The
announcement further stated that Iraq's Revolutionary Command Council, at its meeting of 26 November, adopted the
following resolution:

1. Iraqi Jews who left Iraq since 1948 are hereby entitled to
   return home.
2. All Iraqi Jews returning to Iraq under this resolution shall
   enjoy all lawful rights of Iraqi Citizens under law.
3. The Iraqi Government shall guarantee to the returning Jews
   full constitutional rights enjoyed by Iraqi citizens. This will
   include equality and a secure life free from any sort of
   discrimination.
4. This resolution shall be published in the Official Gazette and
   shall be enforced by the Ministers concerned.[60]

As a result of this advertisement, the *Jewish Chronicle* published a cartoon showing a group of people behind bars with
hangman's nooses dangling above them and, in the foreground,
a door marked 'Iraqi Embassy' with a notice pinned to it saying
'Welcome Home Jews'.[61] Under the heading of 'Furore follows
Iraqi advertisement', the *Jewish Chronicle* wrote of 'bitter controversy' and 'a protest demonstration outside the London office
of the *Guardian*'. The report added that *The Times* had censored
the entire middle section of the advertisement while the *Observer*
'refused to publish the full text but limited the cuts to the most
offensive references to Zionism as a racist movement'. Mr Peter
Preston, editor of the *Guardian*, told the *Jewish Chronicle*
that 'while he was personally critical of the United Nations
resolution equating Zionism with racism and had expressed that
view editorially, he felt that all the advertisement did was to
repeat the Arab arguments already stated in the UN General
Assembly,' and he added: 'I also felt that I should allow our
readers to judge for themselves the Iraqi offer on the basis of the
entire advertisement and not merely on selected passages.'[62]

Those newspapers which had published the Iraqi advertisement were inundated with irate letters from Zionists. Under the
heading of 'Zionism and the protocols of Baghdad', the *Guardian*

published a selection of these; one, from Mr Percy Gourgey, claimed that 'many thousands of Jews were expelled from Iraq between 1948 and 1951',[63] and Mr Mordechai Raveh, who described himself as 'Academic Representative, Israel Universities Study Group for Middle Eastern Affairs', listed the sufferings of the Jews in Iraq between 1935 and 1937, but he failed to mention the very much larger number of non-Jews who had also suffered, and he added: 'Since then, the remnant of the Iraqi Jewish community has been living in conditions of great hardship and constant fear. It is unlikely that many Jewish refugees from Iraq will accept President al-Bakr's offer.'[64]

As most of the writers of letters to the newspapers referred—often in terms of considerable inaccuracy—to the events of 1969, it is worth reviewing these. In view of the revelations which have been made in recent years about CIA and Israeli attempts to undermine Iraq in the 1960s, plus the catastrophic effects on Arab morale generally, following the 1967 war, as well as a great deal of internal turbulence, the situation which developed in Iraq was, perhaps, a logical outcome of these events.

According to the *Jewish Chronicle*, 'Persecution reached its peak in 1968 when scores of Jews were jailed on the discovery of a local "spy ring". Nineteen were hanged in the public squares of Baghdad. . . .'[65]

At the time, it was reported that nine Jews and five non-Jews, whose names were all given, had been hanged in Baghdad and Basra on 27 January 1969, and that the four-man revolutionary court had earlier convicted them and two others of espionage. One of the other convicted men, Sadiq Jaafar al-Haadi, had had his sentence commuted to life imprisonment because of the assistance he gave 'in exposing the alleged spy network', and the report quoted the Israeli newspaper, *Maariv*, which often reflects the more conservative Israeli opinion, as saying: 'For this legalized murder, the Iraqis will pay the full price.'

The trials had begun on 4 January, after more than one hundred people had been rounded up, accused of taking part in a spy network working for Israel, as a consequence of reports from Baghdad the previous summer that a Soviet naval vessel, on a visit to Basra, had intercepted several 'unusual' radio messages and had warned the Iraqi authorities.

The findings of the court were that the defendants had trans-

mitted reports about Iraq's military strength to Israeli agents and
they had sometimes operated through Iran. It was alleged that
the ring had relayed messages over a powerful radio transmitter
hidden in a church in Basra where the network's headquarters
had been established, and occasionally through ships leaving the
port. It was also alleged that some reports were passed through
the American consulate in Abadan.

Of the first group of those accused, ten men, including six
Iraqi Jews, were acquitted, two were sentenced to three years'
imprisonment and two, both of them Iraqi Jews, to six months'
imprisonment.[66] It was then reported from Jerusalem that Mr
Levi Eshkol, Israel's Prime Minister, had said that the hangings,
which had taken place, showed what the Arab régimes, which he
compared to the Nazis, had in mind for the Jews if they could
only do as they pleased. He declared that the one and only crime
of the nine executed Jews was being Jews. He said that only
Israel and its might stood between the planning of genocide and
its perpetration, and he demanded that the 'entire world should
act . . . in order to avert further acts of murder, to save the
families and protect the Jewish remnant. If there is a conscience
in the world,' he added, 'let its voice be heard now.'[67]

The *Baghdad Observer* pointed out that if, as had been claimed,
the sole objective was to execute Jews simply because they were
Jews, then a number of those Jews involved in the same case who
were acquitted would not have been acquitted. For example, the
newspaper wrote, one of those who was acquitted was the brother
of Ezra Naji Zilkha, the alleged leader of the spy-ring. 'Besides',
the account added, 'those who were executed included persons of
all faiths, Muslims, Christians and Jews.'[68]

Iraq's ambassador in Britain wrote of 'a well-organized Zionist
campaign against Iraq, using the espionage trials as a cover and a
pretext for a vicious campaign against my country which is trying
to defend itself against foreign schemes and conspiracies.'[69]
Three days later, a leading article in *The Times* referred to the
Israeli Premier's 'embittered protest at the treatment not simply
of Jews in Iraq but of Jewish communities wherever they remain
in the Middle East and however distant they may be from the
modern state of Israel.'[70]

Without exception, the protests, both in 1969 and 1975, made
no mention of the fact that non-Jews had also been executed, and

there was a strange logic in some of them. For example, a letter from 'The Committee for Iraqi Jewish Refugees', which gave no address and no names of individual office-bearers or members, commented: 'Any returning Jew can be accused of "Zionism" and hanged. We have not forgotten the barbaric hangings of 1969 ... Iraqi Jews cannot return in great numbers to become once again a helpless, captive community any more than Palestinians can return to Israel, which they seek only to undermine and destroy. The general exchange of refugees is a final, historical fact. ...'[71]

One account which did take notice of the general turbulence and unrest in Iraq was written by Robert Stephens and E. F. Penrose who pointed out that, after the coup of 1963 when Qasim was killed and Arif came to power, several thousand communists and alleged communists had been 'summarily executed', and the account continued:

> The grisly Baghdad executions have naturally aroused international anxiety about the 2,300 Jews still in Iraq. The executions should probably be seen, however, not as evidence of a genocidal threat to the small remnant of the once-flourishing Jewish community but rather as an extreme symptom of the turbulence which has been characteristic of Iraqi politics ever since Iraq was established as an independent State after the First World War, a turbulence recently intensified by the fear and frustration created through the Arab East by Israel's victory in the 1967 war.
>
> Iraq was one of the Arab States that the Great Powers arbitrarily carved out of the Arabic-speaking provinces of the Ottoman Empire in order to try to reconcile their promises of Arab independence in World War One with their own strategic and economic designs.
>
> For the British, who gave themselves a mandate over it, Iraq was a rich prize because of its oil potential. ...[72]

At the time of the trials in Baghdad, John Pardoe, Liberal member of parliament for Cornwall North, wrote: 'The charges sound trumped-up even by Middle Eastern standards. The very idea of any ex-president of the Lebanon [this referred to Mr Camille Chamoun who, with other Lebanese personalities, was accused of taking part in a plot to overthrow the Baathist régime] conspiring with Israel to overthrow any Arab régime would, in the light of recent events, be laughable, were it not for the fact that three of the seven accused Jews had been sentenced to death as a result. . . .'[73]

In an article which described Camille Chamoun as 'the right-wing Christian leader', Robert Fisk wrote that when the Lebanese president, Emile Edde and the Patriarch of the Maronite Church met the Zionist leader, Chaim Weizmann, in Paris in 1937, Edde had publicly expressed the hope that 'a new Jewish state's first treaty of friendship with a foreign nation would be with Lebanon. . . . The Christians controlling Lebanon understood the nature of the Israeli state. It, too, was holding back the Muslim Arabs. . . .'[74]

As was described in the preceding chapter, Israel was anxious to cause as much trouble for Iraq as possible because of Iraq's stance on the Palestine issue, while Mr Chamoun's attitude towards Israel and the Palestinians became very clear at the time of the civil war in Lebanon. Writing about the 'hard-line rightists, led by the ex-President Mr Camille Chamoun', Jim Muir reported from Beirut on Israeli training, arms supplies and artillery support in South Lebanon for the Rightists and added: 'But Mr Chamoun may be gambling on greater Israeli involvement to save "Christian civilization" should it come to a showdown with the Syrians.'[75] A few months later, it was revealed that Israel had provided Lebanese Christians with from thirty to thirty-five million dollars' worth of direct aid during the war. This aid included the supply of one hundred and ten tanks, five thousand machine-guns and twelve thousand rifles. Israeli officers had been living in Christian communities 'to provide liaison', and about one thousand five hundred Lebanese were given military training at Israeli army bases. Active Israeli involvement had been launched early the previous year after a secret meeting at sea when Yitzhak Rabin, then Israel's Prime Minister, and Shimon Peres, his Defence Minister, had met the Lebanese Christian leaders, Camille Chamoun and Pierre Gemayel, the head of the extremely right-wing Phalangist Party.[76] A Palestinian guerrilla attack in Israel during which thirty-four people were killed was used as a pretext for what The Times described as a 'massive revenge raid on Lebanon', in the course of which about one thousand Lebanese civilians (this figure was given by Western diplomats) were killed and more than one hundred thousand people rendered homeless.[77]

Bearing in mind the US official admissions of CIA involvement in the affairs of Iraq, it is interesting to recall that, on 12 February 1976, before evidence of Israeli support for the Phalangist militias was made public, the *Guardian* revealed that American weapons had been captured at the beginning of 1976 when Phalangist positions in West Beirut were overrun by the Palestinians, who claimed that the Popular Front for the Liberation of Palestine was in possession of boxes of ammunition and arms stamped 'US Army' and that these could be produced. Bassam Abu Shareef, the PFLP's official spokesman, also said he had information that two CIA officers stationed at the US Embassy in Beirut had supplied ten million dollars to Michel Samaha, one of the Phalangist leaders, and he said: 'The CIA have definitely played a part in the Lebanese crisis.' The Phalangists had been supplied with hundreds of boxes of ammunition and brand-new arms, including M16s, anti-tank missiles and mortars, all of US manufacture.

The *Guardian* report added that he said: 'We dare them to deny this, and we believe they should hold an open investigation into it.' Although evidence of Israeli support for, and co-operation with, the Phalangists, does not prove the claims that Israel had Lebanese collaboration for its alleged subversive activities in Iraq, it demonstrates, at least, that the accusations were not quite as far-fetched as they were thought to be at the time. The further claim of CIA involvement seemed to point to the same kind of pattern as that which had already been established in Kurdistan. Perhaps, if the situation had been allowed to get out of control in Iraq during that period, the country might now be in ruins, as Lebanon is at the present time.

An Iraqi government official in Baghdad said: 'You people in the West always judge us by your own standards. We don't pretend that we have a Western-type democracy. But you don't have the kind of problems that we do; for example, nobody in Britain tries to overthrow the government by violent means as they do here. Why do we have public hangings? Because our people are not very sophisticated and they find it difficult to accept abstract ideas so that, if you tell them someone has been executed, they don't grasp it in the same way as they do when they actually see it for themselves—and also it acts as a deterrent. We are sure that what we are doing is for the good of all the people in the country and we're determined that nobody is going to spoil the very real progress we're making.'[78]

Certainly, from 1974 until the time of writing, Iraq has succeeded in maintaining an unprecedented stability. A number of Jews in Iraq stressed to the author that life has improved immeasurably for them. Tawfiq Sofer, a Jewish businessman in Baghdad, has two brothers, Akram and Abdallah, who live in one of the most expensive residential areas of London. They run an import-export business and they have asked their brother to make his home with them but he has refused. 'Why?' he says, 'because I am an Iraqi. Baghdad is my home and I like the life here. I visited London for a holiday a couple of years ago and I am planning to go again, but only for a holiday,' and he produced some photographs to be delivered to his brothers in London. These pictures were taken at a party to celebrate the barmitzvah (confirmation) of a friend's son, attended by members of the Jewish community, at which the thirteen-year-old barmitzvah boy was pictured cutting an enormous, tiered iced cake, like a wedding cake.[79]

Writing to protest about the 1975 United Nations Resolution which equated Zionism with racism, Mr M. S. Basri, former president of the Jewish community of Iraq, wrote of the immense contribution made by Iraqi Jews to their country, 'in trade, literature, the arts, journalism, the law and other fields of activity', and he asked: 'How have they been rewarded for their loyalty? In 1947, Zionism, along with communism, was made a criminal offence for which the death penalty was applicable.' Unlike other Jews who had written to the newspapers to protest about events of the past in Iraq, however, he did make the point that, in his opinion, not only Jews had suffered, for he wrote:

> It is to the credit of the noble Iraqi people that, despite the persecutions of the authorities, they remained friendly to the Jews and went out of their way to help them in the face of defamation and reprisals. In the meantime, thousands of Muslims and Christians were terrorized, tortured and liquidated by the Chief of the Security Police, General Nadhim Kzar, who was himself subsequently tried summarily for high treason and executed in June, 1973, after an abortive coup to overthrow the régime.[80]

Following the hysterical reaction to the invitation from the

Government of Iraq to the Jews to return home, Muhammad Tarbush, a Palestinian postgraduate student at Oxford (whose elderly parents' numerous pleas to the Israeli Government in the early 1970s to allow them to return to their homeland to spend their remaining years there were treated with contempt) wrote, in a letter to the *Guardian*, that: '. . . no Palestinian I know would subject your paper to any form of abuse were you to accept an advertisement from the Israeli embassy inviting the Palestinians to return home.'[81]

MOROCCO TODAY

Conversations with leaders of the Jewish communities of Casablanca and Marrakesh conveyed the distinct impression that the majority of 'establishment' Jews in Morocco were supporters of Israel but, bearing in mind the fact that Morocco was an Arab country, it seemed advisable, for the sake of the Jews, not to mention such matters publicly.[82]

Later, however, it became obvious that the official Moroccan attitude towards Israel was somewhat different from that of other Arab countries in spite of the fact that Morocco had come in for its share of vituperation. An Israeli writer stated, for example, that: 'Morocco had a Jewish community of about three hundred and fifty thousand in 1948. The overwhelming majority of Jews (some ninety per cent) lived in cities, and a tiny minority lived in villages in the Atlas mountains. When Moroccan Jewry is mentioned in Israel, however, it is nearly always said that "they lived in caves". This is true of only a few thousand Jews from the Atlas Mountains, constituting about one per cent of the total Moroccan Jewish community. . . . Today, there are three hundred and eighty thousand Moroccan Jews in Israel. . . .'[83]

An article by Elie Teicher, in an Israeli newspaper, described how some two hundred Jews of Moroccan origin were leaving Israel for good every month. Most of them, it was said, settled among their families in France, and the number of young emigrants who were unmarried and had completed their military service was 'remarkable'. Those Jews who had returned to Morocco were writing to their relatives in Israel and emphasizing that their situation had improved in 'the new homeland', and they were enjoying excellent working and housing conditions.

I

The heads of a family which consisted of sixty persons said that they planned to liquidate all their assets and to return to Morocco as soon as possible, and they added that many more would follow them.

The writer of the article visited one group of Jews who were preparing to return to Morocco and he found that five families lived in one extremely overcrowded flat where they shared one lavatory. There were big holes in the walls which had been covered with rags and newspapers but, 'even on a hot June day, a harsh chill reigns in the house. It is not hard to figure how one really freezes here in mid-winter. Asthmatic coughs are heard on all sides. There is misery everywhere.'

A spokesman for those who were emigrating said that the economic aspect was not the major cause of emigration. 'The main point,' he said, 'is that we are regarded as third-class citizens. We are defective merchandise. The Ashkenazi Jews have constructed a régime of persecutions against us and arrests for no reason, a rule of the white rich over the black poor.' Then he said, 'Besides, why do you Ashkenazim make such a fuss when we return to Morocco? When Jews return to Germany, where six million Jews were murdered, you swallow it, and say nothing. So why all this fuss when we go back to Morocco? There was no Holocaust there. On the contrary, Jews were treated with respect . . . you should know that we have always managed well with the Arabs. They are fine people. It is only with the Ashkenazim that we never managed.'

Another of the Moroccan Jews added: 'We are fed-up with this country. For twenty-eight years, you have been demolishing us and we still haven't done a tenth of what the blacks have done in the United States. You should thank us for that. But now, it's enough. We are going back to Morocco. Why Morocco? Because the State of Israel can persecute us in every country in which there is an Israeli consulate. We know that Israeli embassies in every country will exert pressure on the local government in order to have us sent back. In Morocco, thank God, there are no Israeli representatives. We are leaving in tens and hundreds and, soon, it will be thousands. We have received letters from friends who settled in Casablanca. Things are fine for them.' He added: 'Note it down, Mr Journalist. Moroccans are emigrating even though professional Moroccan [Zionist] leaders declare that no

Moroccan family has emigrated' (this claim was made repeatedly in the Israeli press and on television and radio).

A bystander said: 'Only one kind of Moroccan does not emigrate,' and when the journalist asked what kind, he replied: 'Moroccan university graduates, simply because there are no such Moroccans. You have taken care of that. You took away our property, our rights, our self-respect. That's enough. Now, you will have to manage without us.'[84]

A few months later, Edwin Eitan, *Yediot Aharonot*'s correspondent in Paris interviewed Professor André Chouraqui, former deputy mayor of Jerusalem and, as has been explained in a preceding chapter, an Algerian-born Jew, who was returning to Israel after a three-week visit to Morocco as the guest of King Hassan. Professor Chouraqui said that the king had put his own car at the disposal of himself and his wife as a sign of friendship and honour, and that, during a two-hour meeting, the monarch spoke of friendship between Arabs and Jews and expressed the hope that the old days of co-operation and friendship would return. The king paid all the Chouraquis' expenses, which included luxury accommodation in various Moroccan hotels where guests and staff knew that Chouraqui was an Israeli, holding an official position in Israel.

He met scores of Cabinet Ministers and senior civil servants and made extensive visits to Jewish centres, institutions and homes, as well as attending the synagogue in Fez. After the visit, he met the Israeli Ambassador in Paris, Mr Mordechai Gazit, to whom he gave a report about his tour of Morocco. When he was asked whether he had not hesitated about accepting the invitation or about 'wandering through Casablanca', Professor Chouraqui replied: 'In Israel, we are living in a ghetto; we have created a completely false picture of the Arabs and the Arab world. People knew who I was, but I felt safe everywhere.'[85]

The following year, after a visit to Morocco, Kathleen Bishtawi wrote: 'Morocco maintains perhaps the lowest rating in the hostility stakes towards Israel', and she also described the attitude of Moroccan Jews towards Israel and quoted Serge Berdugo, the vice-president of the Casablanca Jewish Council, who said that: 'All Jews everywhere are for the existence of Israel', and added that Moroccan Jews supported its existence.[86]

I*

Some Moroccan Jews said that in their opinion King Hassan had issued his invitation to the Jews to come back because there was virtually no middle class in the country, and they believed that he had felt it would be economically advantageous to encourage Jews with entrepreneurial skills to return. Certainly, there are stark contrasts in the Jewish community as well as among the Muslim population. There are rich Jews, who live in luxurious villas in the hills above Casablanca or on the coast at Rabat or among the mountains of Marrakesh, but there are also about one thousand Jews in Casablanca who are destitute and dependent on welfare payments (which come out of Jewish community funds derived from taxes imposed on the sale of kosher meat, etc.). Jewish officials mentioned that the percentage of poverty among Jews is much lower than among the country's Muslim population, and they explained that some of the rich Jews are on terms of friendship with members of the royal family—in fact, Mr David Amar, the head of the Jewish community, was appointed to this post by the king. The very rich Jews, however, are unpopular among their poorer brethren who say they are 'uncharitable'. The twenty-one Jewish schools (which teach both Hebrew and Arabic), synagogues, old people's homes and vocational training centres are run or supported by various Jewish charities and, throughout the country, there are kosher restaurants and butcher's shops.[87]

It was reported that the king had spoken of his hope for 'an alliance between the Arab world on the one hand and Israel and world Jewry on the other',[88] and it was also revealed that the Moroccan Government had invited four leading US rabbis to tour Morocco where they visited numerous Jewish communities; they also conferred with Muslim religious leaders and intellectuals, and they visited the royal mosque in Rabat, an honour which had previously been granted to only one non-Muslim, President Valéry Giscard d'Estaing of France. One of the rabbis remarked that perhaps the most significant aspect of the visit was the fact that they were 'not exactly anti-Israel', and the king told them that he hoped they would 'help to build bridges between Muslims and Jews and between Moroccans and Americans'. The rabbis had been invited by the Ministry of Tourism to investigate the possibility of organizing tours by American Jews to Morocco.[89]

It was reported, too, that 'a delegation of high-ranking officials from an Arab country [Morocco, by all accounts] ... visited Israel ... to investigate possibilities for greater co-operation between the two countries', and that 'talks had gone beyond topics strictly related to the economic sector and had been of important political significance.'[90] In addition, there have been rumours that Moshe Dayan, Israel's Foreign Minister, and Yitzhak Rabin, the former Prime Minister, had made secret visits to Morocco,[91] and, shortly afterwards, it was announced that a rabbi from Jerusalem had been invited to go to Morocco to advise the government there on setting up kosher hotels; he was named as Rabbi Binyamin Pery, head of religious activities and Jewish dietary requirements at Jerusalem's Plaza Hotel, who had been approached by the Moroccans when he was in the United States on behalf of the Jerusalem Hotel Association. He said that the Moroccan Government was planning to set up four kosher hotels and he hoped that Jewish tourists would visit Israel as well as Morocco.[92]

THE ARAB JEWS IN ISRAEL

Many myths have been perpetrated about the Arab Jews in Israel (who, as has been explained are generally known as 'orientals' or 'Sephardim', terms which also embrace, for example, Jews from Iran, Turkey and India). They are slighted and scorned and treated with contempt although, in the main, their disabilities arise from the blatant discrimination which they receive and the fact that the most privileged treatment is accorded to Jews of European origin.

Thus Israel's former chief of staff, General Mordechai Gur, in an interview given to *Al Hamishmar* (a 'socialist' Zionist paper) said that many years would have to pass before Israel's 'oriental' Jews, even those who had completed their education, would attain the ability to compete with the mentality and technology of the West, and that only very few of them would ever reach any high rank. The heads of the newspaper's editorial board decided to delete this passage from the article, although General Gur had not asked them to do so. His words had, however, been recorded by the interviewers who revealed that he had also said that, when he was commander of the Gaza Strip, he had studied the mentality of the Arabs there and had reached the conclusion that another twenty or thirty years would have to pass before the Arab mentality would change. He added that the sad thing about this was that the Arab Jews, also, would not close the gap within the next twenty to thirty years.[93]

The picture presented to outsiders which portrays Israel as a democratic, egalitarian society without distinctions of class or ethnic background among its Jewish inhabitants (the Arabs, of course, come into a different category altogether) is a false one; and the extent of Israeli racialism is often surprising to those who encounter it for the first time, but its forms are the classic ones. Non-European Jews, who constitute about seventy per cent of Israel's Jewish population, suffer from an interlocking network of social disabilities. Their housing is bad, their wages are low and they are the first to be laid off in times of recession. Even those who do prosper encounter difficulties when they attempt to buy property in middle-class districts because Ashkenazi Jews refuse to sell for fear of bringing down the value of the property.

Fewer than ten per cent of university graduates are of non-European origin and, in addition to poor social conditions, the main obstacle put in the way of the 'orientals' is the high fees imposed on secondary school and university students. Besides, equal qualifications do not guarantee equal success in Israel, and there is a policy of making life difficult for non-Western graduates and employees. In 1962 a North African Zionist leader remarked that there were more North African Jewish students at the Sorbonne in Paris than North African Jewish students at the Hebrew University of Jerusalem.[94]

When attending a parent-teacher meeting at a Jewish religious school in Rehovot, the father of a fifth-form pupil was surprised to learn that all the pupils in his son's class were 'oriental' Jews, while the pupils at the second fifth form at the same school were primarily of European origin. The father asked the form teacher for an explanation of the segregation, but he received no reply so he spoke to the headmaster, Mr Yeremiyahu Pepper, who explained to him that research had shown that children from 'oriental origins' were slow learners who had difficulty in absorbing information and that, therefore, segregation was in their own best interest.

These children had, of course, been born in Israel, and the

blatant ethnic discrimination was upsetting to many of them because the gulf that already existed between ethnic groups in
Israel was reinforced by this educational apartheid which resulted in open resentment and tension. Angry parents organized
a series of protests, but the headmaster was unmoved by them.
Girls from the 'oriental class' asked journalists not to publish
their names as they were afraid of retaliation by the headmaster.
A boy whose parents had immigrated to Israel from Morocco
demonstrated how effective the brainwashing had been on the
Arab Jewish children, as well as the others, because he explained
that people of European origin were indeed more gifted and more
cultured than oriental Jews. 'Our parents came from countries
that had no culture', he said apologetically. But when asked to
explain in which way the culture of those who had come to
Israel from Poland was superior, he had no answer.[95]

The great majority of Jews from Arab countries live in new
townships and villages which were established (on the sites of
demolished Arab villages) after 1948, although some immigrants
from Yemen, Morocco and Kurdistan live in long-established
urban areas, but their homes are invariably in slums or poor
housing conditions. Even when they settled in the larger cities,
the poverty of the immigrants meant that they had to remain in
the decaying outskirts. Because of the ethnic segregation which
exists, most primary schools have children with mainly western
or 'oriental' backgrounds but seldom both. However, in the case
of schools which had pupils of both types, it was said that 'the
incompatibility of educational backgrounds and potential' created
problems because the 'slower' children (i.e., the 'orientals')
could not keep pace with the 'brighter' ones (i.e., the westerners).

Secondary school education in Israel is not free and it is
difficult for 'oriental' families to find money to pay the fees as
their income, generally, is below the national average.[96] The fiction is maintained in Israel that the 'orientals' are backward because they come from underdeveloped countries, but, in fact, it
has been the Zionist system which caused their difficulties.
When they arrived in Israel, they were given sub-standard
housing, denied adequate welfare services and forced to accept
poorly paid jobs. They were unable, therefore, to afford to pay
for the education of their children who, from the beginning,
were penalized by living in crowded conditions where it was im-

possible to do homework. Ashkenazi children are not 'brighter', but they are more privileged in that their parents form the highly paid élite who can provide them with all the facilities for study and can also afford the school fees.

Children learn Ashkenazi history down to the finer points of ghetto life but virtually nothing of the history of the Middle East in the last five hundred years. Above all, the children of 'oriental' Jews are taught to feel ashamed of their 'primitive' background and to aspire to 'western' standards. The primary purpose of the continual degradation of non-European Jews is to create a manual working-class that knows its place and there are three types of employee in Israel (categorized on ethnic lines); Ashkenazi, Sephardi and Arab—in that order.

The 'orientals' are frequently accused of not posessing a 'pioneering spirit', but, in fact, although they set up hundreds of settlements, the Zionists failed to provide the Sephardim with funds, land and equipment in the same manner as they had the European Jewish settlements, and so they were forced to turn to labouring jobs and consequently moved to towns where they had to live in slums; Zionist propaganda, however, claimed that they had left new houses because they were unused to living in decent conditions. After 1948, a 'pure' Ashkenazi administration was established although one token Sephardi was appointed, generally as Minister of Police (Shlomo Hillel, a former Police Minister, was an Iraqi Jew who had been sent to Baghdad as a Zionist emissary). This practice was especially useful when Sephardi demonstrators were being beaten up by the police as they could not, then, be accused of prejudice. When David Ben Gurion was advised to add another Sephardi to his Cabinet, he replied angrily: 'The State of Israel will not become a Levantine state.' (The word 'Levantine' is used in Israel as a highly derogatory adjective to describe an oriental person of no culture. It has the same semantic connotations as 'wog' has in English.) This statement did not provoke any public outcry.[97]

Nevertheless, Menachem Begin informed his Likud group 'that it must choose a Sephardi' as Israel's president to succeed President Katzir, and he supported the candidature of Egyptian-born Professor Chavet (Shweika).[98] The reason why it was deemed necessary to have a Sephardi president was because the Likud grouping (of which Prime Minister Begin's right-wing

Herut party is a component) was elected by virtue of the votes of the 'oriental' Jews who had become disillusioned with the spate of financial scandals and revelations of corruption among the ranks of Israel's former rulers. There was a great deal of controversy about Chavet's nomination; he was referred to by Charlie Biton, an 'oriental' Knesset member, as 'a Sephardi Uncle Tom', and, eventually, Chavet withdrew. The *Jerusalem Post* suggested that Begin should apologize to Professor Chavet 'for subjecting him to the indignities heaped upon him by a bemused public not in the mood to humour the Prime Minister in his vagaries.' Professor Chouraqui had also been suggested as a possible candidate, but rumours that he was 'anti-orthodox' were spread; it was also alleged that he had lived in a monastery for a while, and denials were of no effect. Eventually, it was decided that Yitzhak Navon, a Jew of Turkish extraction, was the best candidate, after all, although he had also had his detractors.[99]

The reason why Sephardi Jews are hardly represented in the Knesset is because members are nominated by the parties which are run by Ashkenazi Jews whose finance comes from international Zionist funds, and the handful who do manage to obtain nomination from their bosses are almost invariably 'Uncle Toms'.[100]

The 'oriental' Jews traditionally voted *en masse* for Mapai (the Israeli Labour Party) which was in power for twenty-nine years and was thus in a position to provide a stable plank for Zionism. Only a small number of people outside Israel are aware that this stability was not based on a solid, democratic system, but on intimidation and corruption. The ruling party controlled the government, the Zionist colonization machinery and the trade unions and it was able, therefore, to exercise a great deal of control over many voters. The most underprivileged section of Israel's Jewish population (it is only necessary outside Israel to use this terminology because, inside Israel, all references to 'the population' mean the Jews and the Arabs come into a separate category)—the 'oriental' Jews—were literally dragooned into voting for Mapai. When the elections, which brought the right-wing Likud group to power, were held, the 'orientals' voted for Likud in protest against the excesses of Mapai. Begin had, of course, been courting the 'orientals' so as to get their votes and, as soon as he took office, he showed his gratitude for their support by abolishing subsidies on basic foodstuffs and by raising prices by thirty per cent and more.[101]

The racialist prejudices of Ashkenazim towards non-European Jews, which have existed since the early days of Zionist colonization, are not widely known outside Israel, but there are many examples of an attitude which was typical of the outlook of the European immigrants. For example, a Rumanian woman, who had been in Israel for three months, said: 'When I sold my house in Ploetsi, I wasn't told I'd have to live with Africans. The Jewish Agency should take us away from here, say to Tel Aviv.' Even among Israel's intellectual élite, there was a tendency to declare that the Yemenites or Moroccans belonged to 'an alien tribe'.

A life-long militant Zionist declared indignantly: 'What have I in common with the coloured horde that is invading my country? Racially, most of them are of non-Jewish origin, and they belong to a completely different world culturally. Their entire mentality, their civilization—if they have any—is not mine.' Another 'highly cultured' Israeli Zionist wrote of visiting an office where 'oriental' girls were working and feeling as if she were 'in a zoo'.[102]

All the immigrants from non-Western countries have been labelled *anashim primitiviim* (primitive people) in a manner which is both degrading and sneering. A North African quickly learned that if, in Morocco, he was a Jew, in Israel he was stigmatized as a 'Moroccan', and the non-European newcomer came to feel that influence, power and resulting privilege were the prerogative of one layer of Israeli society: the Europeans of Ashkenazi background.[103]

One Israeli, A. Hoder, pointed out that Israel's whole immigration policy is discriminatory and he explained that this was not only because non-Jews, especially Palestinians born in the country, have great difficulty in securing permanent residence in Israel and even more in becoming citizens, but also because of ethnic discrimination practised against Jews themselves. For example, a distinction is made between 'white' Jewish immigrants to Israel and 'black' ('oriental') Jews who are referred to as coming from 'developed' and 'under-developed' countries, but the hypocritical nature of this division becomes clear in the case of Jewish emigrants from France.

The French Jews are divided into 'French from the north' and 'French from the south' but the division is not at all geographical.

The 'southern' French comprise those coming from North Africa who are French nationals by birth or naturalization, even if they had lived in Paris or any other part of northern France, while those who speak Yiddish, even if they had lived in Marseilles or somewhere else in the south of France, are automatically included among the 'northern' French. Thus the 'northern' French are settled in Tel Aviv, Haifa or Jerusalem, but the majority of the 'southern' French Jews are shunted off to distant development towns such as Dimona, Hatzor or Keryath Shmonah, where the greater part of the population comes from the Orient. In these development towns where the 'orientals' are placed, the infant mortality is thirty-one per cent above the national average and, in Beisan, it is over seventy per cent which is more than double the infant mortality of Herzlia which is situated on the coast and inhabited mainly by western Jews.[104]

It was reported that nine-five per cent of all juvenile delinquents imprisoned in Israel's Tel Mond jail were 'oriental' Jews and that most of them belonged to families which had immigrated from North Africa. These facts were revealed in a study by Bracha Robinek, a graduate of Tel Aviv University, and her co-authors were Professor Michael Hen and Dr Orit Ichilov from the faculty of education of Tel Aviv University. All the prisoners questioned felt very strongly that they suffered from discrimination and were alienated from general society. The prisoners, who were between fifteen and nineteen years of age, were convinced that Jews of European origin were more likely to suceed in their work and studies than 'oriental' Jews.[105]

A. Hoder described how 'Mrs Golda Meir, on whom one can always count to say something shockingly stupid, declared, during a solemn reception at which she was made an honorary citizen of Haifa, that every loyal Jew must learn Yiddish [the language of Eastern European Jews, which is derived, mainly, from German] and that without Yiddish, one is no Jew,' while, when Soviet Jews began to arrive in Israel in the early 1970s, it was said that: 'Once again, real Jews are coming here. . . . These are people of superior caste who will give us heroes. . . .'[106]

When, at the end of 1970, the first Soviet Jews arrived, they were given television sets, washing-machines, refrigerators and furniture, all at heavily subsidized prices. An average family of three persons was provided with a three-room flat and an un-taxed car, which meant that the immigrants paid less than a quarter of the standard price and, in the largest Russian immi-grant concentration in Tel Aviv, Nveh Sharett, the number of private cars per family exceeds the average in the United States. Besides, in spite of the vociferous campaign conducted on their behalf in Europe, the Soviet Jews scorned no comforts in Israel; in fact, they demanded them and threatened to return home if denied them.

On the other hand, the wages of the average 'oriental' family were between four and five hundred Israeli pounds, which spelt poverty and meant that eight to ten persons had to live in rooms of thirty to forty square metres (the Soviet immigrants' three-room flats were eighty square metres) where two or three children would sleep in one bed, or on the floor.

A new quarter, the Nveh Sharett, was built opposite the most miserable slums in Tel Aviv, and the Soviet Jews treated their new 'neighbours', who had lived in the area for many years, with loathing and contempt. They refused to believe that these slum-dwellers were Jews and exclaimed, 'they are Arabs!' At the beginning of 1971, a group of Nveh Sharett residents drew up a list of 'complaints' and 'demands' and presented this to the authorities with the threat that, if satisfaction was not received, they would return to the Soviet Union.[107] The petition published in *Haaretz*, 22 March 1971, declared that: 'A large proportion of new immigrants from developed countries . . . are returning to their countries of origin or are planning to do so. . . . All the new immigrants living in our street came here moved by the same desire, to contribute to the building of a homeland for our people. . . . It has become obvious to us that awaiting this future means living among some people whose conceptions grow less and less civilized and more and more Levantine, and that we shall have to choose between duty to the nation and duty as head of a family. . . .'

Such threats are very effective in Israel and some of the de-mands were met. The schools in the area were segregated accord-ing to discriminatory criteria and the 'blacks' were refused admittance to 'white' clubs and were often turned away from the newly built swimming-pool at Nveh Sharett.[108]

A. Hoder has written: 'The establishment does not believe in the myth it created and on which it rests, namely the myth of one Jewish people. It believes in Jews who speak Yiddish, Jews who come from Europe. Jews coming from the East are valued only as cannon fodder, manual workers, first-class Arabs, as human "material" of inferior "quality"—anything other than free and equal human beings.'

To the amazement of the white establishment, Hoder continued, it had suddenly become apparent that the 'black' Jews could see and understand what was happening to them, and this was illustrated by an article written by Yehuda Nini, a former commandant of units of Arab Jews that were specially trained for sabotage and espionage, who pointed out that the large number of these Jews who had given their lives for Israel had died in vain because their sacrifice was made for the Ashkenazi Jews and not for their own community. He also accused Israeli judges of being racists and swindlers because: 'Let an oriental commit the smallest crime, and even if acquitted, he gets thrown into prison. Let an Ashkenazi contravene the law and eyes are shut to it and he is even acclaimed publicly. . . .'[109] A spate of personal attacks and collective hatred was immediately launched against Mr Nini, but the task of denigrating him was not easy because, according to the newspaper, *Haaretz* 'Mr Nini, a native of Yemen, does not live on the fringes of Israeli society; he was one of the cadres of National Defence, was secretary to the late Minister of Education, Zalman Aran, and a graduate of the university, a professor of literature and member of diverse radio and television commissions. These harsh words were not spoken over Radio Cairo nor written in the organs of "Matzpen" [Israeli Marxist Socialist Organization] nor did they come from Moscow. It was not the journal of the "Black Panthers" [an organization which fights for the rights of 'oriental' Jews] that published the article but the *Shedemoth Review*, the respectable organ of the political orientation of the kibbutzim.'[110]

A. Hoder further explained that it was claimed that Mr Nini was 'worse than Matzpen', and, in general, when anything was disagreeable to the régime, it was assumed that, if it was blamed on Matzpen 'agitators' or 'the left', 'people would accept anything and everything, hunger, oppression, discrimination and the spread of corruption in ruling circles.'[111]

Yehuda Nini had also described the official attitude towards non-Europeans in the Israeli army, for there was a widespread myth that 'in the army, everything is fine,' and there, 'all soldiers are equal', but in reality, there are few places in Israel where discrimination is so blatant. For example, among the numerous Israeli Generals, there is not a single non-Ashkenazi to be found. The number of 'black' officers with the rank of colonel or lieutenant-colonel is very small, and also, in ranks below that of major, the number of 'black' officers is estimated by reliable sources as being below ten per cent (although, at the time, the proportion of non-Europeans in Israel's military service age-group was said to be seventy per cent). Practically all the 'orientals' in the army work as cooks, orderlies, officers' chauffeurs, cleaners, sweepers, greasers and in other menial occupations.[112]

A Sephardi Jew has written:

> As a consequence of mass immigration into Israel and the policies of the Zionist movement and the State of Israel, the Sephardi Jewish communities . . . have been utterly uprooted. They have lost their countries, their property, their folklore, their customs, their language—in fact, the whole of their cultural heritage.
>
> They have lost their economic and social status and the sum total of their deprivations has led to a loss of identity and self-respect. They are fed with the most ferocious forms of European nationalism and the cheapest aspects of Americanism. The Zionist response to the Sephardi plight has been that the disparities in the standard of living between different types of Jews were inevitable and would narrow as these Jews from 'backward' countries were assimilated to the higher standards of their new country. . . . No amount of myth-making, however, can hide the fact that the gap between the Jewish haves and have-nots is widening. The Arab countries produced huge numbers of Jewish doctors, engineers, writers, teachers, top civil servants and so on, and 'orientals' have had no trouble in Europe and America. Let us ask the Israeli Government how many of the children of these people, born and educated in Israel over the last twenty years, have achieved comparable status.[113]

Although there is no evidence, even in Zionist sources, to suggest that Jews were 'expelled' from Arab countries (the majority of Jews expelled from Egypt at the time of Suez held foreign passports and they were treated like other foreign—mainly French and British—nationals who were also expelled), a report headed 'Jews expelled from Arab lands ask compensation' described how the Israelis say that 'if Palestinians are entitled to compensation then so are the Jewish refugees from Arab countries who have found a home for themselves in the state of Israel.' The report added that this claim had been made by the World Organization of Jews from Arab Countries, which had been founded in November 1975, and represented 'Jewish refugees now living in fourteen countries', who had elected two co-chairmen, Leon Tamman from Britain and Mordechai Ben Porat from Israel. The latter said: 'We demand that as part of any peace negotiations, our claims should be considered. The property which the Arab governments have sequestered from us exceeds by far that which the Arab refugees left in Israel.' (There was, at the time, no documentation to support such a claim and it may be hard to sustain it, in view of the repeated Zionist declarations that Jews in the Arab countries 'lived in poverty'. It is obvious that the validity of such a claim could be argued in view of Baruch Nadel's statement that the Zionist organization, of which Mordechai Ben-Porat was an important member at the time, arranged with the Arab governments the departure of the Jews for Israel, and, in exchange, handed over the property of the Jews although, of course, it was in no position to take such a step.)

Israel's former Foreign Minister, Yigal Allon, confirmed the support of the Israeli Government for the claims of WOJAC in an official statement, as did the Justice Minister, Haim Zadok, in the Knesset. The report added, however, that WOJAC had not yet made a list of Jewish property in Arab lands, but Mr Ben-Porat estimated the total at 'many billions of dollars'.[114]

Nowadays, there is fairly widespread recognition that a terrible injustice has been done to the Palestinian Arab people by the Zionist occupation of their country. There has been, however, little awareness outside Israel of the equally tragic fate of, and the crime committed against, the Arab Jews. One day, perhaps, these two unhappy groups will be able to live together in peace and security in a part of the world to which they both belong.

REFERENCES

1. Testimony of Ronald Shaoul, London, 24 July 1978.
2. Cohen, *Jews of the Middle East, op. cit.,* p. 79.
3. *Ibid.,* p. 44.
4. Information obtained by the author in Beirut, September to October 1975.
5. John Bulloch, *Death of a Country: The Civil War in Lebanon,* Weidenfeld and Nicolson, London, 1977, p. 93.
6. Petran, *op. cit.,* p. 199, citing Testimony before the United Nations Special Committee to Investigate Israeli Practices Affecting the Human Rights of the Population of the Occupied Territories in 1971 and the UN Human Rights Committee in 1969. The account states that: 'Israel has refused to permit these UN committees to visit the Occupied Territories.'
7. Edouard Saab, 'Quneitra offre un spectacle de désolation', *Le Monde,* 4 July 1974; Irene Beeson, the *Guardian,* 22 July 1974; *The Times,* 10 July 1974; Alain Cass, the *Financial Times,* 18 September 1974; Marion Woolfson, *Time Out,* 30 August 1974; *Voice,* London, 10 October 1974.
8. *New York Times,* 28 January 1971.
9. *Ibid.,* 4 February 1972.
10. 5 June 1974.
11. 5 June 1974.
12. 10 June 1974.
13. 13 June 1974.
14. *Globe and Mail,* Toronto, 8 January 1972.
15. *Ibid.,* 14 January 1972.
16. *Ibid.*
17. Statement of Jewish Religious Council of Syria, June 1972.
18. Poster attached to a letter from E. Wierschowska, Board of Deputies of British Jews, to Jewish organizations, 5 August, 1972.
19. T. C. F. Prittie and R. I. Jones, 'Jews in the Arab World', in *Britain and Israel,* September 1972.
20. Martin Gilbert, *op. cit.*
21. Investigation by the author in the course of several visits to Syria between 1972 and 1976.
22. Schechtman, *op. cit.,* pp. 164–5.
23. 15 March 1974.
24. 30 July 1974.
25. 21 April 1974.
26. *Ibid.,* 28 April 1974.
27. *Ibid.,* 5 May 1974.

28. *Ibid.*, 5 May 1974.
29. Impressions of the author, Damascus, April–May 1974.
30. Research report of the Institute of Jewish Affairs in association with the World Jewish Congress, London, 10 July 1974.
31. Paul Martin, 2 July 1974.
32. *Sixty Minutes*, CBS Television Network, 8 June 1975.
33. *Ibid.*
34. Letter from Arthur Hertzberg, President, American Jewish Congress to Mike Wallace, CBS, New York, 20 May 1975.
35. *Sixty Minutes*, *op. cit.*
36. Herzberg, *op. cit.*
37. Information supplied by Robert Chandler, CBS, New York, 3 October 1978.
38. *Guardian*, 23 July 1974.
39. IJA report, *op. cit.*
40. *Guardian*, 23 July 1974.
41. 7 May 1976.
42. *Ibid.*, 14 May 1976.
43. *Ibid.*
44. Letter to the General Secretary of the Conference of American Catholic Archbishops, 26 March 1976.
45. *Jewish Chronicle*, 9 June 1978.
46. *Ibid.*, 10 June 1977.
47. *Ibid.*, 20 January 1978.
48. *Ibid.*, 28 July 1978.
49. *Ibid.*, 23 June 1978.
50. 29 December 1976.
51. *Guardian*, 29 December 1976.
52. 30 December 1976.
53. 14 October 1977.
54. *Jewish Chronicle*, 28 July 1978.
55. *Ibid.*, 8 September 1978.
56. *The Times*, 6 September 1978.
57. *Al Qabass* (Kuwaiti newspaper), 22 February 1976.
58. 4 December 1975.
59. Advertisement in the *Guardian*, 4 December 1975.
60. *Ibid.*
61. 12 December 1975.
62. *Ibid.*
63. 6 December 1975.
64. Letter in *The Times*, 6 December 1975.
65. 19 December 1975.
66. *The Times*, 28 January 1969.
67. *Ibid.*
68. Cited in *Iraqi Jews Speak for Themselves*, Dar al-Jumhuriyah Press, Baghdad, 1969, p. 46.
69. Letter in *The Times*, 25 January 1969.
70. 28 January 1969.

71. Letter in the *New Statesman*, 19 December 1975.
72. *Observer*, 2 February 1969.
73. Letter in *The Times*, 24 January 1969.
74. *The Times*, 7 October 1978.
75. *Guardian*, 30 March 1977.
76. *Ibid.*, 16 August 1977.
77. *The Times*, 15 March 1978; *ibid.*, 5 April 1978; the *Guardian*, 23 March 1978.
78. Interview with Mr Zuheir Qadari, Director of Foreign Affairs of the Iraqi Government, 24 April 1978.
79. Information imparted to the author, Baghdad, 2 May 1978.
80. Letter in *The Times*, 24 November 1975.
81. 9 December 1975.
82. Impressions of the author, Casablanca and Marrakesh, May 1977.
83. Baruch Nadel, *Yediot Aharonot*, 23 July 1976.
84. *Haaretz*, 6 June 1976.
85. 17 March 1977.
86. *The Middle East*, London, May 1978.
87. Impressions of the author. See Marion Woolfson, 'A Moroccan Move that may have embarrassed the Israelis', *The Times*, 5 August 1977.
88. *Jewish Chronicle*, 10 June 1977.
89. Stephen Hughes, 'Morocco: The Right of Return', *Middle East International*, August 1976.
90. *Yediot Aharonot*, 12 May 1977.
91. *The Middle East*, *op. cit.*
92. *Caterer and Hotelkeeper*, London, 24 August 1978.
93. *Haaretz*, 21 May 1978.
94. 'Israel's Sephardic Jews', *Middle East International*, March 1978.
95. *Haolam Hazeh*, 15 December 1976.
96. Hayyim Cohen, 'Integrating Israel's Underprivileged Immigrants', *Wiener Library Bulletin*, Vol. XXV, No. 3/4, New Series, No. 24, 1972, pp. 6–8.
97. *Middle East International*, March 1978.
98. *Jewish Chronicle*, 10 March 1978.
99. *The Hebrew Christian*, Ramsgate, Summer, 1978, pp. 87–8.
100. *Middle East International*, March 1978.
101. *Ibid.*
102. Schechtman, *op. cit.*, pp. 343–4.
103. *Ibid.*, pp. 347–9.
104. 'Russian Jews, Black Jews and non-Jewish Jews' in 'The Zionist State and Jewish Identity', *Israca*, No. 5, January 1973.
105. *Al Hamishmar* (Israeli newspaper), 16 April 1978.
106. *Israca*, *op. cit.*
107. *Ibid.*
108. *Ibid.*
109. 'Reflections on the Destruction of the Third Temple', *Shdemoth*, No. 41, Spring, 1971, cited by A. Hoder, *op. cit.*

110. *Israca, op. cit.*
111. *Ibid.*
112. *Ibid.*
113. Ezra Ben Hakham Eliyahu, *Middle East International*, March 1978.
114. *Christian Science Monitor*, 6 June 1977.

Index